DICTIONAR
IDIOMS

D0868497

DICTIONARY OF IDIOMS

IDIOMS

IDIOMS

IDIOMS

IDIOMS

New edition

W. S. Fowler

Nelson

Thomas Nelson and Sons Ltd
Nelson House   Mayfield Road
Walton-on-Thames   Surrey KT12 5PL

Thomas Nelson (Hong Kong) Ltd
Toppan Building 10/F
22A Westlands Road   Quarry Bay   Hong Kong

Monarch Books of Canada
5000 Dufferin Street
Unit K
Downsview
Ontario
Canada M3H 5T5

First published 1972

Revised edition 1982
Reprinted 1983, 1984, 1985, 1987, 1989

Also by W.S. Fowler
First Certificate English *Books 1-4*
Proficiency English *Books 1-4*
Practise your English

(with John Pidcock and Robin Rycroft)
First Certificate English *Book 5*
Proficiency English *Books 5*
Incentive English *Book 1-3*
Incentive Themes

(with Norman Coe)
Nelson English Language Tests *Book 1-3*
Test Your English *Books 1 and 2*
Quickcheck Placement Tests

ISBN 0-17-555381-5
NCN 75-EDR-8979-04

Photoset by Tradespools Limited, Frome, Somerset.
Printed in Hong Kong

How to use this Dictionary

The items in this book are arranged alphabetically under the key word in the phrase.

Key words are shown in capitals e.g. **FORCE** and are arranged alphabetically.

Idioms are in **bold** and are positioned in the left hand margin under the key words. Phrasal verbs are listed under the verb not the preposition.

Phrases employing a noun and a verb (e.g. fall between two stools) are listed under the noun.

Prepositional entries show all the meanings of the preposition.

Examples of usage are preceded by a † mark and are in italic. Where there is speech within an example each speaker is marked with a).

Abbreviations

adj.	adjective(-al)	*p.p.*	past participle
adv.	adverb(ial)	*predic.*	predicative
adv. part.	adverbial particle	*prep.*	preposition(al)
anom. fin.	anomalous finite	*pron.*	pronoun
anom v.	anomalous verb	*prop. n.*	proper noun
aux. v.	auxiliary verb	*reflex.*	reflexive
conj.	conjunction	*rel.*	relative
inf.	infinitive	*v.*	verb
int.	interrogative	*v.i.*	verb intransitive
n.	noun	*v.t.*	verb transitive

Preface

This **Dictionary of Idioms** has been compiled specifically to meet the needs of foreign students of English. It does not therefore claim to include every idiom in the language. On the contrary, it seemed to me in compiling it that it was much more useful for the purpose to select the most commonly used expressions and phrases in modern English, than to include a much wider range that would be of doubtful value to the foreign learner.

By *idiom* we mean a commonly used phrase or expression. In compiling this Dictionary, however, I have concentrated on what I consider to be of most practical use to the student; consequently, I have included all common phrasal verbs (e.g. put up with, run over) in the variety of meanings and contexts in which they appear and have also paid particular attention to the different ways in which modals (may, should, can etc.) are used. On the other hand, while I have retained the kind of cliché found every day in newspapers such as *the rat race* or *lame duck*, I have omitted proverbs, unless they are a feature of everyday speech, and such clichés of comparison as *as light as a feather*, which means no more than *very light*.

It is sometimes difficult to judge whether colloquial expressions can be called slang or not, and consequently to advise foreign students on usage. What is most important, however, is the durability of the expression. Many students who are keen to speak the language in its most up-to-date form often learn such phrases on visits to Britain and do not realise that the expressions frequently disappear or change their meaning within a few years. For this reason, anyone imitating the English used in the stories of Somerset Maugham, for example, sounds strange to a native speaker, because he makes such extensive use of colloquial expressions used fifty years ago which are no longer current. I have therefore been sparing in the inclusion of phrases that have entered the language in the last twenty years.

Contextualisation is of vital importance in learning new lexical items of any kind in a language. Throughout this Dictionary my aim has been not only to define the meaning of the expression but also to give an example of how it is used and as far as possible to suggest any limitations that might apply to the usage socially. The correct use of an idiom in a language depends, after all, not only on knowing what it means but when to use it effectively.

W S FOWLER

ABACK *adv.*

be taken aback Be surprised † *I was so taken aback that I didn't know what to say.*

ABIDE *v.t. & i.*

can't abide Cannot stand, endure † *I can't abide him.*

abide by a promise Keep it † *We can trust him to abide by his promise.*

abide by the consequences Endure them † *If he persists in that attitude, he will have to abide by the consequences.*

ABOUT *prep.*

1 Concerning † *He wants to see you about your advertisement.* **2** In various directions; to various places around † *He spent a whole year travelling about America.* **3** In various places † *The papers were scattered about the room.* **4** In someone's personality, manner, etc † *There's something about him that frightens me.* **5** On one's person † *I am sure I have my pen about me somewhere.* **6** Doing † *What are you about?* † *Take this to the post office, and while you're about it buy me some stamps.*

how about? what about? What do you think of; what is your opinion of † *How about coming to the cinema with me?* † ⟩ *Who else shall we invite?* ⟩ *What about Charles?*

about to *prep.* Just going to † *I was about to ring you when your letter arrived.*

ABOUT *adv.*

More or less; approximately † *There were about 100 people at the wedding.* † *He will arrive about six o'clock.*

ABOVE *prep.*

Higher than; better than; beyond † *He has a flat on the floor above ours.* † *Her cooking is above average.* † *Caesar's wife should have been above suspicion.*

not above Not too good, honest, proud to † *He is not above using unfair means to get what he wants.*

above all Most important of all † *Be honest, above all with yourself.*

ABOVE *adv.*
Earlier (in a letter, book, etc) † *As stated above, we are in agreement with your proposal.* [ALSO: **the above** *n.* Used in letters where a subject heading is given † *With reference to the above . . .*]

ABSOLUTELY *adv.*
1 Completely † *You are absolutely right.* **2** (as answer to question) Certainly † 〉 *Have I your agreement that this will not happen again?* 〉 *Absolutely.*

ACCORD *n.*
of one's own accord Without being asked † *You need not have tried to persuade me. I would have done it of my own accord.*

ACCORDING TO *prep.*
1 On the authority of; as stated by † *According to the weather forecast, we can expect snow tonight.* **2** In conformity with † *Everything went off according to plan.* **3** In proportion to † *The hotel charge you according to the size of room you require.*

ACCOUNT *v.t. & i.*
account for 1 Explain † *How do you account for the difference between his story and yours?* **2** Give a reckoning of † *I can account for every penny I have spent.*

ACCOUNT *n.*
by all accounts According to what everyone says † *By all accounts, it was the coldest night of the winter.*
by one's own account According to one's own story † *She says she thought she saw him, but by her own account she could have been mistaken.*
on no account For no reason, in no circumstances † *You must take great care of the prisoner and on no account let him out of your sight.*
on one's own account Independently; without help from others † *He left the company last year, and went into business on his own account.*
give a good account of oneself Justify oneself; do something to the best of one's ability † *Although he lost the fight, the challenger gave a good account of himself.*
put (turn) to account Use for personal advantage † *He should be able to turn his knowledge of French to account in the export business.*
settle (square) accounts with Pay or receive money owing or settle a moral debt; obtain revenge † *I've been looking for a chance to square accounts with him since he cheated me.*
take into account Take into consideration † *We must take Smith into account when we make up the list of people we are going to invite.*

ACROSS *prep.*
1 From one side to the other † *Go across the road to the butcher's.* 2 On the other side of † *The station is across the river.*

ACT *n.*
put on an act Behave in an affected, dramatic way † *Don't take her seriously. She is just putting on an act to get her own way.*

ACT *v.i. & t.*
act up Behave in an annoying, unpredictable manner (used of children when they behave badly to gain attention, of machines not working properly etc).

ACTUALLY *adv.*
In fact † *She's a relative of mine – my cousin, actually.*

AD LIB *v.* or *adv.* (from Latin)
Speak freely from memory or without preparation † *The leading actor forgot his lines in the second scene and had to ad lib for a while.* † *He left the notes for his speech at home and was forced to ad lib* (or *speak ad lib*).

ADD *v.*
add up (to) 1 Amount to † *He made a number of criticisms, but they didn't add up to much.* 2 Make sense † *The evidence just doesn't add up.*

AFFAIR *n.*
have an affair with Be emotionally involved with (usually when one of the people concerned is married to a third person) † *They say he is having an affair with his secretary.*

AFIELD *adv.*
far afield Far away from home (only in this construction) † *We stayed in the village, and never went far afield.*

AFOOT *adv.*
In preparation (usually in secret) † *I've heard there's a scheme afoot to build a new road through here.*

AFTER *prep.*
1 Following in time or order † *Would you mind coming back after dinner?* † *Put the object after the verb.* 2 Behind † *When you go, close the door after you.* 3 In view of † *After the bad service I had last time I stayed at that hotel, I decided not to go there again.* 4 In spite of † *After all his effort, he still failed to pass the examination.* † *You ought to have told me. After all, I am your father* (In spite of all other considerations ...). 5 In pursuit of † *The police are after me.* † *He left his umbrella behind, so I ran after him to return it.*

AGAINST *prep.*

1 In opposition to † ⟩ *What did the Vicar say about sin?* ⟩ *He was against it!* (Used in this sense with verbs like 'protest', 'write', 'speak', etc.)
2 Indicating impact † *He hit his head against the wall.* **3** Indicating contact † *He was leaning against the wall.*

AGE *n.*

awkward age Adolescence (because people at this age are often difficult to understand, deal with).

ages A very long time † *I haven't seen her for ages.*

AID *n.*

in aid of For, to be used for † *We are making a collection in aid of the hospital.* † *What's that in aid of?* (What is the use or value of that?)

AIR *n.*

in the air 1 Uncertain † *My plans are in the air at the moment.* **2** Rumoured; being spread about † *It's in the air that our office is to be transferred to Manchester.*

clear the air Remove doubt, suspicion by stating one's point of view openly † *A frank discussion of our problems will help to clear the air.*

give oneself airs Behave in a manner intended to suggest to others that one is superior or exceptional in talent, social position † *She has no reason to give herself airs, just because her husband is the Mayor.*

ALL *pron.*

all in 1 Exhausted † *After the game I felt all in.* **2** Everything included † *The holiday will cost £65 per person, all in.* Hence **all-in price, all-in wrestling.**

all in all Considering everything, as a whole † *We had some rain at the beginning of the holiday, but (taking it) all in all the weather was quite good.*

for all I know(care) Indicating ignorance, lack of interest or concern † *I have no idea where he is. For all I know, he may be in China?*

not all that (+ adj.) Not so (+ adj.) as suggested, believed † *The critics have been very hard on the film, but I didn't think it was all that bad.* † *Of course he's a good speaker, but he's not all that good.* [ALSO: **not as** (+ adj.) **as all that** Not as . . . as has been suggested.]

not at all 1 In no way † *He worked late last night, but he doesn't look at all tired.* **2** Don't mention it (formula meaning you need not apologise or thank me) † ⟩ *It's very kind of you to help me.* ⟩ *Not at all.*

ALL *adv.*

all along From the beginning † *I knew all along that he couldn't be trusted.*
all for Totally in favour of † *I'm all for the idea.*
all right 1 Satisfactory † *The customer has sent these shoes back, but I was*

sure they were all right. **2** In a satisfactory state † *He had a headache this morning, but he's all right now.* † *Are you all right for money? I can lend you some if you need it.* **3** Expressing lack of objection or need for concern † *All right, I'll do as you say.* † *It's all right. There's nothing to worry about.* **4** Very well (agreement) † *) I'll meet you at 7 o'clock.) All right.* **5** Very well (before a threat or to express impatience or annoyance) † *All right, if that is your attitude, you must take the consequences.* **6** Going in the right direction † *Am I all right for the Houses of Parliament if I follow this road?*

all-round *adj.* General, including a variety of † *He has a good all-round knowledge of the work.* [ALSO: **all-rounder** *n.* Person with ability to do a number of jobs satisfactorily.]

all the same Nevertheless † *Of course he's been very busy. All the same, he should have answered your letter.*

all the same to (all one to) It makes no difference to † *It's all the same to me whether you go or stay.*

all there Mentally alert (mentally deficient in negative) † *He looks as if he isn't all there, poor fellow.*

all told In total † *A lot of people came to the exhibition – over a thousand, all told.*

all up with At an end (referring to a person's life, prospects, etc) † *The doctor says there is nothing he can do. I'm afraid it's all up with him.* † *Once the police discovered the letter he had written, it was all up with him.*

all very well Satisfactory within certain limits, as far as it goes † *You have offered to pay me what you owe. That's all very well, but how soon will you be able to do it?* [ALSO: **all well and good** Satisfactory, even though it may not completely fulfil hopes or expectations † *If you can deliver half the goods I ordered, all well and good.*]

ALLEY *n.*

a blind alley Something without prospect for the future † *His present job is a blind alley. He has no hope of promotion.*

ALONE *predic. adj. & adv.*

let alone Not to mention, without referring to † *He has enough difficulty in getting the money for food, let alone spending it on holidays abroad.*

let (leave) well alone Do no more, in case one spoils what has already been done. † *He won't like it if you interfere. Let well alone.*

ALONG *prep.*

From one end to the other, or part of the way † *I was walking along the road when I met her.*

along with Together with † *Put it over there, along with the others.*

ALONG *adv.*
Indicating movement † *Come along! I can't wait any longer.* † *She was pulling him along by his hair.*

ALSO-RAN *n.*
Person or animal taking part in a race or contest without success † *I didn't win any of the three prizes. I'm afraid I was just an also-ran.*

AMONG(ST) *prep.*
1 Surrounded by; in the middle of † *He left his castle and went out to live among the common people.* [NOTE: It must be followed by a plural noun or pronoun – *Switzerland lies* between *France, Italy, Austria and Germany.*] 2 Included in a group of things † *I found this letter among some old papers.* 3 One of † *Hemingway is among the greatest American novelists.* 4 Indicating division, distribution † *He left his property to be distributed among his children.*

ANGLE *v.i.*
angle for Use hints, tricks to get something † *When she mentioned her new dress, it was obvious that she was angling for compliments.*

ANSWER *v.t. & i.*
answer back Answer rudely or impudently.
answer for 1 Make oneself responsible for † *I will come myself, but I can't answer for the rest of the family.* 2 Be held responsible for † *It was his advice that caused all the trouble. He has a lot to answer for.*

ANYTHING *n.*
anything but Not in the least (when used alone or with a word that implies certain qualities) † ⟩ *Did you enjoy yourself at the party?* ⟩ *Anything but. It was an awful bore.* † *The climb proved anything but easy* (i.e. very difficult).

APART FROM *prep.*
1 Other than † *Who else is coming, apart from your brother?*
2 Independently of; as well as † *Moving house is difficult. Apart from the legal business, there is all the packing to be done.* [NOTE: 'Apart' is really an adverb and in some sentences, therefore, 'apart from' means 'separate from' † *Her flat is apart from the rest of the house.*]

APOLOGY *n.*
an apology for A very poor example of † *There is scarcely a bubble to be seen. It is an apology for champagne.*

APPLE *n.*
the apple of one's eye The favourite; person loved most dearly † *Don't criticise his daughter in front of him. She's the apple of his eye.*

upset the (someone's) apple cart Spoil the (his) scheme † *If we can buy the shares before him, it will upset his apple cart.*

APRON *n.*

tied to her apron strings Completely under her (mother's, wife's) control † *You never see him at the pub unless his mother is away. He is tied to her apron strings.*

ARM *n.*

keep (someone) at arm's length Avoid familiarity with him † *He is not to be trusted; keep him at arm's length.*

arm-in-arm *adv.* Used of two persons walking side by side, with the arm of one round the arm of the other.

up in arms Protesting strongly (not necessarily carrying weapons) † *People are up in arms about the proposal to build an airport here.*

AROUND *adv.*

to have been around To have travelled widely and therefore acquired knowledge, sophistication † *He's been around. He knows the world.*

AS *conj.*

as for As far as you are concerned (implying contempt) † *The others are too young to know any better, but as for you, John, you ought to be ashamed of yourself.*

as if Used in exclamations to express disbelief or annoyance or to emphasise the opposite attitude from the verb following † *You must be joking! As if he could really have said that!* † *He's given me this pile of letters to type. As if I hadn't got enough to do already!*

it's not as if Also used to emphasise opposite of following verb, but frequently in double negative construction † *He has only himself to blame for what happened. It's not as if I hadn't warned him* (I had warned him frequently).

as it is As the situation is at present, things being as they are † *The market is bad enough as it is, without a strike to make things worse.* † *I would like to have seen you today. As it is, I will wait until tomorrow.*

ASK *v.t. & i.*

ask after Ask about † *I saw Mrs Jones in the supermarket. She asked after you* (asked how you were).

ask for Used sarcastically to mean invite something unpleasant † *So you refuse to apologise. Very well, you've asked for it!*

if you ask me In my opinion (implying 'if you were to ask me, I would say') † *He is very bad-mannered, if you ask me.*

AT *prep.*

1 Indicating place † *He is at his office.* [NOTE: 'At' is generally used for small towns, villages; 'in' for cities, countries, etc. Usage depends on importance of place to speaker *Darwin lived at Downe, a small village in Kent,* but *I'm so glad you have come to live in our village.* Also note *at the corner of the street, in Oxford Street,* but *get off the bus at Oxford Street* meaning the Oxford Street stop.] **2** In the direction of (used with verbs such as 'shoot', 'aim', 'throw,' etc (*See* **to 2**). **3** Indicating attempt to reach, understand something † *I had to make a guess at the meaning of the word.* **4** Indicating distance † *Hold it at arm's length.* **5** Indicating a point or period (*See* NOTE) of time † *I will see you at 2 o'clock.* [NOTE: 'At' is also used for festivals *at Christmas, at Easter,* but use *on a day, in a month, year.* Also note *at breakfast* but *in the morning,* and *at night* but *in (during) the night* † *It's very noisy at night, because there are so many planes passing overhead.* † *I woke up in the night. I thought I heard a noise.*] **6** Indicating age † *He left school at (the age of) 18.* **7** Indicating order, sequence † *He passed his driving test at the second attempt.* **8** Indicating frequency, or repetition † *At times (sometimes) he used to go for long walks.* † *Buses pass the end of the road at regular intervals.* **9** Doing (implying disapproval) † *What is he at? He should have been back long ago.* [ALSO: **at it** Engaged in some activity † *They're always at it, arguing night and day.*] **10** Indicating rate or movement or price † *He was driving at forty miles an hour.* † *Petrol at thirty new pence a gallon.*

ATTENTION *n.*

pay attention to Take notice of † *Pay attention to me!*

pay (one's) attentions to (a woman) Be kind and polite (to her) in the hope of gaining (her) affection or liking.

AU PAIR *predic. adj.*

Arrangement by which a person lives with another's family in a different country and helps with the work in return for board and lodging. Now used as a noun to mean any foreign girl working in a household on these terms (while studying the language, for example).

AUNT *n.*

aunt Sally Target for abuse (often used for an argument deliberately introduced so that it may be demolished).

AVERSION *n.*

pet aversion Someone or something one particularly dislikes † *Don't talk to me about him! He's my pet aversion.*

AWAKENING *n.*

rude awakening Sudden realisation of something unpleasant † *It was a rude awakening for him when he discovered the factory was to be closed down.*

AWAY *adv. part.*

1 To or at another place. **2** Continuously, not allowing interruption † *He was working away, taking no notice of the rest of us.* **3** Indicating loss, disappearance † *You can't explain it all away by saying it was an accident* (cause doubts and questions to cease).

AWFUL *adj.*

Really inspiring awe, terror, but colloquially used to mean very bad, terrible † *The concert was awful.*

AWFULLY *adv.*

Very † *I'm awfully pleased to meet you* ('very' is always the better word to use). *Thanks awfully* (Thank you very much).

AXE *n.*

have an axe to grind Private aims (for advantage, revenge) † *Like all politicians, he says he wants to do good for people, but I think he has an axe to grind.*

BABY *n.*

hold the baby Be left to carry out, bear the responsibility for something difficult or unpleasant † *The manager made the decision and then left me to hold the baby.*

baby-sit *v.i.* Look after small children (for pay) while parents are away for a short time. [ALSO: **baby-sitter** *n.* Person who does this.]

BACK *n.*

the back of beyond Somewhere a long way from centres of civilisation (usually suggesting inconvenience, lack of facilities) † *I am glad to be working in London again. My last job was in the back of beyond.* [ALSO: **the backwoods** Used in the same context.]

with (have) one's back to the wall (Be) in a difficult position or situation, from which there is no retreat † *There is no way out. We have our backs to the wall.*

break the back of Complete the most important part of (a piece of work) so that what remains is easy; destroy the main element of resistance.

put one's back into Use all one's energy in order to do something † *If we put our backs into it, we'll finish the job this afternoon.*

put someone's back up Make him uncooperative or resentful † *The new manager put my back up as soon as he arrived. He spoke as if we hadn't done any work before then.*

BACK *adj.* (used attrib.)

get one's own back Get one's revenge † *I'll get my own back (on you) one of these days.*

BACK *v.t. & i.*

back down Give up a strong or obstinate attitude † *The union have refused to back down over their wage claim.*

back out (of) Withdraw from (a scheme, agreement, etc) † *He wants to back out of the contract.*

back up Support † *Ask him for a rise in salary. I'll back you up.*

BACK-DATE *v.t.*

Date at a time in the past (generally in connection with wage agreements, etc) † *The nurses have been awarded a pay rise, back-dated to 1st January* (i.e. the new rate will be paid as if the award had been made on 1st January).

BACK-FIRE *v.i.*

Cause a noise through too early explosion of gas in cylinder of car, but also used of plans going wrong, suddenly producing a result contrary to what is desired † *The plot back-fired because one of the conspirators betrayed the leader to the police.*

BACKLOG *n.*

Accumulation of work which has not been done † *I'm going to the office on Sunday to try to clear off the backlog of correspondence.*

BACK-PEDAL *v.i.*

Retreat from (a proposal) after showing interest † *He said he liked the idea at first, but now he's back-pedalling from it.*

BACK-ROOM *n.*

back-room boys People concerned in a project (especially scientists etc, working in a laboratory) whose contribution is not publicised † *The successful flight of the new plane is largely due to the work of the back-room boys.*

BACKSTAIRS *adj.*

Underhand; involving intrigue † *He owes his job to backstairs influence.*

BACKWATER *n.*

Place or situation not affected by advanced ideas or change † *He spent his life in a quiet backwater, untouched by events in the capital.*

BACKWARDS *adv.*
backwards and forwards Going from one place to another and returning (suggesting repetition, monotony) † *He goes backwards and forwards to London on the train every day.*

BACON *n.*
save someone's bacon Be the means of escape from a difficult situation † *It's a good thing you managed to repair my car. You saved my bacon.*

BAD *adj.*
too bad 1 A great pity †) *I've lost my job.*) *I'm very sorry. That's too bad.* (Sometimes used without emphasis to mean *too bad for you, but not necessarily for me*). 2 (of someone) Used to express disappointment, irritation with the other person † *You promised to clean the house while I was out, and you've done nothing. That's too bad of you.*

not too bad Quite good (understatement, suggesting 'better than might have been expected').

BADLY *adv.*
badly off Poor; short of money, ideas, staff, etc (*See* **well off**) † *They're very badly off for typists. They have to write their letters by hand sometimes.*

BAG *n.*
in the bag Already certain to be achieved † *The majority of people like him. His election is in the bag.*

BAKER *n.*
baker's dozen Thirteen.

BALL *n.*
on the ball Well-informed and quick to take advantage of it † *He's on the ball. You won't find him making a fool of himself.*

play ball (with) Cooperate † *We need the Council's approval for this scheme. Do you think they'll play ball (with us)?*

start (keep) the ball rolling Begin (maintain) a discussion, sequence of events, etc † *To start the ball rolling, I shall ask Mr Taylor to review what happened at the last meeting.*

BALLOON *n.*
the balloon goes up The critical moment occurs † *I was on holiday when the balloon went up* (when war was declared, for example).

BANDWAGON *n.*
get (jump) on the bandwagon Recognise the popularity and success of a person or plan, investment and support him (invest) in the hope of personal gain † *Once it was clear that he would be elected, all the uncommitted politicians tried to jump on the bandwagon.*

BANK *v.t. & i.*

bank on Place all one's hopes on † *I am banking on an increase in salary at Christmas.*

BANK *n.*

break the bank Strictly, win all the money held by a casino in playing roulette, etc, and therefore stop the game, but used generally in the sense of using up all the money available † *I ought not to have bought it, but I don't suppose it will break the bank.*

BAR *prep.*

bar none Without exception † *This is the best hotel I have ever stayed in, bar none.* [NOTE: 'Bar' is found as a preposition only in this phrase and 'all over bar the shouting' (*See* **shouting**).]

BARGAIN *n.*

into the bargain As well; in addition † *I waited for him for half an hour. By the end of it, I was in a bad mood, and freezing cold into the bargain.*

BARGAIN *v.i. & t.*

bargain for Be prepared for; expect † *I hadn't bargained for her mother coming to the cinema with her.* † *He thought the judge would not punish him severely, but he got more than he bargained for* (he was unpleasantly surprised).

BARK *n.*

his bark is worse than his bite He threatens people, but is unlikely to carry out his threat.

BAT *n.*

off one's own bat Without help, often without others knowing about it † *I never gave him permission to make the arrangements. He did it off his own bat.*

BAY *n.*

at bay Cornered by one's enemies and forced to defend oneself † *The police feared that the criminal, finding himself at bay, would try to shoot his way out.* [ALSO: **keep (hold) at bay** Keep enemies at a distance, prevent them from destroying one.]

BE *aux. v.*

[NOTE: Apart from being used to form the continuous tenses of other verbs and the passive voice, the auxiliary verb is used in various ways with *to* infinitive. These are listed below.] **1** Expressing orders, prohibitions (= must/must not) † *You are to report to the Commanding officer.* † *This exit is not to be used except in case of emergency.* **2** Expressing intention, mutual arrangement † *The happy couple are to spend their* *honeymoon in Paris.* † *We are all to meet at my house at 7 o'clock.* **3** In questions, asking for instructions † *Am I to go with him?* (Is it your wish that I should . . .). **4** Expressing possibility (= can/may) † *Men with long hair are to be seen everywhere nowadays.* **5** Indicating destiny † *It was to be the last time he saw his native city (although he did not know this at the time).* **6** Indicating purpose † *This letter is to inform you that your complaint has been noted.* **7** (**were**) In conditional sentences, indicating supposition † *If I were to offer you the job, would you accept it?* † *Were I to offer you the job, people would accuse me of favouritism.* [NOTE; The second example, employing inversion of subject and verb, implies that the possibility of the job being offered is more remote. Each supposition here is more remote than *if I offered you the job* or *suppose I offered you the job.*

BE-ALL *n.*

be-all and end-all (only in this phrase) The supremely important thing † *It would be nice to have a new house, but it's not the be-all and end-all of our lives.*

BEANS *n.*

full of beans Full of vigour and energy † *You're full of beans this morning, running up the stairs.*

BEAR *v.t. & i.*

bear down on Approach quickly, threatening punishment † *I had just picked an apple from the tree when I saw the farmer bearing down on me.*

bear on Have relation to † *That bears on what you were saying about the problem.* [ALSO: **have a bearing on** The same meaning, though the relationship is usually less obvious.]

bear out Confirm (a statement) † *I knew nothing about it, I promise you. John will bear me out* (or *bear out what I am saying*).

bear up Not show feelings of pain, despair † *Bear up! The worst is over now.* † *She has borne up bravely throughout her illness.*

bear with Be patient with † *Bear with me for a while. It's not easy to explain what happened.*

BEAT *n.*

off-beat *adj.* Unconventional, unusual † *He is an eccentric person, rather off-beat.* † *I know an off-beat little restaurant that might interest you.*

BEAUTY *n.*

the beauty of it The point of a conversation, story, that gives it interest † *They made a mistake about the meeting-place. The beauty of it was that each went to the other's house at the same time.*

BED *n.*

get out of bed on the wrong side Said of someone who is bad-tempered in the morning † *What's the matter with you? Did you get out of bed on the wrong side?*

BED-SITTER *n.*

(short for 'bed-sitting-room') Room used for living in and sleeping in.

BEE *n.*

a bee in one's bonnet A fixed idea; an obsession † *All his political speeches are about race relations. He has a bee in his bonnet about them.*

make a bee-line (for) Follow a straight line (to a place) in order to get there as quickly as possible † *She made a bee-line for me as soon as she saw me.*

BEFORE *prep.*

1 Earlier than † *I loved you before I saw you, when I first heard your name.* 2 As a preparation for (usually with gerund) † *Before having dinner, let's have a drink.* 3 In front of † *A comes before B.* † *Dukes come before earls.* † *I will place your request before the Committee.* [NOTE: 'Before' is only used in preference to 'in front of' when referring to list or order of arrangement, social precedence, etc, or when physical position is not emphasised.] 4 In the presence of † *I'll repeat what I said before anyone you care to name.* 5 Rather than † *Before consenting to that, I'd kill myself.*

before long Soon.

BEG *v.t. & i.*

go begging Be wasted, because no one wants it † *It's a shame to see all these things going begging.*

BEGIN *v.t. & i.*

to begin with In the first place † *There are a number of reasons why I won't agree. To begin with, the plan will not be economical.*

BEHIND *prep.*

1 At the back of (often implying hidden by and therefore secrecy) † *There's a tennis court behind those trees.* † *Who is behind this plan to build a new factory?* (Who supports it?) *I don't trust his expression of friendship. I'm sure there's something behind it* (some secret or dishonest motive). 2 Later than † *These orders are a month behind schedule.* 3 In the past † *Let us put our troubles behind us and face the future with confidence.* 4 Remaining after † *He is dead, but the poetry he has left behind him will live for ever.* 5 Not as advanced as (in learning etc) † *He is behind the rest of the class.* 6 Indicating that one has passed through † *Shut the door behind you as you go out.*

BEHIND *adv.*

In arrears with, late with † *I know I'm behind with my rent.* † *We can't get enough staff, and so we are terribly behind (with our work).*

BELL *n.*

that rings a bell That calls something to mind † *Grimdyke? That rings a bell. I once knew someone called Grimdyke.*

BELOW *prep.*

Lower than (in position, value, status, in a scale, etc) † *People were singing and dancing in the street below our window.* † *The temperature fell below zero.*

BELOW *adv.*

1 At a lower level. 2 Lower down on a page, or later in a book, paper, etc † *The scheme is referred to in detail below.*

BELT *n.*

below the belt Unfair(ly) (of blow or attack) † *You should have not mentioned his getting drunk in front of his wife. That was hitting below the belt.*

BEND *v.t. & i.*

bend over backwards Do everything possible (to help make things easy for someone) † *We have bent over backwards to try to understand his point of view.*

BENEATH *prep.*

1 Underneath (usually not clearly visible, because obscured by something on top) † *The book is on my desk beneath some papers.* 2 Below (used figuratively to suggest inferiority) † *Your actions are beneath contempt* (so despicable that they do not even justify contempt). *He thinks the rest of us are beneath his notice* (we are not important enough to him for him to notice us).

BESIDE *prep.*

1 At the side of † *Come and sit beside me.* 2 Compared to † *He has not done badly, but he seems unambitious beside the previous manager.*

beside oneself Without any control of one's actions because of emotion † *She flung her arms around her son, beside herself with happiness.*

BESIDES *prep.*

as well as † *Besides John, there is the rest of the family to consider.*

BESIDES *adv.*

Moreover † *I haven't time to read the book, and besides, the subject doesn't interest me very much.*

BEST *adj.*

all for the best Eventually with good results, though they may not seem likely now † *It is very annoying, when one suffers a disappointment, to hear someone say, 'It is probably all for the best.'*

at best The best possible result that can be expected under the circumstances (implying that worse results are more probable) † *Her husband's death has left her without any money. At best, she will have to sell her house.*

at the best of times Even when circumstances are most favourable † *It is hard to find a good secretary at the best of times.*

the best part of The greater part of (used of time) † *I have been waiting for you for the best part of an hour* (more than half an hour).

have the best of it Win (an argument, contest, etc) † *It was an interesting discussion, but I think we had the best of it.*

make the best of (a bad job) Achieve the best results possible in a difficult situation; resign oneself to being incapable of achieving more than a limited amount † *He phoned at the last minute to say he couldn't come to dinner, so I made the best of a bad job and ate his portion myself* † *It's no use talking about what we ought to have done. We did nothing and now we must make the best of it.*

to the best of As well as one can, as far as one knows † *I shall serve you to the best of my ability.* † *To the best of my knowledge, he has not worked here for over ten years.*

BET *v.i.*

I bet I am sure (and would be prepared to wager money that I am right) † *I bet he didn't tell his wife that he went to Paris for the week-end.*

BETTER *adj.*

get the better of Defeat (particularly outwit in negotiations, argument, etc) † *He is a good businessman. One would have to be very clever to get the better of him.*

better off Richer (*See* **well off, badly off**).

BETWEEN *prep.*

1 Within time, distance, amount specified † *Where were you last night between 8 o'clock and midnight?* 2 With one thing on one side and another on the other side † *Come and sit here between Mary and me.* 3 Implying emotional connection † *How can you speak of leaving me when so much has passed between us?* † *There is no love lost between them.* (They do not like each other.) 4 Implying intervention † *They suddenly called off the wedding. I think her mother came between them* (used her influence to separate them). 5 Implying combined effort † *Between us we ought to be able to resolve the problem.* 6 Implying shared effort, money † *The work of the office is shared between the three of us.*

between ourselves, between you and me In confidence † *Between ourselves, I think he's fallen in love with you.*

BETWEEN *adv.*

in between *prep. & adv.* Used, with meaning of **between** *prep*. **2** but suggesting repetition † *There are garage spaces in between the houses* (or adverbially, *houses with garage spaces in between*).

few and far between At wide intervals, scarce † *Petrol stations are few and far between on these country roads.*

BETWIXT *prep.*

betwixt and between (only used in this expression, almost always adverbially) Neither one thing nor the other, but somewhere between; incomplete † *I'm neither for nor against your argument but find myself betwixt and between.* † *Nothing is settled yet. It's all betwixt and between.*

BEYOND *prep.*

1 Further than; out of reach of (in place, capabilities, etc) † *Don't go beyond the trees. I don't want to lose sight of you.* † *His lecture was beyond me.* † *He tried my patience beyond endurance* (to a point which was more than I could stand). **2** Other than † *I know nothing about him beyond what you told me.* **3** Above (also in the sense of 'out of reach of') † *He behaved perfectly. His action was beyond reproach.*

BIRD *n.*

Once used to suggest a wise or cunning old man in phrases like 'a wise old bird', 'a wily bird', but now commonly used to mean girl or girlfriend.

a bird in the hand is worth two in the bush (proverbial) It is wiser to hold on to what one already has, rather than risk it in attempting to gain more.

kill two birds with one stone Achieve two different ends by the same action † *We'll talk about out holiday plans when you bring back the records I lent you. In that way, we can kill two birds with one stone.*

BIT *n.*

a bit (+ adj.) Rather; a little † *I'm going to bed early. I feel a bit tired.*

a bit of a (+ n.) Rather a † *I'm sorry he's coming. He's a bit of a bore.*

bit by bit Little by little; gradually † *Bit by bit, he managed to repay everything he owed.*

every bit as (good) as Quite as (good) as; equally (good) † *Brown's mustard is every bit as good as Green's.*

not a bit of it Not at all; on the contrary (contradictory, not a polite reply) †) *I suppose he was angry when you told him about it.*) *Not a bit of it. He just laughed.*

bits and pieces (always plural) Odds and ends; a variety of small objects. Often used to mean small household tasks or chores † *The cupboard is full of bits and pieces. I intend to sort them all out one day.* † *I've got a few bits and pieces at home to get on with.*

BITE *v.t. & i.*
Be attracted to (a proposition etc, implying something not really in one's interest, like a fish biting the bait) † *We've made the proposition very attractive to him. I think he will bite.*

bite off more than one can chew Undertake a task beyond one's ability, capacity † *They accepted every order that came to them and now they can't fulfil them. They've bitten off more than they can chew.*

once bitten, twice shy Proverbial expression, meaning 'once one has been deceived, one will be twice as careful the next time one finds oneself in a similar situation' † *The last time I bought some apples from him, half of them were bad. I won't deal with him again. Once bitten twice shy.*

BLACK *n.*
in the black In a sound financial position, not owing money (*See* **red**) † *The firm must cut its expenditure in order to stay in the black.*

in black and white In writing, print † *His promise over the telephone is not enough. Tell him we want it in black and white.*

BLACK *v.t. & i.*
black out 1 Faint, suffer loss of memory † *I must have blacked out when the car crashed because when I woke up I was in hospital.* [ALSO: **black-out** *n.* Loss of memory.] **2** Shut off all electricity, or cover up all lights (to try to avoid bombing in war, etc). [ALSO: **black-out** *n.*]

BLANK *n.*
a (complete, total) blank Empty (used particularly of the mind) † *I don't remember anything. My mind's a blank on the subject.*

draw a blank Get nothing (as a result of looking for something) † *The police have been looking for the criminal all over London, but so far they have drawn a blank.*

BLANKET *n.*
a wet blanket Someone who prevents others from enjoying themselves (in company) by being gloomy † *You mustn't invite him. He's sure to be a wet blanket.*

BLESSING *n.*
a blessing in disguise Something that proves fortunate, though it was thought at first to be unlucky † *It was a blessing in disguise that I lost my job. I got a better one the next day.*

BLOOD *n.*

in the (one's) blood Part of one's character or personality because of family or national background † *Riding is in her blood. Her family have bred horses for generations.*

in cold blood Without emotion; deliberately † *It's one thing to kill a man in a fight, in self-defence, another to shoot him in cold blood.* [ALSO: **cold-blooded** *adj.* Callous; unemotional.]

cause bad blood between Cause people to dislike each other † *There was an argument over land between the two families which caused bad blood between them.*

blood is thicker than water (proverbial) Family ties are stronger than those with other people (and therefore people usually support their relations against others) † *He knew that his brother started the fight, but in court he blamed the other man. Blood is thicker than water.*

BLOW *v.i. & t.*

blow over Pass (used of storms, trouble disappearing) † *They had a terrible row but by tomorrow the whole thing will have blown over.*

blow up 1 Explode, destroy with explosives † *Someone had placed a bomb on board, and it blew up the plane.* 2 Inflate, expand † *Father is in the next room, blowing up balloons for the children's party.* † *I want to blow up this negative to make a (photographic) print six inches by ten inches.* 3 Start (of storms) † *A storm blew up without warning.*

BLUE *adj.*

blue Depressed † *I felt blue this morning so I bought a new hat to cheer myself up.*

BLUE *n.*

the blues Condition of being depressed or folk music expressing this condition.

out of the blue Unexpectedly † *A letter arrived out of the blue from some friends in Canada, inviting me to stay with them.* [ALSO: **a bolt from the blue** An unexpected event, causing surprise or shock.]

BLUFF *n.*

call someone's bluff Force him to show whether what he states or pretends to be the case is really so (from playing cards) † *The garage said they couldn't repair my car until next week, so I called their bluff by threatening to go elsewhere.*

BOARD *n.*

above board Honest, open, legal † *They can be trusted in any negotiation. They are always fair and above board.*

on board On a ship (or aeroplane) † *How many passengers are there on board?*

go by the board Be abandoned † *The changes in the regulations for bridges mean that our plans will go by the board.*

BOAT *n.*

(all) in the same boat In the same difficult situation † *We are all in the same boat, so the best thing we can do is to help one another.*

miss the boat (*See* **bus**).

rock the boat Upset the smooth progress of (a negotiation, etc), cause disagreement between partners † *Everything was going very well until Smith refused to support the rest of us. It's typical of him to rock the boat.*

burn one's boats (always plural) Leave oneself without any means of retreat (originally meaning a deliberate action to force oneself to go forward, but now often used to imply rashly exposing oneself to trouble) † *I told him I would never work for him again. So there's no going back. I've burned my boats.*

BOG *v.t.*

be (get) bogged down (usually passive) Be stuck at some point in negotiations, production, etc, and unable to make progress † *The committee got bogged down by little points of detail and never reached a decision on the main issues.*

BOIL *v.i. & t.*

boil down 1 Amount to † *They say they don't like the scheme, but what it boils down to is that they are too busy to give it real attention.* **2** Condense † *Your article is much too long. Can you boil it down to 500 words?*

BOLSTER *v.t.*

bolster up Give support to (Government, structure, etc) in danger of collapsing † *What's the point of trying to bolster up a group of people who won't even help themselves?*

BOLT *n.*

a bolt from the blue (*See* **blue**).

shot one's bolt (used in past tense only) Made one's final effort without success † *If he had won that game, he might have had the strength to go on. But he's shot his bolt now and is certain to lose.*

BOMBSHELL *n.*

A sudden surprising event, piece of news † *My son rang up to say he had just got married to a girl we have never heard of. It was such a bombshell!*

BONE *n.*

have a bone to pick with Have a cause for argument, disagreement with

20

† *I have a bone to pick with you. Why weren't you at work yesterday?*
[ALSO: **a bone of contention** Subject producing disagreement.]

make no bones about Not waste time by introducing a subject with polite phrases
† *I'll make no bones about it. Your behaviour has been disgraceful.*

BOOK *n.*

a closed book A subject one knows nothing about † *I'm afraid biochemistry is a closed book to me.*

in my book In my opinion † *In my book, a man can never have an excuse for hitting a woman.*

be (get) in someone's good (bad) books (always plural) Be in (out of) favour with someone † *He brought the teacher some flowers, wanting to be in her good books.*

bring someone to book Find evidence to convict, arrest † *He escaped detection for years but he was eventually brought to book.* [ALSO: **book** *v.t.* Write down someone's name with the intention of making a charge against him † *The policeman booked me for speeding.*]

go by the book Follow instructions and refuse to use one's own initiative † *It is best to go by the book in the army. Then you can never be accused of doing anything wrong.*

suit one's book Be convenient to † *It suits his book to be pleasant to us. He knows we are good clients of his firm.*

BOOK *v.t. & i.*

Reserve (seat in the theatre, table at restaurant, etc) (commonly used with 'up') † *I am going to book up for the concert.* † *I'm sorry. The play is completely booked (up)* (there are no seats left). † *I'm afraid I can't accept your invitation. I am already booked up on that evening* (I have an engagement).

book in Register (by writing one's name in a book) † *Have you booked in at the reception desk?* (registered at a hotel, conference, etc). [NOTE: **booking office** Office where tickets are bought at station, airport. Theatre tickets, etc are bought at the **box office**.]

BOOT *n.*

the boot is on the other foot The responsibility or blame is the opposite of what has been stated † *You say I'm to blame because I dropped the parcel, but the boot's on the other foot. You should have wrapped it up better.*

too big for his boots (always plural) Unpleasantly aware of his own importance † *He has grown too big for his boots since they made him manager.*

BOTHER *v.t. & i.*

can't be bothered Be too tired or indifferent to trouble oneself about a thing

† *I can't be bothered (to ring him) at this time of night. I'll do it tomorrow.*

BOTTLE *v.t.*

bottle up Control emotion, feeling (usually with sense of giving way to it at a more appropriate time) † *He bottled up his hatred of her while she was there, but as soon as she had gone, he called her a lot of names.*

BOUND *n.*

out of bounds (always plural) Outside limits one is allowed to enter † *The village near the camp was declared out of bounds to the soldiers.*

BOUND *part. adj.*

bound for Going in the direction of † *That ship is bound for New York.*

bound to 1 Certain † *Ask John. He's bound to know where it is.* 2 Obliged † *Don't feel bound to come if you don't really want to.*

bound up in Involved in, very busy with † *He is so bound up in his work that he never stops thinking about it.*

bound up with Closely connected with † *His life has always been bound up with the family business.*

BOW *v.i. & t.*

bow out Accept one's retirement, dismissal gracefully † *It's time for me to bow out (of public life) and make way for a younger man.*

bow to (wishes, knowledge, opinions of others) Submit to, accept † *I thought she was a relative of his. But I bow to your superior knowledge of the family.*

BOX *n.*

box number Used for an advertisement in a newspaper when the advertiser does not wish to give his name and address.

box office Office where tickets for theatre, cinema, etc, are bought (*See* **book**).

BRAIN *n.*

have something on the brain Be obsessed with an idea, subject † *He blames everything that goes wrong on the taxes. He's got taxation on the brain.*

beat one's brains (always plural) Make a great effort to find the answer to something or remember † *I can't remember her name. Well, it's no good beating your brains over it.*

pick someone's brains Make use of his (specialised) knowledge in order to find the answer to a problem † *I've come to pick your brains. You're a metallurgist, and I've been asked this question about steel.*

BRAINWASH *v.t.*

Remove ideas from someone's mind and substitute others (by means of constant mental pressure) † *Everyone is changing to this product. They must have been brainwashed by all the advertising.*

BRAINWAVE *n.*

A sudden bright idea † *I did not believe I would ever find an answer to the problem and then I suddenly had a brainwave.*

BRANCH *v.i.*

branch out Expand in a new direction † *A big modern company needs a variety of interests, so we've branched out into new fields.*

BRASS *n.*

get down to brass tacks State the real reasons for talking; begin bargaining, etc † *You've hinted that you would be willing to sell it. Let's get down to brass tacks. How much do you want for it?*

BREAD *n.*

know which side one's bread is buttered Know which of two groups arguing, etc has more to offer for one's support; know where one's best interest lies † *You didn't expect him to support you against his boss, did you? He knows which side his bread is buttered.*

bread line Line of people waiting for charity, food, but used to mean extreme poverty † *There's no reason to be so mean. We're not on the bread line yet.*

BREAK *v.t. & i.*

break oneself of (a habit) Make a successful effort to give it up † *I smoke far too much. I wish I could break myself of the habit.*

break down 1 Separate † *We can break the process down into four stages, and then it will be easier to understand.* 2 Stop, especially because of mechanical failure † *My car broke down, and I had to walk.* † *Negotiations have broken down.* 3 Collapse. † *Her health broke down under the strain* † *She broke down when she heard the news* (i.e. She burst into tears and wept uncontrollably). [ALSO: **breakdown** *n.* 1 Report indicating different stages in detail. 2 (Mechanical) failure. 3 Collapse of health (nervous breakdown).]

break in 1 Enter a building by force † *Some burglars had broken in* (but into *the house*) *and stolen her jewels.* [ALSO: **break-in** *n.* Forced entry.] 2 Train a horse (by breaking its will to be independent).

break in on Interrupt (people), disturb their privacy (usually by forcing entry) † *The police broke in on them while they were planning the robbery.*

break into 1 Enter by force (*See* **break in**, above). 2 Interrupt (a conversation, discussion, etc). 3 Suddenly start (laughing, singing, running) † *Without warning, he broke into song.* † *When he saw me following him, he broke into a run.*

break off 1 Stop speaking suddenly † *He broke off in the middle of a sentence and looked round.* 2 End (a relationship) suddenly † *He broke off his*

23

engagement to her the day before the wedding. **3** Stop temporarily (for a rest, etc) † *Let's break off (work) for a while and have a cup of tea.*

break out 1 Escape (from prison) † *He has broken out of prison and is making his way towards London.* **2** Start, appear † *War broke out the following day.* † *A rash broke out all over his face.* † *He broke out in a rash.* **3** Speak impulsively, violently † *'You've no right to say that!' he broke out.* [ALSO: **outbreak** *n.* Sudden appearance of something dangerous (fire, violence, disease, etc). **break-out** (USA) *n.* Escape of several prisoners at once.]

break through Force a way through an obstacle. [ALSO: **breakthrough** *n.* Successful development in commerce, technology, etc, overcoming previous difficulties † *The discovery of penicillin was an outstanding breakthrough in the war against disease.*]

break up 1 Smash, split † *Help me to break up these old boxes. We can use them for firewood.* **2** Disperse, separate † *The police broke up the crowd of demonstrators.* † *The meeting broke up at 10 o'clock* (The people separated and went home). *The school breaks up three days before Christmas* (The pupils go home for their holidays). [ALSO: **break-up** *n.* Destruction by dispersal.]

break with 1 End a friendship with † *We could no longer agree. I had to break with him.* **2** Separate oneself from † *It is hard to break with old ties, and leave a place you are fond of.*

BREAK *n.*

Opportunity to do better † *The poor man was waiting outside my office. 'Give me a break,' he said.*

a bad (lucky) break A piece of bad (good) luck † *It was a bad break for him that he was suddenly taken ill just before he was to go on holiday.*

BREATH *n.*

take one's breath away Surprise so much that one cannot speak † *When my girlfriend suddenly told me that she was going away for a year, it took my breath away.*

BRICK *n.*

drop a brick Do or say something inappropriate without realising it (particularly by offending or embarrassing someone else in the company) † *I've just dropped an awful brick. I said, 'Who's that fat lady?' to the man next to me and he said, 'My wife.'*

BRIEF *v.t.*

Give someone necessary information about a subject so that they can act on it (particularly make speeches, do business, etc) † *The Prime Minister is going to brief the Cabinet on the latest situation in the Middle East.* [ALSO: **brief** *n.* The information given † *The minister departed from his* *brief (He stopped using the information of official speech prepared for him, and spoke on his own account).]*

BRIEF *adj.*

in brief In a few words (used to cut short a long detailed explanation) † *There are strikes in the factories, outbreaks of violence in the streets. . . In brief, the country is in a serious position.*

BRING *v.t. & i.*

bring about Cause (gradually) † *His kindness brought about a change in her attitude towards him.*

bring in 1 Produce, yield † *His shares bring (him) in an income of £1000 a year.* 2 Introduce (a new fashion) † *This is the biggest change in women's clothes since they brought in the mini-skirt.* [NOTE: Ford *brought* the motor-car *into* popular use.]

bring on Be the cause of † *He was caught in the rain for an hour last night. That must have brought on his cold.*

bring out 1 Demonstrate (by examples) † *His book brings out the difficulties which face people beginning a new life in a strange country.* 2 Publish † *We hope to bring out your book before Christmas.*

bring round 1 Convert † *It won't be easy to bring him round to our way of thinking.* 2 Bring back to consciousness (after fainting, etc) † *Throw a little water on her face. Perhaps that will bring her round.*

bring to Persuade (usually used reflexively) † *I could never bring myself to do anything so dishonest.*

bring up 1 Raise (a subject) † *The meeting was nearly over when he brought up the problem of the new wage rates.* 2 Rear a child † *Her parents died when she was very young, and she was brought up by her aunt and uncle.* † *What a well brought-up child!* (well-behaved, because of her parents' example, etc). 3 Vomit † *He has stomach trouble. He brought up all his dinner as soon as he had eaten it.*

BROAD *adj.*

it's as broad as it's long It makes no difference either way † *Is it better to go by train or by car? It's as broad as it's long. They both take the same time from here.*

BROKE *adj.*

Without any money † *I can't lend you anything. I'm broke myself.*

BROOM *n.*

a new broom A new man in authority who is certain to change things (in order to demonstrate that authority).

BROWN *v.t. & i.*

browned off *adj. part.* Bored, fed up † *I'm browned off, sitting here all day with nothing to do.*

BRUNT *n.*

bear the brunt (used only in this phrase) Be at the main point of an attack; suffer the main consequences † *As the main shareholder in the company, he will bear the brunt of the loss.*

BRUSH *v.t.*

brush aside Take no notice of objections, opposition † *He brushed aside our arguments as if they had no importance.*

brush up Study in order to achieve previous competence † *I shall have to brush up my French before we go to Paris. It's so long since I spoke the language.*

BUCK *v.i. & t.*

buck up **1** Hurry up † *Buck up! We shall be late.* **2** Cheer up; restore spirits, strength † *Have a whisky! It will buck you up.*

BUCK *n.*

pass the buck Pass on the unwanted responsibility for something † *He hates taking decisions. He always passes the buck (on to someone else).*

BUCKLE *v.t. & i.*

buckle down Use one's energy to work hard (particularly when this involves concentration) † *The examinations are in two weeks' time. You will have to buckle down (to your work) if you want to pass.*

BUILT-IN *adj.*

Constructed as an integral part † *The flat has built-in furniture* (wardrobes set in the wall, for example). † *The scheme has a number of built-in advantages which ensure it against failure.*

BUILT-UP *adj.*

built-up area Densely populated area, with a large number of buildings on it.

BULK *n.*

the bulk of The greater part of or number of † *The bulk of our produce is despatched by road.*

in bulk In large amounts † *As wholesalers, we don't deal in small quantities. Everything is ordered in bulk.*

BULL *n.*

like a bull in a china shop Clumsily, awkwardly in a situation where care is required † *Don't rush into the negotiations like a bull in a china shop.*

take the bull by the horns Face a difficult situation and use direct measures to overcome it † *I can't wait for you to mention the matter to him. I shall take the bull by the horns and confront him with it myself.*

BUS *n.*

miss the bus (boat) Lose an opportunity † *If he really wanted the house, he* *should have told me. Now he has missed the bus, because I've sold it to someone else.*

BUSH *n.*

beat about the bush Talk about a subject without coming to the real point at issue † *Let's not beat about the bush. The important thing is this . . .*

BUSINESS *n.*

no business to No right to † *You have no business to question me about my private life.*

a (bad) (terrible) business An unpleasant or troublesome matter † *Three cars crashed into each other outside the house this morning. It was a terrible business.* † *It's such a business clearing up the house after a party.*

mind one's own business Keep to one's own affairs and not interfere or ask personal questions † *He asked me if I was married, so I told him to mind his own business.* [ALSO: **send someone about his business** Tell him not to intrude, interfere.]

BUSINESS-LIKE *adj.*

Practical; efficient; systematic † *I like to see things done in a business-like manner even in my own home.*

BUT *prep.*

Except † *He is never content with anything but the best* † *He was the last but one to leave the class.* † *This television set has given me nothing but trouble since I bought it.*

anything but The opposite of † *She looks anything but well* (She looks ill).

but for If it had not been for † *But for you (keeping us waiting) we should have arrived on time.*

BUT *adv.*

Only † *We can but try to make him see how unreasonable he has been.*

all but Almost † *We're all but finished now. We'll be ready in a moment.*

BUTT *v.i.*

butt in Interrupt rudely † *Don't butt in like that when I'm in the middle of a conversation.*

BUY *v.t.*

buy off Get rid of someone by paying them † *He threatened to tell the police about me so I had to buy him off.*

buy out Pay a rival to give up business, etc † *We bought out some of the smaller companies to reduce competition.*

buy up Buy as much as possible of something (in order to dominate the market, use it for a different purpose) † *The Council have bought up all the property in this road for a new housing development.*

BY *prep.*
1 Near; beside † *He has a house by the sea.* 2 Indicating direction of movement, means of travel † *Did you come by (way of) Dover or Folkestone?* † *We came by train.* 3 Past † *He went by the window while you were talking.* 4 During a period of time (only 'by day' and 'by night'). 5 Not later than † *She said she would be back by 10 o'clock.* 6 Indicating measure, period of time for buying and selling † *Coal is sold by the ton.* † *He is paid by the hour.* 7 Indicating agency † *This picture was painted by my uncle.* 8 According to † *By my watch, it is 10 o'clock.* † *By that line of reasoning, we should be unwise to consider it.* 9 Indicating difference in price, size, etc † *The price has gone up by 10 per cent.* † *We won the game by two goals to one.* 10 Indicating a part of the body or object in order to define a general statement more precisely † *He took me by the shoulders and shook me.* 11 Implying 'as a result of' † *He found out by accident.* † *He sent it to the wrong address by mistake.* 12 Indicating manner of addressing someone † *He calls his secretary by her Christian name.* 13 Indicating a series or succession of people or things at a time † *She sold all her possessions, one by one.*

by oneself 1 Alone † *I am going up to my room. I want to be by myself.* 2 Without help † *Look, Johnny has put the (toy) car together again (all) by himself.* † *I can manage by myself, thank you.*

by and by After a time, one day † *I must go now, but I'll be in your neighbourhood again by and by.*

by and large Taking everything into account † *Of course he has his faults, but he's a good fellow, by and large.*

BYGONES *n.*
let bygones be bygones (only used in plural and in this form) Let past sorrows, offences be forgotten † *Shake hands and agree to let bygones be bygones.*

BY-PASS *v.t.*
1 Take a different road in order to avoid a town (to save time, difficulty, etc) † *We'll by-pass London to avoid the traffic.* [ALSO: **by-pass** *n.* Road built to avoid main traffic centre (town, etc), joining older roads which run through it.] 2 Avoid, ignore (a problem) † *You can't by-pass a moral issue of such importance.*

CAKE *n.*

a piece of cake Something (task, etc) easily done † *That won't give me any trouble. It will be a piece of cake.*

CALL *v.t. & i.*

call for 1 Need, demand (frequently with object and verb in passive voice) † *Building a new bridge will call for a large sum of money.* † *The opposition leader called for an election (to be held).* 2 Collect † *The dustmen call for the rubbish once a week.* † *I'll call for you at 6.30 and we'll go out.* [ALSO: **called for** *part. adj.* Required, necessary (usually within the limits of responsibility) † *He did all that was called for, but showed little interest in the work.*]

uncalled for *part. adj.* Undesirable, as well as unnecessary † *Your unpleasant tone is quite uncalled for.*

not called for Unnecessary, but not undesirable † *He was willing to help but his services were not called for.*

call in 1 (*at* a place, *on* a person) Visit (indicating that one entered the building) † *I called in (at your office) (on you) this morning, but they told me that you were out.* 2 (money) Cause to be collected † *The Government called in all ten shilling notes and issued 50 pence coins instead.*

call off Cancel (an arrangement, meeting, etc) † *She gave him back his engagement ring and called off the wedding.*

call up 1 Telephone (often 'call') † *Someone called me (up) after midnight last night.* 2 Order (someone) to join the armed forces † *He was called up the day the war began.* [ALSO: **call-up** *n.* Order to join the army (often used adjectivally) † *He got his call-up papers on the same day as I did.*]

CALL *n.*

a close call A narrow escape from disaster † *The car almost ran me over. It was a close call.*

CALL-BOX *n.*

Public telephone booth † *He hasn't a 'phone at home. He is speaking from a call-box.*

CALL-BOY *n.*
Boy at theatre who warns actors when they are due to go on stage.

CALL-GIRL *n.*
Prostitute who arranges meetings by telephone.

CAN *n.*
carry the can Be forced to take the blame for something someone else has done † *It was the manager's fault, but I shall have to carry the can in his absence.*

CAN (COULD) *anom. fin.*
1 Expressing ability or capacity (including *know how to* as well as *be able to*) † *I can run faster than you.* † *He can speak French.* † ⟩ *Can you swim?* (Do you know how to?) ⟩ *Yes, but I can't swim as well as you* (I am not able to). [NOTE: 1 The future and perfect tenses here are formed with *able to*. The use of the present tense for the immediate future, however, is also possible with *can* † *I am not sure if I will be able to afford a holiday next year.* † *I regret that I have been unable to find any reference to your letter.* † *You can't come today, then. Can you come tomorrow, instead?* 2 There is a distinction between the use of *could* and *was able to* in the past tense here. *Could* expresses ability, capacity possessed in the past in general terms, but *was able to* must be used in reference to something attained through capacity in a specific instance. A good guide to the difference is that *managed to* (+ infinitive) or *succeeded in* (+ gerund) can be substituted for *was able to* but not *could* in such sentences † *He could read before he was five years old.* † *He could run very fast when he was young.* † *Because he could swim, he was able to reach the shore when the ship sank.* 3 *Could* is used instead of *can* to indicate ability or capacity in present time when the speaker wishes to be polite or is expressing doubt, uncertainty † *Could you help me with this case?* † *I couldn't promise that all the figures will be accurate.*] **2** Indicating that one is sometimes capable of, able to. Here *could* is always used in the past † *She can be very irritating. She could be annoying as a child.* **3** Indicating possibility (*See* **may** (**might**)). *Can* (affirmative) indicates a possibility that is always present, but *may* is used in a specific case † *We think of Spain as enjoying a beautiful climate all the year round, but it can rain very heavily there in the autumn* (similar to **2** above). † *It may rain this afternoon. Could* in the present is used to indicate that the possibility is less likely (*See* **might**) † *This could (might) be the opportunity you have been looking for* (It is just possible that it is). [NOTE: 1 In the interrogative, *can* enquires after possibility and *may* is not used † *Can it be true?* (*Could it be true?* again indicates greater doubt.) 2 In the negative, *can't* expresses impossibility, where *may not* means perhaps not † *It can't be true. He would never have*

done such a thing. † *It may or may not be true. We can't know for certain until we have all the facts.* 3 *Can have* + past participle forms the present perfect tense, and *could have* the present perfect in the past † ⟩ *Why hasn't she arrived? Can she have mistaken the meeting-place?* ⟩ *She can't have mistaken it. I gave her clear directions.* † *When he discovered America, Columbus could not have foreseen that it would one day become a richer continent than Europe* (i.e. it was impossible at that time for him to have foreseen). *When he set out on his voyage, Columbus could not foresee what lay ahead of him* means *He was incapable of foreseeing. (See* **can 1**).] 4 *Can* is used in questions to express astonishment, impatience, despair, etc. It is stressed in these cases † *What can he mean? It seems nonsense to me.* † *Where can he be? He should have been here half an hour ago.* 5 *Can* is interchangeable with *may* to express permission or right. *May* is generally considered to be more precise, but *can* is as commonly used, more commonly in the negative † ⟩ *Can I leave the office an hour early this afternoon?* ⟩ *No, you can't.* † *You cannot use a train ticket on the buses when the trains are not running* (i.e. you are not allowed to). 6 *Can, could* are commonly used with verbs of the senses in place of the simple present and past tenses † *I can hear someone knocking at the door.* † *I could see the mountains from my bedroom window.* 7 *Could* is used in the present to mean 'feel inclined to' † *I could kill him.* † *I could dance for joy.* [NOTE: In the past, this idea is expressed by *could have* † *He looked so pleased with himself that I could have murdered him.*] 8 *Could* forms the conditional tense and *could have* conditional perfect tenses in conditional sentences † *If you lent me the book I could return it to you in a day or two.* † *If you had told me the date was inconvenient, I could have changed it.* 9 In reported speech, *could* replaces *can* and *could* and *could have* remain unchanged.

CANDLE *n.*

burn the candle at both ends Work and enjoy oneself without resting † *If he goes on burning the candle at both ends, he will be ill.*

CAP *n.*

cap in hand Humbly † *He lost his temper and then had to go cap in hand to apologise.*

set one's cap at (only of a woman) Make it plain to a man that she would like to become friendly with him † *She set her cap at Johnny, but he took no notice of her.*

CARD *n.*

on the cards Quite likely † *It's on the cards that the trains will be late because of the fog.*

play one's cards well (right) Do business, handle negotiations with good judgement † *If we play our cards right, they are sure to agree.*

put (lay) one's cards on the table Show one's intentions openly † *I'll be frank with you and put my cards on the table.*

CARE *n.*

care of (written c/o) Used on letters sent to people without a permanent address † *Write to me care of the British Institute.*

take care of 1 Pay attention to † *Take care of the pennies and the pounds will look after themselves.* 2 Deal with; look after † *The porter will take care of the luggage.* † *Are they taking care of you?* (i.e. paying attention to your needs)

CARE *v.i.*

care for 1 Look after (a person) † *When her parents died, there was no one to care for her.* 2 Like † *I don't care for cigars unless I've eaten a good dinner beforehand.* 3 Love † *She never knew how much he cared for her.*

CARRY *v.t. & i.*

be (get) carried away Become so excited that one loses self-control † *He got so carried away when his team won the game that he threw his arms round the man next to him.*

carry off 1 Win, take away † *He carried off first prize.* 2 Bring to a successful conclusion in spite of a mistake † *He lost his place in the middle of his speech, but carried it off so well that no one noticed.*

carry on 1 Continue or resume † *He carried on working although he was tired.* † *Carry on reading from where you left off.* 2 Conduct business, etc † *He carried on a profitable business as a butcher.* 3 Behave † *The way he carried on, you would think he owned the hotel.*

carry on (at) Complain noisily † *He was carrying on (at me) in a most unpleasant way.*

carry on with (a person) Flirt with, have an affair with † *I heard she was carrying on with a married man.*

carry out Do; put into practice † *He carried out efficiently everything he was asked to do.* † *It is one thing to plan a new town, and another to carry out the plan.*

carry through 1 Take something to a successful conclusion in spite of difficulty † *He carried the project through in spite of the Minister's opposition.* 2 (of a person) Enable him to survive until he can rest or get help † *If I take two aspirins now, they will carry me through the evening.*

CART *n.*

put the cart before the horse Do things in the wrong order † *She arranged the wedding date before he gave her the engagement ring. That's putting the cart before the horse.*

CASE *n.*

in case As a precaution, because of a possible event † *Take this money in case you need it* (because you might need it).

in case of In the event of † *In case of fire, ring 999.*

in any case Whatever happens or may have happened † *I think I told him to do it, but in any case he should have seen for himself that it was necessary.*

in that case If that is so †) *I'm not going.*) *In that case, I won't go, either.*

CASH *n.*

cash down Money paid at the time of buying something † *He doesn't accept cheques. He insists on people paying cash down.*

cash on delivery (C.O.D.) Money paid when goods are delivered † *Will you pay in advance or C.O.D.?*

CASH *v.t. & i.*

cash in on Take advantage of special knowledge or experience to get money † *He heard the company had found oil and cashed in on it before it was announced in the newspapers.* † *He has cashed in on his success as a footballer by letting his name be used in advertisements for boots.*

cash up Count money taken in bank, shop, etc (usually at end of day, week) † *The banks close at 3 o'clock, but the staff have to stay on to cash up.*

CASTLE *n.*

castles in the air (in Spain) Imaginary plans, conceptions arising from daydreams † *He tries to escape from his problems by building castles in the air.*

CAT *n.*

let the cat out of the bag Disclose information at the wrong moment † *Don't tell him. He's sure to let the cat out of the bag.*

(not) room to swing a cat (Not) enough space for anyone to be comfortable † *He lives in a tiny flat. There's not room to swing a cat in it.*

CATCH *v.t. & i.*

catch on 1 Become popular, become the fashion † *Corduroy trousers did not catch on like jeans.* 2 Understand † *I caught on after she had explained it to me a second time.*

catch out Detect (someone) in an error, usually by means of a trap † *The policeman made the suspect tell his story several times in the hope of catching him out.* † *The third question in the examination will catch a lot of people out.*

catch up (in) Become trapped or involved in † *Women must wear caps in this job, because their hair could be caught up in the machine.* † *Through mixing with dishonest people he was caught up in the crime.*

catch up (with) Get level with (when one has been left behind) † *Walk on ahead of me. I'll catch you up (catch up with you).*

catch up on As **catch up with,** but used in the narrower sense of doing things
one has not had time to do † *I shall have a lot of work to catch up on
when I get back from my holiday.* † *Being confined to bed with a broken
leg at least allows me to catch up on my reading* (read books I would not
otherwise have time to read).

CATCHING *adj.*

Contagious (particularly of illness, but also of habits, errors) † *Measles is
very catching.* † *The habit of calling Western countries 'the free world' is
catching. The Americans began it and now it is often heard in England.*

CATCHWORD *n.*

Slogan, phrase which is fashionable † *When I was young, 'votes for
women' was the feminist catchword. Now it is 'freedom from marriage'.*

CERTAIN *adj.*

for certain Without doubt † *I don't know for certain if he's coming.*
make certain 1 In order to be sure † *I think the train leaves at 8 o'clock, but
I'll ring the station to make certain.* **2** Make sure of getting † *I made
certain of the seats by booking them in advance.*

CERTAINLY (NOT) *adv.*

Yes (no), of course (not) (indicating indignation or politeness) † ⟩ *Would
you like to come?* ⟩ *Certainly.* † ⟩ *Will you lend me £100?* ⟩ *Certainly
not.* † ⟩ *Do you mind waiting for me?* ⟩ *Certainly not.*

CHAIN *n.*

chain reaction Originally a chemical reaction by which products are formed
which cause further changes to take place, but used generally to mean
events resulting from a common cause which interact to produce a series
† *The announcement that petrol tax would be doubled set up a chain
reaction as motorists rushed to buy petrol and garages became short of
supplies.*

CHANCE *n.*

by chance Unexpectedly, without having planned it † *We met in the street
yesterday, quite by chance.*
on the chance of In case † *I waited outside on the chance of seeing you* (in case
I should see you). [ALSO: **on the off-chance** Just in case † *I didn't expect
to see you, but I came on the off-chance.*]

CHANGE *n.*

Coins of small value or the difference due when one has paid with a coin
or note of greater value † *I haven't any change. I'll have to give you a
pound note.* † *I gave you a pound note, so you owe me twenty pence
change.* [ALSO: **get no change out of** Be unable to obtain help, information,

etc from † *I asked the telephone operator if she could tell me my friend's number if I gave her the address, but I got no change out of her. She said she wasn't allowed to tell me.*]

for a change Contrary to what usually happens † *The sun is shining, for a change.*

ring the changes Rearrange (usually within a limited range for the sake of variation) † *Governments often ring the changes within a Cabinet and move the Ministers to different Departments.*

CHAPTER *n.*

(give) chapter and verse (for) (Give) exact reference (for) in a book, file, etc † *I can't give you chapter and verse for the regulation, but I know it exists.*

CHASE *n.*

a wild goose chase A search, journey, which is certain to fail † *Why didn't you make sure that the goods had reached the depot, instead of sending me there on a wild goose chase?*

CHASE *v.t.*

chase up Find out why something has not been done and try to get it done quickly † *The copies have not arrived. Chase them up!* or *Chase the printers up* (i.e. find out the reason for the delay and make them hurry).

CHECK *v.t. & i.*

check in Register on arrival at a hotel, airport, etc. [ALSO: **check out** Hand in keys, etc on leaving.]

check off Mark on a list as having been found correct † *I'll read out the list of items in stock, and you check them off one by one.*

check (up) (on) Often used where 'check' (examine to see if something is accurate, true) is sufficient in itself † *The police checked (up) (on) his story.* [NOTE: 'Check up on' is necessary when it means find out all relevant information about people (e.g. to see if they are implicated in a crime) † *The police checked up on a number of suspects.*] [ALSO: **check-up** *n.* Examination (often medical) to see if everything is correct † *I'm going to the hospital, but don't be alarmed. It's only a check-up.*]

CHEEK *n.*
(*See* **face**)

CHEESE-PARING *n.*

Miserly economy which will produce very small savings [ALSO: **cheese-paring** *adj.*] † *When we changed our telephone number, the boss made us use up the old writing-paper and write the new number in. He enjoys cheese-paring (or making cheese-paring economies).*

CHICKEN-FEED *n.*

A small sum of money by comparison with other sums; small reward for effort † *Compared to what he earned when he was famous, what he gets now is chicken-feed.*

CHILD *n.*

be with child Be pregnant.

child's play Something very easy for someone to do † *His new job will be child's play to him. He is used to that sort of work.*

CHIP *n.*

have (carry) a chip on one's shoulder Carry a grudge (against society, individuals) and therefore be defiant or sullen in manner † *He was very badly treated by his firm and has a chip on his shoulder.*

CHOCK *n.*

chock-a-block *adj.* Packed together, overcrowded † *There were only four carriages on the train this morning, instead of the usual eight. We were chock-a-block.* [ALSO: **chock-full** *adj.* As full as possible † *He was chock-full of excuses* (i.e. made a large number of them).]

CHOP *v.t. & i.*

chop and change Change continually † *I wish he would make up his mind, instead of chopping and changing.*

CLEAN *adj.*

come clean Confess, be frank † *Why don't you come clean? We know you're lying.*

CLEAR *v.t. & i.*

clear away Remove † *When we had cleared away the undergrowth, the ground was bare.*

clear off Go away † *Clear off and don't come back.*

clear out 1 Empty in order to throw away things no longer wanted † *I must clear out my desk.* 2 Leave (*See* **clear off**). [NOTE: 'Clear out' is used if the person is inside a building. The meaning can also be extended to 'leave employment' † *Clear out! You're not wanted here any more.*]

clear up 1 Become clear † *The weather may clear up after lunch.* 2 Resolve † *Once we know the answer to that question, we'll be able to clear up the whole matter.* 3 Tidy, make clean † *She cleared up (the room) after the children's party.*

CLICK *v.i.*

1 Spontaneously establish good relations † *We clicked the first time we met.* 2 Suddenly go well † *We had a lot of trouble with the project at first, but then everything clicked.*

CLIMB *v.t. & i.*

climb down Adopt a humbler attitude, recognising a mistake or strength of opposition † *He climbed down when he saw that we were determined to resist his demands.*

CLIMBER *n.*

(often 'social climber') Person who tries to advance his position by making friends with powerful people.

CLOCK *n.*

put (turn) the clock back Cause to revert to a previous state of affairs † *We must move with the times. We can't put the clock back to the nineteenth century.*

CLOCK *v.t. & i.*

clock in Record time of arrival at work [ALSO: **clock off, clock out** Record time of leaving work.]

CLOCKWORK *n.*

like clockwork With mechanical efficiency; perfectly † *The factory has run like clockwork since he became manager.*

CLOSE *v.t. & i.*

close down 1 Stop operating (in business), stop production completely † *The factory has closed down (for the time being) because there are not enough orders.* 2 Stop transmitting (of a broadcasting station) † *That is the end of the news. We are now closing down until 6 o'clock tomorrow morning.*

close in (on) 1 Come nearer; surround † *The hunters closed in on the animal.* 2 Grow shorter † *The days close in in November.*

close with Settle an agreement with † *As soon as I received their offer, I closed with them.*

CLOSE-FISTED *adj.*

Mean, miserly † *He is so close-fisted that he wouldn't give a penny to a starving child.*

CLOUD *n.*

under a cloud Under suspicion; in disgrace † *Nothing was proved against him, but ever since he has been living under a cloud.*

with one's head in the clouds With one's thoughts elsewhere, not concentrating † *He doesn't know what is going on around him. He's got his head in the clouds.*

CLOVER *n.*

be (live) in clover In great comfort, in a very satisfactory situation † *He's in clover now. He has his own office and a good expense account.*

COAT *n.*

cut one's coat according to one's cloth Adapt what one spends to income; limit ambition to what may be achieved † *We would like to spend our holidays abroad, but we have to cut our coat according to our cloth.*

COLD *adj.*

leave one cold Make no impression on one † *In spite of the publicity for it, the scheme leaves me cold.*

be left (out) in the cold Be excluded from, left out of something † *When they chose a new board to run the firm he was left out in the cold.*

COLLAR *n.*

white-collar *adj.* Professional, working in an office, as distinct from **blue-collar** workers (factory workers) † *There is said to be a white-collar revolution in Trade Unions, as more and more professional people join them.* † *She is keen on her son getting a white-collar job.*

COLUMN *n.*

fifth column Group within a group or country working to destroy it (by betraying it to the enemy) † *The Union leader said there was a fifth column among the members who were in league with the management.* [ALSO: **fifth-column** *adj.*]

dodge the column Avoid an unpleasant duty † *Everyone must take it in turn to guard the camp. I won't have you dodging the column.*

COLOUR *n.*

off colour Not very well † *I'm not really ill. I'm just a bit off colour.*

under colour of Under the pretext of † *Under colour of observing the rules of the society strictly, they tried to keep him out.*

give colour to Imply evidence to support † *His nervousness when the police questioned him gave colour to the accusation against him.*

in one's true colours As one really is † *It was not until he gained power that he showed himself in his true colours.*

COME *v.i.*

come about Happen (usually suggesting an unexpected series of causes) † *How did that come about? Something strange must have occurred.*

come across Find, without having looked for † *I came across this old diary in my desk.*

come back Return. [ALSO: **come-back** *n.* Return after absence to field of previous success † *She hasn't appeared in a film for several years but now she is planning a come-back.*]

come by Obtain (by chance) † *No one knew how he came by the money.*

come down (in the world) Fall (to lower social station). [ALSO: **come-down** *n.* Humiliation; anti-climax † *What a come-down for him to be playing a small part in the film, after having been such a great star.*]

come down on Descend on to accuse, punish † *The Government will come down heavily on anyone who evades paying taxes.*

come in 1 Become fashionable † *People say short skirts will come in again.*
  2 Take part in, have a share in † *You've given everyone else something (to do). Where do I come in?*
come in for Receive † *He came in for a lot of criticism because of his policy.*
come in handy (useful) Prove useful † *Keep the bag. It may come in handy some day.*
come into (money) Inherit † *He came into a fortune when his aunt died.*
come into one's own Be at one's best, show one's ability to the best advantage
  † *He was nervous at the beginning of the game, but later he came into his own.*
come of Result from † *You've burnt your fingers! That's what comes of being careless.*
come off 1 Happen † *When is your visit to Paris coming off?* 2 Succeed † *I don't know if the experiment will come off, but it's worth trying.*
come on 1 Progress † *Johnny is coming on very well at school.* † *The flowers are coming on nicely.* 2 Hurry up (often imperative) † *Come on! I can't wait all day for you.* 3 Used in imperative as challenge † *If you want to fight over it, come on, then!*
come on to Start to (usually of weather) † *It's coming on to rain.*
come out 1 Appear; become known; be published † *The stars come out at night.* † *The flowers have come out* (are blooming). † *We knew the truth would come out in the end.* † *When is your book coming out?* † *He always comes out well in photographs.* 2 Be removed (of stains) † *The stain came out when I washed it.* 3 Fade (of dye) † *All the colour came out in the wash.* 4 Be resolved (mathematical) † *I've been working on this equation for an hour, but it doesn't come out.*
come out in Develop (of diseases showing in the skin) † *He came out in spots (in a rash, etc).*
come out with Say unexpectedly † *I never imagined he would come out with the story in front of everyone.*
come over Take possession of (of feelings, behaviour) † *What came over you? How could you be so rude?*
come round 1 Come a short distance to visit † *Come round and see me after dinner.* 2 Recur † *I always feel cheerful when Christmas comes round.*
  3 Change views and give up opposition † *He'll come round (to our point of view) if you give him time.* 4 Recover consciousness after fainting
  † *Throw some water over his face. Then perhaps he'll come round.*
come up Appear, arise † *Do you think this question will come up in the examination?*
come up against Encounter (difficulty, opposition) † *We came up against an insoluble problem.*
come up to Reach † *I was very disappointed in it. It didn't come up to expectations.*

come upon Find, meet unexpectedly † *We suddenly came upon a party of climbers on an excursion.*

if it comes to that If that is the state of affairs; if that is your argument † *You complain of having too much to do. If it comes to that, we're all busy.*

COMMON *n.*

in common Equally shared.

in common with Like † *In common with other people of my generation, I find these restrictions irritating.*

have in common with Have similar interests, personality, experience † *We have nothing in common. I have a great deal in common with him.*

COMMON *adj.*

common ground Basis for discussion, etc, shared by both, all.

common knowledge Something known to everyone.

COMPANY *n.*

in company With a number of other people, at a social gathering † *He is pleasant when you meet him on his own, but very shy in company.*

(get) in (to) good (bad) company (Be) with good (bad) people † *His father was worried that he would get into bad company in the big city.*

in good company (only) In the company of people of similar tastes (often humorous) † *Neither John nor I plays bridge, so if you can't play you'll be in good company.*

in company with Together with † *We welcome the ambassador from France in company with his wife and daughter.*

keep someone company Stay with him (often to prevent him from being lonely) † *Her neighbours often keep her company in the evenings.* [ALSO: **for company** As a companion † *She has only her cat for company since her daughter moved away.*]

the company someone keeps The kind of people he is often seen with † *It is said that you can judge a man's character by the company he keeps.*

part company Separate, go different ways † *If you continue to contradict me, we'll have to part company.*

COMPLETE *adj.*

complete with Including (often indicating that accessory items are included in a single price) † *This beautiful house, complete with garage and parkland, will be sold by auction.*

CONCERN *n.*

a going concern Commercial undertaking in full operation and making a profit † *It will take a year before the factory becomes a going concern.*

CONDITION *n.*

in condition In good physical condition, fit. [ALSO: **out of condition** In bad physical condition (used for a person who is healthy, but does not have enough exercise) † *I'm sorry I wasn't able to give you a good game. I'm out of condition.*]

CONFIDENCE *n.*

in confidence Expecting that it will be kept secret † *I'm telling you this in confidence. Don't tell anyone else.*

with confidence With assurance, confidently.

confidence man (frequently 'con man') One who obtains money, etc by deception, pretending to be honest and respectable.

confidence trick Deception employed by confidence man. [ALSO: **con** *v.t.* Trick, deceive in this way.]

CONSEQUENCE *n.*

in consequence As a result † *My train was delayed and in consequence I was late.*

of some (no) consequence Of some (no) importance † *His opinion is of no consequence.*

CONTRARY *n.*

on the contrary Used to express direct contradiction of something † ⟩ *You must have an easy life now.* ⟩ *On the contrary, I'm busier than ever.*

to the contrary To the opposite effect † *I'll arrange the meeting for Tuesday unless I hear from you to the contrary.*

CONVENIENCE *n.*

make a convenience of Take advantage of person's good nature, hospitality, etc † *I once offered to lend him my car and since then he has made a convenience of me by borrowing it regularly.*

all modern conveniences (frequently 'all mod cons') All the appliances, arrangements, etc, which make living comfortable (e.g. central heating, hot water).

COOL *adj.*

Widely used nowadays as a vague term of praise, meaning 'satisfying', appealing to the speaker's mood, temperament, taste (which in his opinion is sophisticated and up-to-date).

COOL *n.*

keep (lose) one's cool Keep (lose) one's temper (and, by implication, reputation for being calm in crisis). [ALSO: **play it cool** Act shrewdly and with self-control.]

COOL *v.t. & i.*

cool down Become less excited *You shouldn't let him annoy you so much. Cool down!* [ALSO: **cool off** The same, with the suggestion of separation

41

from the cause of excitement † *They started fighting, so we had to pull them apart until they had cooled off.*]

CORNER *n.*

a tight corner A difficult situation † *He's a good man to have at your side in a tight corner.*

turn the corner Pass a critical point and begin to improve, recover † *Her life was in danger but now she has turned the corner.*

COST *n.*

at all costs Whatever the cost may be (in money, sacrifice) † *At all costs we must prevent the enemy from reaching the capital.*

at the cost of At the loss of or expense of † *He saved his son's life at the cost of his own.*

to one's cost To one's loss or disadvantage † *It is exhausting as well as rewarding to be Prime Minister, as he knows to his cost. It ruined his health.*

COUNT *v.t. & i.*

count against Be held against; be to someone's disadvantage † *The fact that he has been in prison before will count against him when they sentence him.*

count down Count in diminishing numbers to nought (before a rocket is launched, bomb exploded, etc). [ALSO: **count-down** *n.* Such a count.]

count for Be considered worth † *His opinion should count for something. He has worked here longer than anyone else.* † *Does it count for nothing that I have always been loyal to you?*

count in (out) Include (exclude) someone † ⟩ *Would you be willing to take part in the scheme?* ⟩ *Yes, count me in.*

count on Rely on † *You can count on him to help you.*

COURSE *n.*

in course of In process of † *This road will be closed while the new bridge is in course of construction.*

in the course of At some point during † *In the course of conversation, he asked me if I knew your uncle.*

in (the) course of time Eventually † *In (the) course of time, these problems will be resolved.*

in due course At the proper time, in the natural order of things † *Thank you for your application. We will be writing to you in detail in due course.* † *They were married and in due course Susan gave birth to a son.*

of course (not) Certainly, naturally † ⟩ *Will you be able to come to the meeting?* ⟩ *Of course (I will).* † *Of course I expected him to pass the examination because he had worked so hard.*

COVENTRY *n.*

send to Coventry Isolate someone by refusing to speak to him (as group punishment of individual) † *People who go on working when their Union calls a strike are often sent to Coventry by their workmates.*

CRAZY *adj.*

Mad, but sometimes used favourably to mean agreeably eccentric, original.

crazy about Very fond of † *I'm crazy about you* (I love you so much that it is driving me mad). *She's crazy about the Beatles* (She likes their records very much).

CRICKET *n.*

not cricket Unfair, contrary to fair play (in any game) † *Wasting time is not against the rules of the game, but it's not cricket.*

CROCODILE *n.*

crocodile tears Pretended sorrow † *He shed crocodile tears over the death of his rival.*

CROP *v.t. & i.*

crop up Occur unexpectedly † *We never imagined so many difficulties would crop up.*

CROPPER *n.*

come a cropper Have a violent fall; suffer disaster as a result of recklessness † *He never thinks before he acts. He is bound to come a cropper one day.*

CROSS *n.*

bear one's cross Support a burden of sorrow or suffering † *He was paralysed as a young man, but he has borne his cross patiently.* † *We can't stop him interfering in our work. He's a cross we have to bear* (i.e. an irritation we must put up with).

CROSS-PURPOSES *n.*

be at cross-purposes (with) Misunderstand someone's (each other's) ideas, intentions or consistently take an opposite point of view † *I think we're speaking at cross-purposes.* † *They're always at cross-purposes (with each other).*

CROSS-SECTION *n.*

A representative selection (of people, views, etc) † *We have interviewed a cross-section of the public to get their views.*

CROW *n.*

as the crow flies In a straight line (travel, not mathematical) † *It's only ten* *miles from here as the crow flies, but the road winds so much that it takes half an hour by car.*

CRUSH *n.*

have a crush on Imagine one is in love with (used of adolescents, particularly when they are thinking about older people) † *Half the girls in the class have a crush on the teacher.*

CRY *v.i. & t.*

cry off Withdraw from something one has agreed to take part in † *He promised to come to the party, but cried off at the last moment.*

CRY *n.*

a far cry A long way (metaphorical) † *He's always talking about the need to help under-developed countries, but that's a far cry from volunteeering to go out there.*

CUE *n.*

take one's cue from Watch what someone does and follow his example in one's own actions † *Take your cue from James. He knows what to do on these ceremonial occasions.*

CUFF *n.*

off the cuff Without preparation, previous thought † *Government representatives often regret having spoken off the cuff to journalists.*

CUPBOARD *n.*

cupboard love Affection displayed to get something (of children) † *As soon as she saw the sweets, she put her arms round me. 'That's cupboard love,' I said.*

CURRY *v.t.*

curry favour (with) Try to get someone's approval by flattery, etc † *She brought the teacher some flowers, hoping to curry favour with her.*

CURTAIN *n.*

iron curtain Barrier of suspicion hindering free exchange of ideas, etc, between the West and the Communist bloc in Eastern Europe (sometimes refers to the actual border). Hence **iron-curtain countries** Those countries in Eastern Europe under Communist rule.

CUSTOMER *n.*

Often used simply to mean fellow (always used critically): 'an awkward customer', 'a funny (odd) customer', 'a stubborn customer', etc.

CUT *v.t. & i.*

cut someone (dead) Deliberately ignore him, treat him as if he were a stranger † *People in society were so shocked by her behaviour that many of them cut her dead.*

cut in 1 Interrupt a conversation † *I hope you don't mind my cutting in. I must go now.* **2** Overtake another car in a line of traffic, moving sharply in front of it.

cut off 1 Break connection (on telephone) † *I was talking to a friend, but the operator cut us off (we were cut off).* **2** Isolate (of towns, armies, etc) † *The village was cut off by floods.* **3** Disinherit † *His father disapproved of his marriage and cut him off (or cut him out of his will).* [ALSO: **cut off with a shilling** Reduce someone's inheritance to a minimum.]

cut out Leave out † *Cut out the details and get to the main point.*

be cut out for (to be) Have the natural ability to be † *He's so shy. He's not cut out for (to be) a salesman.*

be (get) cut up Be (get) very upset † *He was cut up when he heard about the accident.*

cut-and-dried *adj.* Decided, and unlikely to be changed † *You must take a decision and stick to it. Then the matter will be cut-and-dried.*

CUT *n.*

a cut above A little superior to (in social class or ability) † *She thought herself a cut above the rest of us because she had been educated at a private school.*

a short cut A quick way or method † *If you turn left here, there is a short cut which avoids the traffic in the town centre.* † *This is a mathematical short cut which is useful for rough calculation.*

cut and thrust Hand to hand struggle (often used figuratively to mean where the action is really taking place) † *University professors are sometimes accused of being too far removed from the cut and thrust of everyday life.*

DABBLE *v.t. & i.*

dabble in Take a superficial interest in; become involved in, without fully understanding what one is doing † *He dabbles in stocks and shares, but that's just one of his many interests.*

DAMPER *n.*

put a damper on Discourage, reduce others' enthusiasm † *My father put a damper on the evening by saying I would have to be home before midnight.*

DANCE *n.*

lead someone a (merry) dance Cause him trouble by making him follow one's lead † *She led him a (merry) dance before she would agree to go out with him.*

DARE *anom. fin.*

1 Have the courage to † *I daren't tell him the terrible news.* **2** Be independent enough to † *How dare you insult me?* [NOTE: 1 In the past tense, *I dared not tell him* and *I didn't dare to tell him* are both found. 2 In the affirmative and also after the past participle, *dare* is usually followed by *to*, except in *I dare say* (*See* below). It is always followed by *to* after the present participle or gerund *daring* † *I haven't dared to tell him yet.* † *He ran away not daring to look back.* 3 The non-anomalous verb *dare* means face the risk of or challenge (someone to do something) † *He will dare any danger.* † *I dare you to climb up the tower.*]

I dare say I think it very likely † *I dare say we shall see you frequently now you are working nearby.* †) *Are you going to the coast this weekend?*) *I dare say.* [NOTE: Used alone, the phrase tends to be non-committal and expresses a vague affirmative, like † *Yes, I think so.*]

DARK *n.*

in the dark In ignorance † *The boss had kept us in the dark about his plans (We were in the dark . . .).*

DARK *adj.*

keep it dark Keep it secret † *I thought you should know about it. But keep it dark, won't you?*

DASH *v.t. & i.*

dash off **1** (**away**) Leave quickly † *Don't dash off (away). I have something to tell you.* **2** Write (a letter, article) in haste † *I dashed off a letter to him at breakfast.*

DASH *n.*

cut a dash Try to impress by spending money extravagantly, wearing expensive clothes † *Let's go out to dinner at the Ritz. We can afford to cut a dash!*

DATE *n.*

out of date No longer fashionable † *He was considered a great man in his time, but his ideas are now out of date.* [ALSO: **out-of-date** *adj.* Old-fashioned.]

to date So far; up to the present † *He promised to reply this week, but we have heard nothing to date.*

up to date Into line with modern practice, up to the present time † *We have revised the dictionary and brought it up to date.* [ALSO: **up-to-date** *adj.*

Modern, in fashion † *This kitchen contains up-to-date gadgets which make the housewife's life easy.* **up-date** *v.t.* Bring up to date (files, information).]

have a date with Go out with (someone of the opposite sex) † *She had a date with James last night.* [ALSO: **date** *v.t.* Arrange to go out with, go out with someone of the opposite sex † *That was Johnny on the 'phone. He wanted to date me.*]

DAUNT *v.t.*

nothing daunted Not discouraged by an obstacle † *When I arrived at the airport, I found that my plane could not take off because of fog. Nothing daunted, I took a car to another airport.*

DAWN *v.i.*

dawn on Become clear to, occur to † *It slowly dawned on him that he had been deceived.* † *It's just dawned on me that I should have sent in my application before last Saturday.*

DAY *n.*

day after day For a succession of days without a change † *It rained day after day, without stopping.* [ALSO: **day in day out** As **day after day**, but implying even more the routine aspect of something † *Day in, day out, he sits in the library studying those papers.* **day by day** As **day after day**, but meaning the succession of days individually (*each* day, rather than *every* day) † *Day by day, her condition improved, until she was eventually able to leave the hospital.*]

a rainy day A time when one is in difficulties (particularly short of money) † *You ought to have saved some money for a rainy day.*

the other day One day in the recent past † *I went to the cinema the other day.*

one of these days One day in the future (used in forecasting something) † *One of these days he will have an accident if he doesn't learn to drive more carefully.*

off-day *n.* Day on which a person works, plays games, etc worse than usual † *I can't understand why he is losing. He must be having an off-day.*

from day to day From one day to the next, each being considered separately † *It is difficult to know how the war is going. The position changes from day to day.*

late in the day Almost too late † *I wish you hadn't sent in your article so late in the day. I don't know if we shall have time to include it.*

call it a day Decide not to work any longer that day † *We'll call it a day now and start again tomorrow morning.*

have one's day Have one's time of success, prosperity (frequently used in the proverbial phrase given in the example) † *He's doing very well at the moment, though I don't believe his good luck will last. Still, every dog has*

his day. [ALSO: **have had one's day** Implying that one's period of success is
over, or that something is no longer fashionable † *The old ideas of class
distinction have had their day.*]

have seen better days Implying that a person has enjoyed more success,
prosperity than now or that a machine, tool, etc used to work better † *I'll
lend you this umbrella, though I'm afraid it has seen better days.*

DEAD *adj.*

go dead Stop transmitting (of radio, telephone) † *The line's gone dead. I shall
have to dial the number again.*

dead beat Very tired, exhausted † *I can't go any further. I'm dead beat.*

make a dead set at Attack directly, go directly towards for some purpose † *As
soon as she saw me, she made a dead set at me.*

DEADLINE *n.*

Time fixed in advance by which something must be done † *As a
journalist, I always have to work to a deadline.*

DEAD-PAN *adj.*

Expressionless (face, look, etc) † *He is very good at playing cards. He has
such a dead-pan face that no one can guess what he has in his hand.*

DEAL *v.t. & i.*

deal with 1 Have relations with † *He is a difficult man to deal with.*
2 Handle, behave towards † *I don't know how to deal with this enquiry.*
† *I have a lifetime's experience of dealing with criminals. I think I
understand them.* 3 Be concerned with † *His article deals with
unemployment and ways of overcoming it.*

DEAL *n.*

a square (raw) deal Fair (unfair) treatment † *He was a good employer. He
always gave me a square deal.*

DEALINGS *n.*

have dealings with Have relations within business † *I've had dealings with
him on many occasions and have always found him honest.*

DEATH *n.*

be the death of someone Make him laugh uncontrollably (sometimes used to
mean cause worry, but almost always said in a good-humoured way)
† *You'll be the death of me one day, the way you talk.*

be in at the death Be present at the decisive moment, the conclusion of
something † *I was in at the death, when the police recaptured the
prisoner.*

DEBT *n.*

in (out of) debt Owing money (no longer).

in someone's debt Owing him gratitude † *You have saved my life. I shall always be in your debt* (or *indebted to you*).

get into debt Borrow money and owe it.

DEFAULT *n.*

by default From lack of opposition † *He won the game by default, because his opponent was ill.*

in default of In the absence of † *We'll have to accept it, in default of anything more suitable.*

DEGREE *n.*

third degree Questioning (of prisoners, etc) involving brutal treatment, torture, etc.

DEPEND *v.i.*

it (all) depends The decision depends on certain factors or considerations
 † ⟩ *Are you going to the dance on Saturday?* ⟩ *It (all) depends. Are you going yourself?*

DEPTH *n.*

be (get) out of one's depth Literally, be in water too deep to stand up in, but frequently used to mean be (get) involved in a situation too complex for one's understanding † *I understood his general introduction, but once he began to use technical terms, I was out of my depth.*

DESIGN *n.*

by design Deliberately, on purpose † *The letter was left on the table by design, so that I could not fail to see it.*

have designs on (always plural) Intend to steal, take † *I think he has designs on your property.* † *The King feared that his brother had designs on his life.*

DESPITE *prep.*
In spite of † *Despite my warning, he continued to break the law.*

DEVICE *n.*

leave someone to his own devices (always plural) Leave him alone to amuse himself, resolve his own problems † *He didn't want to come out with us, so we have left him to his own devices.*

DEVIL *n.*

a devil for Particularly addicted to; unable to resist the temptation to † *My boss is a devil for changing his mind after I have typed a letter and making me do it again!* † *He's a devil for work. He never stops.*

the (a) devil of A very difficult or long (time, journey), job, etc) † *She always takes a devil of a time to get ready.* † *We had the devil of a job to convince him that it wasn't our fault.*

49

talk of the devil Exclamation used when person one has been speaking about appears † *Talk of the devil! Here he comes.*

DIAMOND *n.*

a rough diamond A person who is good-natured and kind in spite of his rough manner.

DIE *v.i.*

die away Become weak and disappear (of wind, noise, etc) † *The shouting gradually died away and everyone waited in silence for him to speak.*

die down Similar to **die away**, but more abrupt and therefore applied to fire, excitement, etc † *There was tremendous public interest in the invention at first, but it died down when the first trials proved a failure.*

die hard Die in spite of great resistance † *Old beliefs die hard in this part of the country.* [ALSO: **die-hard** *n.* Person who sticks defiantly to ideas which are no longer popular, or refuses to be convinced of different views.]

die off Die one by one † *My tropical fish are dying off from some mysterious disease.*

die out Become extinct † *We are afraid that unless we can prevent people from hunting these rare animals, they will die out within a few years.*

be dying for (to do) something Be very keen or anxious to have (do) it † *I'm so thirsty. I've been dying for a drink for the past hour.* † *I'm dying to see the new film at the Majestic.*

DIG *v.i.*

dig (oneself) in Establish oneself securely in a position † *Once I have dug myself in in the firm, they will find it hard to get rid of me.*

DIG *n.*

A sharp push, or, figuratively, a critical remark, aimed at someone † *He has a habit of making sly digs at the people who work with him.*

digs (always plural) Colloquial word (short for 'diggings') meaning lodgings † *I've left my car outside my digs.*

DIGGER *n.*

gold digger Person who digs for gold, but commonly a woman aiming to gain security for herself by marrying a rich man † *I never believed she was in love with him. I always said she was a gold digger.*

DIN *v.t. & i.*

din in(into) Resound, tell someone forcibly and repeatedly to do something † *The noise of the battle dinned in his ears.* † *I have been dinning it into them for days that we must have the order by Friday.*

DIP *v.t. & i.*

dip into 1 (one's pocket for resources, etc) Put one's hand into it and take out money † *My son has spent his student's grant so I shall have to dip into my own pocket to keep him at the University.* 2 (a book) Read passages from it to see if it is of interest.

DISCOUNT *n.*

at a discount At a low price, (considered) of little value † *I sometimes think that the old virtues of respect for one's parents are (held) at a discount these days.*

DISH *v.t.*

dish out Issue (in a careless or clumsy manner) † *Dish out these magazines among the staff, will you?*

dish up Serve up (dinner, facts, information) † *Can't you show more originality? It's no use dishing up these old figures again.*

DISPOSE *v.t.*

dispose of 1 Deal with † *That disposes of the first problem, I think. Let us now consider the second.* 2 Get rid of † *How are we going to dispose of all this rubbish?* † *The President disposed of the opposition by putting them all in prison.*

be disposed to Be willing to † *I am not disposed to argue with you any longer.* [NOTE: **be indisposed** Be unwell † *Unfortunately, Sir John is indisposed. In his absence Mr Frederick Smith will present the prizes.*]

be well disposed towards Be willing to help, friendly towards (someone) † *We were all very well disposed towards her and made her welcome.*

DISTANCE *n.*

keep one's distance Avoid coming close to someone, being closely connected with him † *We had an argument when we first met and since then we have kept our distance.* [ALSO: **keep someone at a distance** Prevent him from approaching, attempting to establish a relationship.]

DITCH *v.t.*

Abandon † *My car broke down, so I had to ditch it and walk the rest of the way.* † *How cruel of him to ditch her like that.* (Here there is a suggestion of breaking promises though not necessarily of a formal engagement.)

DO (DID) *aux. v.*

1 Used to form present and past tenses of verbs in the interrogative and negative. 2 Used for emphasis in affirmative sentences † ⟩ *Why didn't you clean your teeth?* ⟩ *But I did clean them!* [NOTE: 'Do' or 'did' is stressed in this usage. While it is correct here, there is no doubt that many English speakers use it needlessly † *I (do) feel that something should be done.* This is a habit which should always be avoided in writing and has little to recommend it in speech.] 3 Used to add emphasis to an imperative † *Do go on with your story! What happened next?*

DO *v.t. & i.*

do away with Abolish, kill † *This law is out of date. It is time the Government did away with it.* † *He has such a desperate expression that I am afraid he will do away with himself* (i.e. commit suicide).

do by Treat (infrequently used except in expression **hard done by** Badly treated † *He claims that he is hard done by, but he is not treated worse than the rest of us*).

do down Cheat (implying forcing a price down below the real value) † *I won't sell it for a penny less than £5,000. They are not going to do me down.*

do for 1 Be suitable for † *We have been buying presents for the family. That ornament should do for Aunt Jane.* 2 Ruin, finish, wear out (usually passive) † *I know I am done for. No doctor can save me.* † *When he saw the policeman at the door, the thief knew he was done for* (here 'caught'). † *This old coat is done for. It's not worth keeping it any longer.* 3 Manage † *What will you do for money while you are studying?* (How will you manage . . .).

do out Clean out (a room) † *I must do out the kitchen before I go.*

do someone out of Cheat someone of what is due to him † *He used his knowledge of the law to do his nephew out of his inheritance.*

do up 1 Redecorate; restore † *We have had the front bedroom done up. It looks as good as new.* 2 Tie, fasten † *Would you help me to do up this parcel?* † *The dress does up at the back.* 3 Be exhausted (usually passive) † *I'm out of condition. I feel quite done up after running for the bus.*

do with 1 (with 'can', 'could') Need, make use of † *I could do with a pound, if you don't mind lending it to me.* 2 Be connected with † *It is nothing to do with me.* † *He is something to do with insurance.* [ALSO: **have to do with** Be connected with; have dealings with; be concerned in † *Don't have anything to do with him! He's dishonest.* † *Some of you boys have been writing insulting words on the school walls. Did you have anything to do with it?* **done with** Finished † *I am glad that's (over and) done with.*]

do without 1 Manage without † *The baker's shuts early on Wednesday, so we shall have to do without bread this evening.* 2 (with 'can') Manage without (implying independence, resistance to offers of help – often used sarcastically) † *I can do without your assistance, thank you.* † *With him for a friend, you can do without enemies!*

that (it) will do That will be (is) sufficient, enough † *That will do for now. Come back and finish it tomorrow.* † 〉 *I am offering you what I think is a fair rise in salary. Don't you think it is fair?* 〉 *It will do* (said without enthusiasm, as if the speaker hoped for more, but will accept it).

that (it) won't do That will not be (is not) satisfactory, suitable † *That won't do. We must think of something better.* † *It won't do. Have you a larger size?*

it doesn't do It is unwise † *It doesn't do to call your boss names, unless you already have another job to go to.*

nothing doing 1 Nothing happening † *The young people get bored with life in this village. There's nothing doing here.* **2** Used alone as a form of refusal † ⟩ *Will you lend me a pound?* ⟩ *No, I'm sorry, nothing doing.*

it (that) wants (takes) some doing (used impersonally) It requires, takes a great deal of skill or effort. † *He drank ten glasses of beer, one after another. That wants (takes) some doing.*

it's not done It is not socially acceptable † *It's not done for a man to wear a hat in church.*

that's done it That has finished it (mending, breaking, etc) † *That's done it!* (completed the job). *The car should go now.* † *That's (now you've) done it! We shall never be able to stick all those pieces together again.*

DO *n.*

Party, entertainment † *There was a wonderful do at the club last weekend.* [NOTE: **to-do** Row, fuss † *I couldn't see that it was very important, but my wife made a great to-do over it.*]

DO-GOODER *n.*

Person who shows so much enthusiasm for helping others that he irritates them by his attention.

DOG *n.*

a dog in the manger (proverbial expression) Someone who has no need for a thing, but refuses to let anyone else have it † *I thought she would give me her old curtains, but she threw them away. She was a dog in the manger about it.*

go to the dogs Deteriorate † *The papers are always telling us that the country is going to the dogs.*

DOG-EARED *adj.*

(of books) With leaves turned down at the corners because of much use, etc.

DOLE *n.*

be on the dole Be unemployed and drawing money from the State; be on National Assistance.

DOLL *v.t. & i.*

doll (oneself) up Dress in one's best clothes; dress as attractively as possible † *My wife is upstairs dolling herself up.*

DONKEY *n.*

donkey work The dull, repetitive part of a job † *The professor writes the book, but his assistants have to do the donkey work of checking all the references.*

donkey's years A very long time † *I've known him for donkey's years, ever since we were at school together.*

DOOMSDAY *n.*

till doomsday Till the end of the world † *You will be here till doomsday if you are waiting for him to make up his mind.*

DOT *n.*

on the dot Exactly on time † *It is a pleasant surprise to me when my train arrives on the dot.*

the year dot A time so long ago that it is not possible to give the date † *He's been working here since the year dot.*

DOUBLE-CROSS *v.t.*

Trick by pretending to work for one group when one is really working for another † *All the time that he was supposed to be employed by us, he was double-crossing us by selling our secrets to the enemy.*

DOUBLE-TALK *n.*

Deliberate misuse of words to confuse, trick opponents † *'We are dedicated to the preservation of peace,' said the General. It sounded like double-talk to me.*

DOUBLE-THINK *n.*

Ability to believe in contradictory ideas at the same time (implying the mental process required by adherence to rigid party discipline, etc) † *Many Communists in the 1930s had to employ double-think to accept the Nazi-Soviet pact.*

DOUBT *n.*

in doubt Uncertain.

no doubt Certainly; very probably (often used politely when the speaker may in fact not be certain) † *No doubt you have seen the news in the paper.* † *You are all familiar, no doubt, with the main theme of this book.*

DOWN *prep.*

1 Indicating movement to a place at a lower level † *He ran down the hill.* **2** Indicating movement from a place of greater importance, or to a place further south † *This train continues down the line to the suburbs.* † *I am going down to Brighton for the week-end.* **3** Along (a road) † *I was walking down the street when I met him.* (See **up 3**).

DOWN *adv.*

to be (feel) down To be depressed; miserable † *I feel so down today. I don't know what's the matter with me.*

down and out Out of work, and forced to live on charity † *The people who are down and out come to this hostel for a free meal.*

down under Australia, New Zealand.

DOWN *n.*

have a down on Have a prejudice against, dislike for † *He has never been fair to me. He must have a down on me for some reason.*

DOWN-TO-EARTH *adj.*

Practical, realistic † *He's a down-to-earth sort of man. He always says what he means.*

DRAG *n.*

1 Person who hinders another's progress † *His wife has been a drag on him in his career.* **2** Boring person, party; wasteful, time-consuming task † *He's such a drag. Did you have to invite him?* † *When I arrived at the theatre I found I had left the tickets at home, so I had to go back to get them. It was an awful drag.* **3** Clothes worn for female impersonation. Hence *drag artist, drag revue.*

DRAW *v.t. & i.*

draw in **1** Arrive; stop † *The train drew in at the station.* **2** Become shorter † *The days begin to draw in in the autumn.*

draw on Take from † *I shall have to draw on my savings to meet the expenses of the holiday.* † *He has drawn on his own experience in writing his book.*

draw out **1** Prolong (used mainly in passive) † *He drew out the meeting by making irrelevant comments.* **2** Become longer † *The days are drawing out now that summer is here.* [ALSO: **drawn-out** *adj. drawn-out speech.*] **3** Encourage someone to talk about themselves, give an opinion † *I should like to draw him out on the subject of his retirement. He hasn't said anything yet, but I am sure he is not happy about it.* [ALSO: **be drawn** *He refused to be drawn, in spite of my questions* (i.e. he refused to commit himself).]

draw up **1** Stop † *The car drew up outside our house.* **2** Formulate; compile (a list, plan, etc) † *Have you drawn up a list of points for us to discuss at the meeting?*

DRAWING-BOARD *n.*

on the drawing board At the design stage (of plans, projects, etc) † *The new model is still on the drawing board.*

DREAM *v.i. & t.*

dream of Consider † *I wouldn't dream of speaking to him about it without asking you first.*

dream up Invent † *He dreams up the most extraordinary machines, but he never pursues his ideas far enough to see if they will be practicable.* † *It's not convenient for me to see him at the week-end. I will have to dream up an excuse for putting off the meeting.*

DRESS *v.t. & i.*

dress down Reprimand verbally † *He dressed us down in front of the whole class for our carelessness.* [ALSO: (and more commonly used) **give someone a (good) dressing down.**]

dress up **1** Put on special clothes (for a play, etc) † *Our children love dressing up at parties.* **2** Put on one's best clothes or evening dress † *I hate dressing up for dinner.* **3** Add ornaments to (a story, article, etc) † *We shall have to dress up the basic facts to make the proposal more attractive to people.*

dressed to kill (of a woman) Dressed in a way likely to attract attention.

DRIVE *v.t.*

drive at (continuous tenses only) Mean, try to say or imply † *I don't understand what you are driving at.*

DROP *v.t. & i.*

1 Leave a person or thing at a place (when driving a car, etc) † *You needn't come all the way to the house. Drop me at the corner.* † *I dropped a few things at your house this afternoon.* **2** Break off social contact, relationship with someone † *I never thought he would drop her without an explanation.* **3** Leave out of team, group, etc † *He has been dropped from the team next Saturday because he has not been playing well.*

drop off **1** Fall asleep † *The programme on television was so boring that I dropped off in the middle of it.* **2** Become fewer or less † *The demand for this paper has dropped off sharply in the last month.*

drop out Retire from a race, competition, group activity † *We hoped to have three guest speakers at the Conference, but Mr Jones had to drop out at the last minute.* [ALSO: **drop-out** *n.* Someone who cannot or does not want to belong to established society † *Gauguin was a drop-out of a kind. He abandoned his family and went to live on a South Sea Island.*]

DROP *n.*

at the drop of a hat Immediately, without hesitating † *I'd leave my job at the drop of a hat if I could find someone willing to pay me the same money elsewhere.*

a drop in the ocean A very small quantity (by comparison) † *The amount of money I waste is a drop in the ocean compared to what the Government spend on projects which achieve nothing.*

DRY *v.i.*

dry up Become dry (river, well, etc), but also used for speaker, actor, etc, who forgets what he intends to say and stops speaking.

DUCK *n.*

lame duck Unfortunate person, in need of help or incapable of doing his work properly.

DUE TO *adj.*

Caused by † *The accident was due to a fault in the signal mechanism.* [NOTE: *Due to* is frequently used as a compound preposition in place of *owing to* † *The concert has been cancelled, due to the lack of interest shown. Owing to* or *because of* should be used in such cases.]

DURING *prep.*

1 Throughout (a period of time) † *During the day, the street is very busy, but there is not much traffic after dark.* [NOTE: In speaking of the duration of an activity, answering the question † *How long has it been going on?, during* is not correct – *I have been living in London* for *three years.*] **2** At some point within a period of time † *I thought I heard a noise during the night.* † *During our stay in London, we visited the Houses of Parliament.*

DUTCH *adj.*

double Dutch Incomprehensible language † *I know how to add up, but when someone starts talking about applied mathematics, it's double Dutch to me.*

go Dutch Share the expenses of a meal, etc † *She's a very independent girl. When I took her out, she insisted on going Dutch.*

DUTY *n.*

in duty bound Under an obligation † *I feel in duty bound to tell you that you are not the only person we are considering for this job.*

DWELL *v.i.*

dwell on Emphasise; recall at length † *If I have dwelt on this point, it is because I think it is by far the most important one.* † *She dwells so much on the past. She ought to make the most of her life as it is now.*

DYED-IN-THE-WOOL *adj.*

Fixed on one's attitudes and incapable of change † *He's a dyed-in-the-wool optimist. He always believes things are for the best, whatever happens.*

EAR *n.*

in one ear and out the other Implying either that what one says makes no impression or that the listeners are thoughtless, stupid † *I tell them that if* *they don't do their homework they will never pass the examination, but it goes in one ear and out the other.*

turn a deaf ear (to) Deliberately ignore, pretend that one has not heard † *He turned a deaf ear to criticism.*

EARNEST *n.*

in earnest Seriously † *I must speak to you in earnest for your own good.* † *The holiday season doesn't begin in earnest until July.*

EARTH *n.*

what, how, etc on earth? Used for emphasis only † *What on earth do you mean by coming into my bedroom without knocking?* † *How on earth do you expect me to complete the work by Friday?*

come down (back) to earth Stop dreaming and consider something practically † *They were so excited by their success that it was hard for them to come down to earth and accept that there was still work to be done.*

run to earth Track something down; find it after a long search † *I was looking for a medal of this type for years before I finally ran it to earth in a little shop in Soho.*

EARTHLY *adj.*

no earthly good (use) No good (use) at all † *It's no earthly good expecting other people to help you if you won't help yourself.*

not an earthly No chance (hope) at all † *He feels very confident of passing his driving test, but if you had seen him in a car, you'd agree he hasn't an earthly.*

EASE *v.t. & i.*

ease up Work less hard; slow down † *If you don't ease up and stop taking work home at night, you will make yourself ill.*

EASE *n.*

ill at ease Uncomfortable because of embarrassment, mental strain † *He felt ill at ease in the strange surroundings.*

EASY *adj.*

I'm easy I don't mind (which of a number of alternatives happens) † *You take whichever you prefer and leave the other one for me. I'm easy.*

take it easy Relax, stop being tense or control oneself in doing something † *I'm going to shut the office, go down to the beach and take it easy.* † *Take it easy (with the salt)! You'll make the food inedible.*

EASY-GOING *adj.*

(of person) Not troubling much about details, discipline, etc † *My boss doesn't mind if I arrive late. He's very easy-going.* † *You're too easy-going with the children. They do just as they please.*

EDGE *n.*

be on edge Be irritable, in a nervous state † *I was expecting an important letter this morning and it hasn't arrived. I shall be on edge until it does.*

have the edge (on someone) Have a slight advantage (over him) † *It will be a very close fight, but I think the champion will have the edge (on his opponent).*

EFFECT *n.*

for effect In order to make an impression, produce a reaction † *He makes remarks like that purely for effect, to see what people will say in reply.*

in effect **1** In fact; for practical purposes † *Officially we are still an independent company but in effect we belong to Exports Ltd, because they own the majority of the shares.* **2** In operation † *This law has been in effect for five years.* [NOTE: Put into *effect*, come into *effect*, etc.]

of no effect Useless (in doing what was intended) † *The proposals he made were of no effect.*

take effect Come into operation † *His appointment will take effect from the first of May.* [ALSO: **with effect from** Used in the same context to indicate time at which something comes into operation † *With effect from the first of May.*]

to no effect Without producing the result desired † *He argued to no effect. They refused to let him go.*

to that effect With that information; in that connection † *I knew he would be arriving on the 12.00 plane. I received a telegram to that effect.* † *The department is being reorganised. To that effect, I am calling a meeting to discuss possible changes.*

EGG *v.t.*

egg on Urge someone to do something (implying that he is afraid to do it) † *He would never have had the courage to do it if you hadn't egged him on.*

EGG *n.*

put all one's eggs in one basket Risk everything on a single enterprise † *He has invested all his money in a property company. I think he is unwise to put all his eggs in one basket.*

EGG-HEAD *n.*

Intellectual (used critically) † *It's easy for egg-heads in the Universities to talk about the social problems of the workers. They've never done a day's work in their lives.*

EIGHT *n.*

have one over the eight Drink too much, become drunk † *You look as if you've had one over the eight.*

ELBOW-ROOM *n.*
Enough space to move freely † *There are so many people in this bar at lunch-time that they don't even give you elbow-room.*

ELEMENT *n.*
in (out of) one's element In surroundings where one feels at ease, confident of one's ability (ill at ease, lacking in confidence) † *He is the kind of politician who is only in his element in front of a crowd. He is out of his element answering questions on television.*

ELEPHANT *n.*
white elephant Possession, property useless to the owner (and often expensive to maintain) † *He arrived back from abroad to find that he had been left a large house in the country, but it proved a white elephant. He could not afford to keep it up and no one would buy it.*

EMBARK *v.i. & t.*
embark on Literally, to go on board a ship, but widely used to mean begin a career, business undertaking, etc † *He arrived in South America, ready to embark on a new life.*

END *v.i. & t.*
end up Conclude, reach a state finally † *If you go on in this way, you'll end up in prison.* † *We lost our way and ended up miles away from home.*

END *n.*
at a loose end Having nothing interesting to do † *I am at a loose end when the children go back to school.*
end to end With the end of one object touching the end of another † *Laid end to end, those logs would reach the other side of the field.*
in the end Eventually, finally † *I waited for him for over an hour. In the end, I decided that he wasn't coming.*
no end of A large number, large amount of † *We've had no end of complaints since the new system was installed.*
on end 1 Standing upright on the end † *We had to turn it on end to get it through the door.* 2 Without stopping, change † *He plays the piano for hours on end. The road continues straight ahead for miles on end.*
go off the deep end Lose control of one's feelings (in anger) † *I know I was mistaken, but you had no reason to go off the deep end like that.*
keep one's end up Hold one's own; not get the worst of (a fight, argument, etc) † *They had some strong criticisms to make of our proposals, but we kept our end up.*
make both ends meet Limit one's expenditure so that it does not exceed one's income † *The cost of living has risen so quickly that it is almost impossible for us to make both ends meet.*

ENLARGE *v.t. & i.*

enlarge on Explain (what one is saying) at greater length, in more detail † *I have made my views quite clear. I don't think it would help if I were to enlarge on them.*

ENTER *v.t. & i.*

enter for Apply to take part in (an examination, competition) or write down name, etc for that purpose † *I am going to enter for the Proficiency Examination in English.* † *He entered his horse for the Derby.*

enter into 1 Take part in † *I am not prepared to enter into negotiations with them.* 2 Imagine, feel oneself part of † *Unless you are prepared to enter into the spirit of the play, you will never be able to convey the author's ideas to the audience.* 3 Be a part of † *I don't think the possibility of our refusing had entered into their calculations.*

EQUAL *adj.*

be (feel) equal to Have sufficient strength, courage for † *Unfortunately my grandfather did not feel equal to the journey.* † *It will be a great responsibility for him, but I am sure he will be equal to it.*

other things being equal If in every other respect, things are (were) the same † *Other things being equal, he is more likely to get the job than anyone else, because his father worked here* (i.e. If the other candidates' qualifications are the same . . .).

ERR *v.i.*

err on the right side Make a calculation with a safe margin of error, so that although it is wrong, no serious harm will result † *We'll order 50 tins above what we know we can sell. If there is a sudden demand, we shall have erred on the right side.*

EVEN *v.t.*

even up Make equal † *John's brother arrived suddenly, so we invited Mary to even up the numbers* (i.e. make the number of women invited equal to the number of men).

EVEN *adj.*

break even Make neither a profit nor a loss † *We lost money at first but eventually managed to break even.*

get (be) even (with) Have one's revenge (on someone) † *I shall remember this, and one day I'll get even with you.*

EVENT *n.*

in the event As things turned out † *We had hoped to play the match at the beginning of the month, but in the event it rained and we were forced to postpone it.*

61

in the event of Should a certain thing happen † *In the event of my death, my property will pass to my wife.*

at all events Whether that is the case or not † *I'm not sure if he said he was coming tomorrow or not. At all events, I shall see him this evening and can find out one way or the other.*

EVER *adv.*

did (have) you ever? Expression of incredulity † *Well, did you ever hear of such a thing? It's unbelievable!*

as if one would ever Used with same meaning † *Mrs Smith told me she had seen our Johnny throwing stones. As if he would ever do a thing like that!* (i.e. I cannot believe he could).

EVERY *adj.*

every now and then From time to time † *Usually we are left alone in this office. The boss comes in every now and then just to see that we have something to do.*

every so often At regular intervals, but not according to a fixed schedule † *Every so often a man comes to clean the windows. It's about once a month, but you never know which day of the week.*

EVERYDAY *adj.*

Daily, familiar because of its frequency † *When my grandfather was young, it was apparently an everyday occurrence to see people lying drunk in the streets.*

EVIDENCE *n.*

be in evidence Be seen; noticeable † *At one time I often saw him, but he hasn't been much in evidence recently.*

EXAMPLE *n.*

make an example of Punish (severely) as a warning to others † *The judge made an example of the criminal.*

EXCEPT *prep.*

But not; apart from † *Everyone arrived on time except me.* † *I go to London every day except Sunday.*

except for Apart from (emphasising contrast with other things in a statement) † *The book he wrote ten years ago is still reliable, except for the chapter on space exploration.* [ALSO: **except that** Apart from the fact that.]

EXCHANGE *v.t.*

exchange words (blows) Quarrel † *I am sure they are not happy together. I have heard them exchanging words many times.*

EXPENSE *n.*

at someone's expense In mockery of him, using him as an object for laughter or contempt † *He's the kind of person who always makes jokes at other people's expense.*

EXPLAIN *v.t.*

explain away Make a convincing excuse for † *He's a clever politician, but he will find it difficult to explain away his broken promises.*

EYE *n.*

an eye for an eye Revenge equal to the injury suffered (from the biblical † *an eye for an eye and a tooth for a tooth*).

in one's mind's eye In one's imagination † *In my mind's eye I can still see the old house where I was born.*

in the public eye Well known to the general public † *People in the public eye are followed by journalists and photographers wherever they go.*

up to one's (the) eyes in (work, etc) Totally engaged in, extremely busy with † *We are up to the eyes in the preparations for the Queen's visit.*

with the naked eye Without the aid of a telescope, etc † *Many stars are too far away from the earth to be seen with the naked eye.*

have an eye for Have good judgment (in order to choose or find the best, etc) † *More than anything else, a publisher needs to have an eye for what will interest the public.*

have an eye to Have as one's object † *He always has an eye to his own advancement.* [ALSO: **with an eye to (the main chance)** Recognising what is of most benefit to oneself † *He will sell his knowledge for as much as he can get. He is a man with an eye to the main chance.*]

keep an eye on Watch (in the sense of general supervision, while doing something else) † *Keep an eye on the kettle and turn the gas off if it boils before I come back.* † *The police thought the escaped prisoner might try to see his wife, and kept an eye on his house in case he did.*

make eyes at Indicate to person of the opposite sex that one is attracted to him, her † *The man in the corner is making eyes at me. What shall I do?*

open someone's eyes to Cause him to realise † *She's been deceiving him for some time. It's time someone opened his eyes to it.* [ALSO: **close one's eyes to** Deliberately ignore, pretend not to know † *He suspected that she was deceiving him, but closed his eyes to it because he did not want to believe it.*]

see eye to eye (with) Agree (with someone) † *They don't see eye to eye over future policy.* † *He doesn't see eye to eye with his assistant.*

set eyes on See † *I hope I never set eyes on him again.*

take one's eyes off (used in negative) Be unable to stop looking at (someone or something) † *She hasn't taken her eyes off you since she came in.*

turn a blind eye (to) Overlook deliberately (*See* **close one's eyes to**. The

difference is that there is no element of self-deception involved here)
† *The girls sometimes take more than an hour for lunch, but I turn a blind eye (to it).*

EYE-OPENER *n.*

Something that surprises, particularly by providing unexpected knowledge † *Their new factory is quite an eye-opener. Almost everything there is done by machines.*

FACE *v.t. & i.*

face out Continue to defy a person or situation; refuse to admit that one is wrong † *The Prime Minister faced out the storm of criticism which arose from his decision.*

face up to Confront bravely † *You will never solve your problems unless you face up to them.*

FACE *n.*

face to face (with) Confronting; together † *He was face to face with his enemy at last.* † *I would like to bring the two of you face to face so that you could discuss the matter.*

in (the) face of Confronted by; in spite of † *In (the) face of the latest developments in the situation, we must ask the Government for assistance.* † *They captured the bridge in the face of fierce resistance.*

on the face of it Apparently, at first glance † *On the face of it, the project has a good chance of success.*

to someone's face Openly in his presence † *If he doesn't like what I'm doing, he should tell me so to my face, instead of complaining to other people behind my back.*

have the face to Have the insolence to † *I don't know how he had the face to say it.* (This could imply hypocrisy or insolence.) [NOTE: We would not only use *face* in this context. We could say † *What a cheek!* † *He's got a cheek.*]

look someone in the face Look at him without fear or embarrassment (most frequently used in negative † *I was unable to, afraid to, dared not*, etc, to suggest embarrassment) † *If he knew I had taken his raincoat by mistake and then left it on the train, I wouldn't be able to look him in the face.*

lose face   Lose one's dignity, the respect in which one is held by others (used particularly of Governments, officials, etc)   † *The war continued because both sides were afraid that they would lose face by offering peace terms.*

save one's face   Avoid being disgraced, losing one's reputation (completely)   † *They managed to save their faces by saying that they had been let down by their advisers.*

set one's face against   Adopt a fixed attitude against someone or something, refusing to listen to argument in its favour   † *He has set his face against moving, and nothing will change him.*

FACT   *n.*

in fact   **1** Really   † *You must have imagined we were old friends from the way we were talking, but in fact I only met her a week ago.*   **2** Used to introduce a statement of fact   † ⟩ *Have you two met each other before, then?* ⟩ *Yes. In fact, we were at school together.*   [ALSO: **as a matter of fact** As for **in fact** but more common in the second context.]

FAG   *n.*

1 Something tiring, boring   † *I wouldn't like to have to drive 40 miles to work every day. I'd find it a terrible fag.*   [ALSO: **fagged out** Exhausted, very tired.]   **2** Slang word for cigarette.

FAG-END   *n.*

1 The last remaining part of something (e.g. a period of time, activity taking up time) which one wishes was over   † *He came to see me at the fag-end of the day, when I was beginning to put everything away and get ready to go home.*   **2** Cigarette end (*See* **fag**).

FAIL   *n.*

without fail   (only in this expression) For certain, no matter what happens   † *You will have the goods on Friday, without fail.*

FAILING   *prep.*

If this proves impossible; if it does not happen   † *I hope to let you have your car back on Thursday. Failing that, it will be ready by Friday.*

FAITH   *n.*

in good faith   With honest intentions; without suspicion (implying that the result appears otherwise or that the person was deceived)   † *We accepted the order in good faith, but now we find we cannot deal with it.*   † *I paid him the money in good faith, and never imagined he would break his word.*

FALL   *v.i.*

fall away   Disappear   † *The support he was relying on began to fall away as the election approached.*

fall back on   Turn to, when one's first choice is not possible, not available

† *We invited the President to speak, but he cannot come. It is a good thing we have another speaker to fall back on.*

fall behind (with) Fail to keep up (with) (payment, correspondence, etc) † *He fell behind with his rent and the landlord told him to leave.*

fall for 1 Be strongly attracted to someone or something (house, car, etc) † *I fell for her the moment I saw her.* **2** Be convinced by (a story, plan, etc) † *It's a very clever plan. Do you think they will fall for it?*

fall in with Agree to † *He fell in with my suggestion without stopping to consider it.*

fall off Decrease † *Attendance at cinemas has fallen off sharply since television sets became common.*

fall on Attack (usually implying surprise) † *We fell on the enemy while they were asleep.*

fall out (with) 1 Quarrel (implying an end to relationship) † *I never expected them to fall out (with each other). They always seemed so friendly.* **2** Result, turn out † *Everything fell out as we had planned.* [ALSO: **fall-out** *n.* Radioactive dust † *The worst thing about the atomic bomb is not the explosion itself but the effect of fall-out on people far away.*]

fall over oneself (each other) Be very (too) anxious to; do everything in one's power to † *People who ignored him when he was poor are falling over themselves to be nice to him now that he is rich.* † *They fell over each other to get the contract.*

fall through Come to nothing † *He applied for a number of jobs, but they all fell through.*

FAMILIAR *adj.*

familiar with 1 Having good knowledge or experience of † *Are you familiar with the procedure?* [ALSO: **familiar to** Well known to † *The facts of the case are already familiar to me.*] **2** Behaving in too intimate a way towards another person (implying social or sexual impropriety) † *How can he expect his staff to respect him when he is so familiar with them?* † *He drank too much at the party and became very familiar with his boss's wife, so they asked him to leave.*

FANCY *v.t. & i.*

fancy! Imagine! (expression of surprise) † *Fancy meeting you here!* † *Just fancy what would happen if everyone was completely free to do as he liked!*

fancy oneself as Have a conceited opinion about one's own accomplishments † *He is sure to show you his paintings. He fancies himself as an artist.*

FANCY *n.*

take a fancy to Develop a liking for someone or something (e.g. kind of food, car, etc) † *I've taken quite a fancy to the new Vicar.* † *I never used to eat sweets, but recently I've taken a fancy to chocolate.*

FAR *adv.*

by far By a great deal † *He is by far the best pianist I have ever heard.*
† ⟩ *Which book do you think is the better?* ⟩ *This one is the better, by far.*

far from it Used to emphasise a negative statement † *He wasn't the best man you could have chosen. Far from it!* (i.e. implying that there were many better).

go far **1** (of a person) Achieve great success in one's life, career † *He is a bright boy. He will go far.* **2** (of money, food, etc) Buy, feed a lot † *You should have bought more cheese. This won't go far* (will not feed many people). † *A pound doesn't go far nowadays* (does not buy very much).

go too far Go beyond reasonable or socially acceptable limits † *You had no reason to insult him. That was going too far.*

FASHION *n.*

after a fashion In a way, but not satisfactorily † ⟩ *Can your little boy dress himself yet?* ⟩ *After a fashion.*

FAST *adv.*

play fast and loose with Repeatedly change one's attitude towards (implying insincerity) † *You must make him say whether he wants to marry you or not. He has no right to play fast and loose with you (your affections).*

FASTEN *v.t. & i.*

fasten on **1** Fix (one's look, attention, or blame, responsibility for an action) on (someone) † *He fastened his eyes on me with such a pitiful expression that I could not ignore him.* † *The police were able to fasten the robbery on him because his fingerprints were found at the scene of the crime.* **2** Concentrate attention, attack on a particular idea or part of a speech † *He was foolish to promise to provide houses for everyone. His opponents fastened on this point.*

FAULT *n.*

at fault To blame; mistaken † *I am sorry to say that I was the one who was at fault.*

to a fault So (generous, amiable, etc) that the virtue becomes a defect in other people's eyes † *She is generous to a fault. She gives money to anyone who comes to her door.*

find fault with Criticise (implying the intention to discover something wrong, if possible) † *No work of art is perfect. A critic can always find fault with it if he wants to.*

FAVOUR *n.*

in favour of On the side of, agreeing with † *Are you in favour of capital punishment?*

in someone's favour To his advantage, benefit † *His aunt altered her will in his favour.*

FEAR *n.*

for fear of In case (something unpleasant might happen) † *I turned down the radio for fear of waking the baby.*

in fear of Anxious in case (something unpleasant might happen) † *The escaped prisoner waited on the roof while the police searched the house, in fear of being re-captured.* [NOTE: **in fear of one's life** In fear of losing one's life † *He received a threatening letter and is in fear of his life.*]

no fear of No chance, possibility of (something happening) † *My wife thought we would have to cancel our holiday because of the trouble at the works, but there's no fear of that.* [ALSO: **no fear!** Not likely!]

FEATHER *n.*

a feather in one's cap Something (e.g. promotion, honour awarded) one has reason to be proud of.

FEED *v.t. & i.*

be fed up (with) Be tired of, discontented (with) † *I'm fed up with seeing the same programmes on the television week after week.* † 〉*What's the matter with you?* 〉*I'm fed up.* 〉*You're not fed up with me, I hope.*

FEEL *v.t. & i.*

feel for 1 Try to find something with hands, feet, etc, when one cannot see it † *The room was very dark, and he felt for the light switch.* 2 Sympathise with † *Of course I feel for you very deeply, and wish I could do more to help you.* [NOTE: **have a feeling for** Have taste, sensitivity in a certain field † *She has a feeling for antique furniture.*]

feel like 1 Feel as if one were † *I have felt like a new man since I came out of hospital. I feel like a million dollars* (USA) (I feel very well). 2 Be inclined for, be in the mood to (have) † *I feel like jumping for joy.* † *Do you feel like going for a walk?* † *I feel like a cup of tea.*

feel up to Have sufficient strength for, be well enough to † *My mother would have come to the wedding, but she didn't feel up to (making) the journey.*

FENCE *n.*

sit on the fence Avoid taking sides (implying, until one sees which is going to win).

FEND *v.t. & i.*

fend for oneself Provide for oneself, look after oneself † *His parents died when he was a boy, so he has always had to fend for himself.*

fend off Block a blow, attack (by putting up one's arm, for example) † *The dog attacked me, but I fended it off with my umbrella.*

FETCH *v.t. & i.*

fetch and carry for Look after someone's needs, act as a servant to (often used when one is not employed as such) † *I don't think the old lady has a bad life. She has her three daughters to fetch and carry for her.*

FIELD *n.*

have a field-day Take part in an important occasion; make the most of an occasion (political, sporting) † *They are having a field-day at the Town Hall, preparing for the Queen's visit.* † *Jones had a field-day in the game this afternoon and scored six goals.*

FIFTY *n.*

go fifty-fifty (with) Share expenses equally † *It's too complicated to work out how much each of us ate. Let's go fifty-fifty (I'll go fifty-fifty with you).*

FIDDLE *n.*

play second fiddle to Adopt a subordinate position to † *He is tired of playing second fiddle to men with less talent.*

FIGHT *v.t. & i.*

fight off Repel † *I'm not very bright this morning. I'm trying to fight off a cold.*

FIGURE *v.t. & i.*

figure on (USA) Plan to, reckon on † *I figure on leaving the house at a quarter to twelve.*

figure out Resolve, work out a problem or think about it until one understands it † *Would you mind looking at this map? I can't figure out where we are.*

FIGURE-HEAD *n.*

Person in high position who has no real authority † *The President of a company is usually a figure-head. The decisions are taken by the managing director.*

FILL *v.t. & i.*

fill in **1** Complete (a form, etc) by adding details required † *Please fill in the form I have given you.* **2** Give (someone) necessary information to enable him to complete his knowledge or add necessary details to complete a picture, scheme, etc † *Would you fill me in on what's been happening while I've been away?* † *I can give you an outline of what we want, but we'll leave it to you to fill in the details.*

fill out Become or make fatter; expand (an article, report, etc) † *She's filled out a lot since I saw her last.* † *It is a good article, but you should fill out the introduction to make it clearer.*

FIND *v.t.*

find oneself Discover one's true ability † *He is still at school and doesn't know what he wants to do in life. He'll find himself before long.*

find out 1 Discover by means of a conscious effort † *I'll ring the station and find out the times of the trains to London.* 2 Discover to be dishonest, to have done something wrong † *I won't tell the police about it myself, but they'll find him out one day.*

FINE *adj.*

cut it fine Leave oneself with the minimum of time necessary to do something † *We should leave the house at half-past nine. It would be cutting it fine to wait until 10 o'clock.*

FINGER *n.*

have something at one's finger tips Be so familiar with one's work, etc that information is immediately available.

put one's finger on Point out exactly (e.g. where a mistake has been made).

twist someone round one's little finger Persuade him to do whatever one wants (most often used of wives, children, etc, capable of obtaining whatever they want from husbands, fathers).

FIRE *v.t.*

Dismiss a person from employment (*See* **sack**) † *I'm tired of listening to your excuses. You're fired!*

FIRE *n.*

hang fire Be slow to develop † *The negotiations are hanging fire because we are waiting for an impartial report on the future prospects of the company.*

FIRST *adj.*

first thing (in the morning) As early as possible (the next day) † *I'll ring you first thing (in the morning).*

FIRST-CLASS *adj.*

(*See* **first-rate**).

FIRST-HAND *adj.*

Obtained in person from the source † *This is first-hand information. I spoke to the Minister himself.*

FIRST-RATE (SECOND-RATE) *adj.*

Excellent (not very good). [NOTE: *First-class* and *first-rate* are more or less the same, but *-class*, in general, refers more to official classification, while *-rate* implies a judgement † *He has a second-class degree in Mathematics* (i.e. quite good, not inferior). *She stayed at a second-rate hotel* (i.e. where the service, etc was not very good). *Third-rate service* would indicate poor service, but a *third-class hotel* could be good of its kind.]

FISH *n.*

a fish out of water Person unsuited to position, job, etc (particularly as the result of a change in responsibility or environment) † *He's been like a fish out of water since he was transferred to another Department.*

FISH *v.t. & i.*

fish **(for)** Try to get, by indirect methods (particularly information, compliments) † *He doesn't know as much about our affairs as he pretends. I think he is fishing (for information).*

FISHY *adj.*

Suspicious † *There was something fishy about the way he tried to evade your questions.*

FIT *n.*

have a fit React with horror or great annoyance † *Go and have a bath. Your mother will have a fit if she sees you covered in mud.*

by fits and starts Not regularly; spasmodically † *The machine goes by fits and starts, and stops running without warning.*

FIT *adj.*

fit to drop On the point of collapse from exhaustion † *He worked until he was fit to drop.*

FIT *v.t. & i.*

fit in **(with)** 1 Get on, establish satisfactory relations (with) (people around one) † *How are you fitting in (with your colleagues) in your new job?*
2 Suit, go satisfactorily with (of arrangements, plans, etc) † *I'm going on holiday in August. Does that fit in with your plans?* (i.e. in the sense that they want either to go together or avoid going at the same time because of business commitments, etc).

fit out Equip † *The boat was fitted out for a long voyage.* † *We must fit the children out for the summer* (buy them suitable clothes).

fit up 1 Install † *He has fitted up a bar in his living-room.* 2 Equip for a particular purpose † *He has fitted up his spare room as a studio.* 3 Equip with additional items † *He has fitted up his house with wall-lights, extra electrical points, etc.* 4 Equip (a person) with everything necessary for a particular purpose † *The shop on the corner specialises in the kind of thing you want. They will fit you up* (See fix up 3).

FIX *n.*

in a fix In an awkward situation † *I'm in a fix this morning. My secretary has rung to say she cannot come in to work.*

FIX *v.t. & i.*

fix on 1 Decide on † *Have you fixed on a place for your holiday this year?*
2 Fix one's eyes, attention, affections (always plural) on; concentrate on.

fix up 1 Arrange † *I've fixed up the meeting for next Thursday* (or *I've fixed the meeting up with John).* **2** Install; provide † *I've fixed up a bed for you in the spare room.* **3** Supply † *If you want to claim expenses for your journey, go to the accountant and he will fix you up* (supply you with the money, arrange the matter). † *We don't stock pipes here, only cigarettes. The shop on the corner will fix you up.* [NOTE: The emphasis is on settling the particular problem, not on the shop being capable of supplying whatever the customer might want within a specified range of goods (*See* **fit up 4**).] **4** (in passive) Provided with † *How are you fixed (up) for money?* † *Are you fixed (up) for lodgings in the town?* [NOTE: It is more usual to say *fixed up* in the second case, where arrangements are necessary.]

FLAME *n.*

an old flame Former girl-friend (less commonly, former boy-friend) † *I heard that Joan got married the other day. She is an old flame of mine.*

FLAP *n.*

be in (get into) a flap Be (become) nervous, worried and consequently unable to make decisions calmly (usually because of fear that one will be unable to cope with a task) † *The manager is in an awful flap, because the directors of the company are coming to look round the factory next week.*

FLARE *v.i.*

flare up Show a sudden outburst of anger † *You shouldn't be so touchy, flaring up at the slightest thing anyone says.*

FLASH *n.*

a flash in the pan Short-lived success † *My horse won his first race of the season, but I'm afraid it may have been a flash in the pan.*

FLAT *adj.*

and that's flat! That is plainly what I mean (leaving no room for doubt) † *Don't go on trying to persuade me to take part in the play. I won't do it, and that's flat!* [ALSO: **a flat refusal, denial, etc** One that leaves no doubt in the listener's mind.]

fall flat (of plans, speeches, etc) Fail completely to gain approval or interest † *His attempts to convince them fell flat.*

flat out Using all one's energy (or power, in a car, etc) † *I was going flat out but I still could not catch him.*

FLOP *n.*

Failure (particularly used of play, book, party, etc).

FLUKE *n.*

Success or achievement depending on a lucky accident rather than on judgment or ability † *He shot the bird without taking aim. It was a fluke.*

FLY *n.*

a fly in the ointment A disagreeable occurrence (or person) preventing enjoyment from being complete † *We had a delightful picnic in the country. The only fly in the ointment was that we left the tin-opener at home and couldn't open the cans of beer.*

there are no flies on him He is too clever or alert to be tricked.

FOB *v.t.*

fob off (only used in this form) Get rid of (an object of poor quality) by passing it to someone else, or attempt to avoid (person or criticism) with inadequate excuses † *He had expected to be rewarded by being given a position of authority, but instead they fobbed him off with empty honours.* † *Don't let him fob you off with a story like that. You have a genuine complaint and should insist on seeing him.*

FOLD *v.t. & i.*

fold up (of business, job, conference, etc) Close down abruptly, collapse † *The company he worked for folded up, so his job folded up* (disappeared) *with it.*

FOLLOW *v.t. & i.*

follow up Take further action as a result of making progress † *Now that we have established a basis for agreement, we should follow it up by arranging further discussions.*

FOOL *n.*

suffer fools gladly (always plural and normally in negative sense) Be patient with silly or boring people † *He has a brisk, decisive personality and does not suffer fools gladly.*

FOOL-PROOF *adj.*

(of plans, machines) Completely safe, because it is so easy to use that even a fool could not make a mistake † *Unfortunately, no system we have been able to devise is fool-proof.*

FOOT *n.*

fall on one's feet (always plural) Escape by good luck from a difficult situation (and find oneself better off as a result) † *He lost his job because the factory closed down, but he's fallen on his feet. He got a better job elsewhere.*

find one's feet (in) (always plural) Adjust oneself satisfactorily to new surroundings † *Have you found your feet in your new job yet?*

have feet of clay Be unworthy of confidence placed in one, admiration given to one † *The 'great man' was shown to have feet of clay when he betrayed his country to save his own life.*

have (get) cold feet Lack (lose) courage (particularly to perform an action)

† *The bank robbers got cold feet when they saw the policeman and ran away without taking anything.*

put a foot wrong Make the slightest mistake † *If you put a foot wrong in this office the boss gets furious.* [ALSO: **cannot put a foot wrong** Be incapable of making a mistake (frequently because others refuse to admit that one could be wrong) † *His boss has such a high opinion of him that he can't put a foot wrong.*]

put one's foot down Take a firm attitude over something and refuse to give way † *I'm tired of your arriving late to work, and I'm going to put my foot down. The next time you are late, you will be sacked.*

put one's foot in it Say something stupid or embarrassing † ⟩ *Is this your daughter, then?* ⟩ *No, she is my sister.* ⟩ *Oh dear, I've put my foot in it, haven't I?*

put one's feet up (always plural) Relax (not necessarily resting one's feet on a chair, table, etc) † *I've been working very hard. I'll be glad to get home and put my feet up.*

put one's best foot forward Walk as quickly as possible, hurry † *If we don't put our best foot forward, we shall be late.*

set off (start off) on the wrong foot Make a mistake, create a bad impression, at the beginning of an enterprise † *Put on your best suit for the first day at the office. You don't want to start off on the wrong foot.*

FOR *prep.*

1 Indicating destination † *The train for London is leaving from Platform 2.* † *It's time I set out for the office.* **2** Indicating for whom or for what something is intended; point at which one is aiming † *I have brought these flowers for you.* † *I have made a cake for tea.* † *Aim for the centre of the target.* † *He is going to run for President* (attempt to become). **3** Indicating purpose † *What is this for?* † *We have invented a process for making cheaper steel.* **4** On behalf of † *Speak for yourself. The rest of us will make up our own minds.* † *He speaks for us all on this matter.* **5** Representing; employed by † *The Honourable Member (of Parliament) for Birmingham South.* † *He works for the gas company.* **6** In favour of, on the side of † *I'm all for the proposal.* † *Are you for me or against me?* **7** About, with regard to † *I'm concerned for him. I hope he knows what he is doing.* **8** Because of † *Do it for my sake.* **9** As a result of † *Take a holiday. You'll feel much better for it.* **10** In exchange for † *How much did you pay for it?* † *I have translated the letter, word for word.* **11** As a reward, penalty † *He won a prize for English composition.* † *He was sentenced to prison for stealing.* **12** Taking into consideration † *It is very warm for this time of year.* † *He is very intelligent for his age.* **13** Indicating length of time † *I shall be away for a few days.* † *He has known her for several years.* **14** Indicating a point of time in connection with arrangements made † *The wedding has been fixed for 20th of May.* **15** Indicating distance † *We drove for ten miles without passing another car on the road.* † *For miles and miles there was nothing but sand.* **16** Indicating the object of hope, desire, liking, hatred, etc † *We must hope for the best.* † *It's no use wishing for the moon.* † *He developed a great affection for her.* **17** Indicating the object of preparation, planning † *We are getting ready for the holidays.* † *We have plans for a new factory.* **18** Indicating suitability † *Don't eat so much chocolate. It's bad for your teeth.* **19** Indicating a special occasion † *I gave him some gloves for his birthday.* † *We always go to my parents' house for Christmas.* **20** Indicating number in a sequence † *I have spoken to you about it for the last time.* **21** In the pattern *for* + noun/ pronoun + infinitive with *too* including sentences with *too, enough* † *There is no need for him to do anything about it.* † *It's impossible for me to understand him.* † *This case is too heavy for me to carry.*

for all In spite of † *For all his wealth, he lived modestly.*

but for (*See* **but**).

FORCE *n.*

in force In existence according to law or regulation at present † *The new rules have been in force for two or three years.* [NOTE: **put into force** Make the law. **come into force** Become the law.]

FORGET *v.t.*

forget oneself **1** Consider the interests of others rather than one's own † *Every nurse must learn to forget herself and think only of her patients.* **2** Behave in an unsuitable manner, showing lack of respect or control † *You are forgetting yourself. How dare you speak to me in that way?*

FORK *v.t. & i.*

fork out Pay (implies unwillingly) † *I've had to fork out £50 for repairs to my car.*

FORM *n.*

in (good) form **1** In good physical or mental condition for a test † *If he is in form, he will win the game.* **2** Showing one's ability in a lively manner † *He was in good form when he made a speech at the dinner.*

in the form of Shaped in that way, with that appearance.

on form **1** Playing a game, racing, etc, as well as one can † *When he is on form, I have no chance of beating him.* [ALSO: **off form** Playing worse than one usually does.] **2** On the basis of previous results † *On form, they have no chance of winning.*

good (bad) form What is socially accepted as good (bad) behaviour † *It is a matter of good form to thank your host for having invited you to his house.*

FOUL *adj.*

fall foul of Break (the law, regulations); arouse dislike, anger in (someone) (implying accidentally in both cases) † *He left his car outside his house with the engine running, not realising he was falling foul of the law.*

FOUR *n.*

go on all fours Walk on hands and knees, crawl.

four-letter word Obscene word (not necessarily with four letters, but used because the most common examples have four).

FRAME *v.t. & i.*

Make a plan, invent evidence, etc, to make (an innocent man) appear guilty † *When his partner refused to confirm his story, he realised that he had been framed.* [ALSO: **frame-up** *n.* Plan for this purpose.]

FREE *adj.*

free from Without (blame, pain, worry, etc) † *Her husband returned safely and at last she was free from anxiety.* [ALSO: **trouble-free** *adj.*]

free of 1 Exempt from (tax, customs duty, charge, etc) † *You may import one bottle of wine free of duty.* [ALSO: **duty-free, tax-free** *adj.*] **2** Without, no longer tied to † *He was tired of her and wished he were free of her.* [NOTE: The distinction between *free from* and *free of* is not always clear, but in general *free from* implies being freed (set free) by someone else, while *free of* indicates the wish or attempt on one's own part to get rid of ties, responsibilities, etc.]

free and easy Informal, not concerned with ceremony † *There's no need for you to put on a tie. We're free and easy around here* (or *There's a free and easy atmosphere here*).

make free with Use other people's things as if they were one's own (usually without permission) † *When I said he could use my flat while I was away, I didn't expect him to make free with my whisky.*

FREE-FOR-ALL *n.*

A fight, argument in which everyone present joins † *This fellow hit my brother and in no time the row developed into a free-for-all.*

FRIENDLY *adj.*

a friendly (game, match, etc) Not competitive but not necessarily played between friends (can be used in this context as a noun) † *We are going to play a friendly against a team from France.*

FRIGHTFUL *adj.*

Bad (*See* **awful, terrible**) † *What frightful weather we have been having recently!*

FROM *prep.*

1 Indicating starting point in place or time † *The train will leave from*

Platform 6. † *The programme will be broadcast from 5 o'clock to 6 o'clock.* † *He was interested in music from an early age.* **2** Indicating distance † *It is over 100 miles from London to Birmingham.* **3** Indicating absence † *He lives away from home now.* † *William has a cold, so we have kept him away from school.* **4** Indicating the source of something, or person who sent or supplied it † *These oranges come from Spain.* † *This was a present from my cousin.* † *They are going to act a scene from 'Hamlet'.* † *The book contains many characters drawn from life.* † *From my point of view, there is no advantage in it.* **5** Indicating material † *Wine is made from grapes.* [NOTE: *From* is used to indicate the source material when this changes its form in the final product. We say *The chair is made of wood* because the material is still recognisably the same.] **6** Indicating the lower limit of a range of prices † *New houses for sale from £5,000.* **7** Indicating the present or previous state of something being changed † *The price of an egg has gone up from 2p to 3p.* † *Things are going from bad to worse.* **8** Indicating cause or evidence † *He is suffering from lack of sleep.* † *He died from exposure to the cold.* † *From what I have been able to find out, he seems to have been a careful man.* [NOTE: *Die from* implies the effects of an action, *die of* a disease, a broken heart, etc.] **9** Indicating prevention, protection, separation, etc † *He saved the child from drowning.* † *He prevented her from leaving.* † *Take the knife (away) from him.* **10** Indicating difference † *He is quite different from the rest of his family.* † *The problem of immigration must be distinguished from questions about housing and education.* **11** With adverbial and prepositional phrases indicating place † *He threw a stone at me from behind the tree.* † *He saw a man looking down at him from the balcony above.*

FRONT *n.*
in front of 1 Before (in position) † *A garden is in front of the house.* † *I couldn't see what was going on because there was a very tall man in front of me.* [NOTE: The second sentence indicates the difference between *in front of* and *facing*. *Facing* is only used when the people or things face or look towards each other.] **2** Ahead of (in place or time) † *The man pushed in front of me and got on the bus first.* † *We have a long day's work in front of us.*

FROWN *v.i. & t.*
frown on Disapprove of † *The committee would frown on any attempt to change the established procedure.*

FRYING-PAN *n.*
out of (from) the frying-pan into the fire From a bad situation to a worse one.

FULL *adj.*

full of oneself Conscious of one's own importance † *He's become very full of himself since he was promoted.*

full out Using all the power available (of an engine etc) (*See* **flat out**) † *His car can do over 100 miles per hour, if he goes full out.*

full up Completely full † *I'm sorry, but we cannot give you a room for tonight. We are (the hotel is) full up.*

in full Without leaving anything out † *Write your name in full, please. Initials are not enough.* † *I will repay the debt in full.*

to the full As completely as possible † *We did not enjoy our holiday to the full, because we were worried about my father.*

FUN *n.*

make fun of Cause people to laugh at † *It is unkind to make fun of people who are ill.*

FUNERAL *n.*

that's your funeral You will be the one who suffers, not anyone else † *I've given you my advice and if you won't take it, that's your funeral (not mine).*

FUSS *n.*

make a fuss about Complain; cause trouble † *How could she make such a fuss about something so unimportant?*

make a fuss of Give excessive attention to † *Grandparents usually make more of a fuss of their grandchildren than they did of their own children.* [ALSO: **fuss over** *v.t.* Pay unnecessary attention to.]

FUTURE *n.*

in future From this time onwards † *I hope this will be sufficient warning to you. I shall not be so easy-going with you in future.*

in the future At some future time (not necessarily from now on) † *In the future, it may be possible for men to reach other planets.*

GALLERY *n.*

play to the gallery Try to win approval (from people not involved in the argument) by attracting attention, speaking in a loud voice, etc † *He didn't mean to hurt you by what he said. It is simply that he cannot resist playing to the gallery* (by making a joke at your expense, for example).

GAME *n.*

play the game Play fairly, be fair † *You haven't given him the chance to answer your accusation. That isn't playing the game.*

play someone's game Without realising it, help to carry out someone else's plan † *Don't you see that by refusing to take part, you are playing Brown's game.*

what's the (his) game? What is going on? What are his intentions? † *I found a man in my garden last night. 'What's the game?' I said.*

fair game Person or group who may be attacked without fear of legal action (from original meaning of animals which may be hunted lawfully) † *Now that the laws have been relaxed, even the Royal Family are fair game for the newspapers.*

GAME *adj.*

Ready, prepared (for a challenge, invitation) † ⟩ *We are going to have a race to the top of the hill.* ⟩ *All right, I'm game.* † *He's game for anything if there is a prize to be won.*

GAMESMANSHIP *n.*

Tricks used to win games (and now extended to business negotiations, etc) aimed at putting one's opponent off without in fact breaking the written rules of the game, e.g. deliberate coughing when one's opponent is about to play a shot in golf is gamesmanship. (*See* **one-upmanship**).

GANG *v.i.*

gang up (on someone) Join together, usually for a bad motive (to exclude him or do him harm) † *He had to close down his factory, because the big companies ganged up on him (to ruin him).*

GARDEN *n.*

lead someone up the garden path Mislead or deceive him † *She thought he* *intended to marry her, but all the time he was leading her up the garden path.*

GATE-CRASH *v.t.*

Enter (a private party, meeting, etc) without being invited. [ALSO: **gate-crasher** *n*. Person who does this.]

GEAR *n.*

in (out of) gear Used of things working well (badly) in conjunction with others (from the gears of a car) † *There are so many people on holiday that things are out of gear at the office.*

GET *v.t. & i.*

1 Understand; hear † *I don't get you. What are you trying to say?* † *I didn't get the last thing you said. Would you repeat it?* **2** Catch, trap (in an argument, etc) † *That's got you! How are you going to answer that?* **3** Revenge oneself on † *I'll get you for that one day.*

get about 1 Travel † *Do you get about much in your job?* **2** (of an invalid, etc) Move outside the house † *He is much better. He is managing to get about now.* **3** (of news, information) Spread, become known † ⟩ *They tell me you are getting married at Christmas?* ⟩ *How did that get about?*

get above oneself Have an exaggerated opinion of one's ability or social position † *She has taken her children away from the local school and sent them to an expensive school in town. I think she's getting above herself.*

get across Become understood † *It's useless explaining. The idea doesn't get across.*

get across to (someone) Make him understand, obtain his sympathy for oneself or one's opinions † *He tried to get across (over) to the electors the fact that he had their interests at heart.* † *I couldn't get across to* (communicate with) *him.*

get along 1 Make progress † *How are you getting along (on) in your new job?* **2** Manage † *We haven't much money, but we get along somehow.* **3** (with someone) Be on friendly terms with † *He doesn't get along with the people who work with him.*

get at 1 Reach † *The bottle was stuck at the back of the cupboard and I couldn't get at it.* **2** Obtain, find † *I am going to get at the truth if I have to question you for a week.* **3** Suggest, imply † *Tell me exactly what you think. I think I know what you're getting at but I want to be sure I'm right.* **4** Attack in an irritating, spiteful way † *The Minister complained that journalists were getting at him.* **5** Corrupt, make ineffective † *The police say that someone must have got at the witness because he has changed his story of what happened.* † *The horse ran so badly in the race that the owner suspects it was got at* (here, given drugs, etc).

get away (from) Escape (from) † *The thieves got away from the* *police.* [ALSO: **(make) a getaway** *n.* (Make) an escape (from scene of crime, prison, etc).]

get away with Avoid being punished † *He is so charming that he can insult people and get away with it!*

get one's own back Obtain revenge † *He beat me at tennis today, but next time I'll get my own back.* (Compare **get 3**, which is much stronger and implies violence, injury, etc.)

get by Pass (physically overtake or be adequate socially) † *There were so many people in the corridor that I couldn't get by them to reach the classroom.* † *I haven't a new suit to wear, but I'll get by in this one.*

get down 1 Write down † *He spoke so quickly that I couldn't get it (what he said) down.* 2 Depress † *I heard that you had failed your examination, but don't let it get you down.*

get down to (work, business, etc) Deal with it seriously † *We've been making general conversation long enough. Now let's get down to business.*

get off (with) 1 Escape (heavy) punishment † *He could have been sent to prison, but he got off with a fine.* [ALSO: **get someone off** Enable him to escape punishment † *He was accused of the crime, but his lawyer got him off.*] 2 Introduce oneself to someone of the opposite sex and make friends (usually of a girl attracting a man) † *You had a good time at the party, didn't you? I saw you get off with that nice-looking friend of John's.*

get on Make progress, advance (in work, socially, in time) † *He is very intelligent and sure to get on in life.* † *How are you getting on in your new job?* (See **get along**). † *The time is getting on* (passing). *We must go soon.*

get on for (of time) Approach † *He is getting on for eighty (years old).* † *It was getting on for midnight before we left the party.*

get on with 1 Continue doing † *Get on with your work and don't gossip.* 2 Be on friendly terms with (See **get along**).

get out (of news, secrets) Become known (See **get about**). [NOTE: *Get out* implies secrecy. *Get about* refers more to people passing news on from one to the other, than to the fact of its becoming known.]

get out of 1 Escape from, extricate oneself from † *The bird has got out of its cage* (See **get away from**). † *How shall we get out of this mess?* 2 Avoid (a duty) † *You said you would help me to wash the dishes. Don't try to get out of it.* 3 Give up, cure oneself of (a habit) † *I wish he would get out of the habit of staring at me every time he sees me.* [NOTE: We would not say *get out of smoking, get out of drinking too much*; *give up smoking* is usual.]

get over 1 (an illness, disappointment, etc) Recover from † *I've got over the shock now. I feel much better.* 2 Overcome (a difficulty, opposition, etc) † *I hope my explanation will get over your objections to the proposal.*

get over to (someone) Convince him of, make him understand. (See **get across to**).

get round 1 (a problem, the law, etc) Find a way of overcoming, evading
    † *There are a number of difficulties in our way, but we may be able to get round them.* 2 (someone) Persuade, influence (by flattery, making use of his, her affection for one, etc) † *His daughter knows how to get round him.*

get round to Find the time to (do something, deal with someone) † *He often says he is going to write a book, but he never seems to get round to (doing) it.* † *Would you mind waiting for a moment? I'll get round to you when I have served this customer.*

get through 1 Manage to complete (work, etc) † *He gets through a great deal of work.* 2 Pass (an examination, test, etc) † *Do you think he will get through the mathematics paper?* [ALSO: **get something (someone) through** Ensure that it (he) passes through various stages, overcomes opposition; help him to pass an examination † *The Government are trying to get the bill through the different committees that must approve it.*]

get through to Make contact with, establish communication with † *I tried to get through to your office this morning, but the telephone was out of order.*

get together Meet (usually for a common purpose) † *We must get together to discuss this problem.* [ALSO: **get-together** *n.* Meeting.]

get people together Organise a meeting of this kind.

get up 1 Get out of bed † *I get up late on Sundays.* 2 Stand up † *He got up to speak at the meeting.* 3 Develop (of speed, steam, wind, etc) † *The train got up speed once it was out in the country.* † *A sudden wind got up while we were sailing on the lake.* 4 Organise (usually in an informal way) † *We are trying to get up a football team to play against the next village* (implies that there is no regular team).

get oneself up Dress, make oneself attractive (implies criticism or that dress is unusual) † *My wife spends a couple of hours getting herself up before we got out.* † *The children were got up as eighteenth-century aristocrats for the wedding.* [ALSO: **get-up** *n.* Dress † *What an extraordinary get-up! Where does she find clothes like that?*]

get up to 1 Reach (point in a discussion, page of a book, etc) † *Where did we get up to at the end of the last lesson?* 2 Do (implying tricks, mischief, etc) † *You have to keep an eye on the children all the time. You never know what they'll get up to.*

GIVE *v.t. & i.*

give away Disclose; betray † *Promise you won't give away my secret.* † *He swore that he had not been at the scene of the crime, but his fingerprints gave him away.*

give in (to) 1 Surrender, yield † *The general has lost the battle, but he refuses to give in.* † *I will not give in to threats of violence.* 2 Hand in (papers, one's name, etc) † *When you have finished the examination, give your answers in (to the teacher) at the desk.*

give off Send out (smoke, smell, etc) † *When I opened the bottle it gave off fumes and a peculiar smell.*

give on (to) Look out on, overlook † *My windows give on to the square.*

give out 1 Be completely used up † *He tried to climb the mountain alone, but his strength gave out and he had to be rescued.* † *The food for the voyage would have given out if they had not rationed it.* **2** Make known (by public announcement, etc) † *It was given out that the Minister would be coming to the reception.*

be given over to Be abandoned to (used critically) † *He made no attempt to govern the country. He (his life) was given over to idle pleasures.*

give up 1 Resign, abandon † *He has given up his job and retired to the country.* † *Why don't you give up this pretence?* **2** Retire from struggle, contest † *I'm not going to give up as long as I have any chance of winning.* † *I've made three guesses (and they were all wrong). I give up. Tell me the answer.* **3** Sacrifice † *Many men believe that it is no longer necessary to give up one's seat to a woman in a train.* **4** Stop (doing something) † *I have given up smoking several times, but I always start again.*

give up for lost Assume that someone is not coming, or that something is lost † *We waited for three hours, and then gave her up for lost.*

GIVE-AND-TAKE *n.*

Willingness on both sides to compromise † *There has to be a certain amount of give-and-take in a marriage.*

GIVEN *p.p.*

given (that) Assuming or granted (that) † *Given that he had to do the job in a hurry, I still think he should have done it better.*

given to Inclined to † *He is given to making* (inclined to make) *wild statements without any facts to support them.*

given (time, place, etc) Agreed, pre-arranged † *At a given signal, the children left the class and made their way to the playground.* † *The conspirators met at a given time and place to decide what to do.*

GO *v.i.*

go about Do; attempt to do (implying the technique for, approach to job of work, negotiation, etc) † *He is wrong, but I don't know how to go about telling him.* † *That's no way to go about the job. Let me show you.*

go after Try to obtain † *They told me you were going after a job in France. Did you get it?*

go against 1 Be contrary to † *It would go against my principles for me to accept money without having done anything to earn it.* **2** Turn against, prove unfavourable for † *His business was very successful at first, but things have been going against him recently.* † *If the Government's decision goes against us, we will have to abandon the scheme.*

go ahead 1 Proceed without hesitation † ⟩ *Do you mind if I borrow your matches?* ⟩ *Not at all. Go ahead.* [ALSO: **the go-ahead** *n*. Permission to proceed † *We are waiting for the authorities to give us the go-ahead on our project.*] **2** Make progress † *Work is going ahead fast. The house should be finished in a few weeks.* [ALSO: **go-ahead** *adj*. Progressive † *We are a go-ahead company and welcome new ideas.*]

go along Proceed; become more experienced † *There is no scheme for training new employees. They have to learn the job as they go along.*

go along with Agree with; accompany † *I agree with some of what you say, but I can't go along with you entirely.* † *He asked me if I would go along to the meeting with him.*

go at Work at; do (something) with all one's energy † *Look at those men knocking down that house. They are going at it for all they are worth* (i.e. as hard as possible).

go back on (a promise, one's word, etc) Break, retract † *I said I would help him and I will not go back on that.*

go by 1 Pass (of place, time) † *Mr Jones has just gone by (the window).* † *Three hours went by without our noticing.* **2** Act on; judge from † *Can you give us a good rule to go by.* † *If I were you, I wouldn't go by what John says.*

go down 1 (of a ship, etc) Sink. **2** (of the sun, moon, etc) Set. **3** (of wind, prices, etc) Drop, fall. **4** (of speech, performance in theatre, etc) Be received † *I started by saying how happy I was to be in the village. That went down well (with the audience).* **5** Be recorded in books, etc † *This day will go down as one of the greatest in the history of our country.*

go for 1 Attack (physically or verbally) † *She had no right to go for me like that.* **2** Be applicable to † *He will have to work harder, and that goes for all of you.*

go for nothing Be in vain † *All his careful planning went for nothing.* (See **going for a song**).

go in 1 Fit (into space) † *Are you sure you have given me the right key? This one won't go in* (into *the lock*). **2** (of sun, moon, etc) Disappear (behind clouds, etc).

go in for 1 Enter one's name for (competition, examination, etc) † *How many of you are going in for the Proficiency examination?* **2** Take up (a sport, hobby, etc) † *I hear you go in for stamp collecting.*

go into 1 (Details, explanation, etc) Occupy oneself with † *We accept your general argument. There's no need to go into details.* **2** Investigate, examine carefully † *We have had a complaint from a customer, I'm afraid we'll have to go into it.*

go off 1 Explode; make a loud noise † *The alarm clock went off at 7 o'clock and woke us all up.* 2 (of food, performance in game, etc) Deteriorate; become bad † *Milk goes off very quickly in hot weather.* † *The team began the season very well, but went off after Christmas.* 3 (of play, concert, party, etc) Proceed to a conclusion † *I think the evening went off very well* (was a success throughout).

go on 1 (+ gerund) Continue † *I'm sorry I interrupted you. Please go on.* † *I am not willing to go on working here any longer.* 2 (+ infinitive) Say or do next † *After thanking them for inviting him, he went on to say how much he had enjoyed the evening.* 3 (of time) Pass † *As time went on, he got used to his new surroundings.* 4 Behave (implying criticism) † *You go on so calmly, as if nothing was wrong.* 5 Happen † *What's going on? Why is there such a crowd in the street?* [ALSO: **goings-on** *n*. Happenings or behaviour (used critically) † *They were making a terrible noise in the middle of the night. The police shouldn't allow such goings-on.*] 6 Be guided by (of evidence, etc) † *No one saw the thieves' faces. All we have to go on is the number of the car they used.*

be gone on Be fascinated by, very much attracted to † *She's completely gone on him.*

go out 1 (of fire, light, etc) Be extinguished † *You have let the fire go out.* 2 Cease to be the fashion † *People said the mini skirt would soon go out.* 3 Meet people in society, go to social functions, etc † *We don't go out very much. It's difficult to find someone to look after the children.* [NOTE: **go all out** Use all one's energy, initiative, etc (to achieve something) † *He went all out to win the race (contract).*]

go over 1 Examine carefully (of details, papers, etc) † *I'd like to go over the plans for our new office with you.* 2 Repeat; study carefully † *I have now explained to you how the system works. Let us go over the main points once again.*

go round Cater for the needs of everyone concerned † *There's not enough food to go round.* † *Will there be enough copies of the speech to go round?*

go through 1 Examine carefully (of papers, plans, etc) † *Let us go through the programme for the conference to see if we have forgotten anything.* [NOTE: The difference between this example and *go over* 1 above is that here one is concentrating on the correctness of every detail, while *go over* suggests checking main points already agreed, or likely to be agreed.] 2 Suffer † *She has gone through a great deal since we last met.* 3 Pass; reach a conclusion (of negotiations, proposals, etc) † *The deal I was arranging has gone through, so we can begin work tomorrow.*

go through with Carry out (threat, promise, etc) † *The Government threatened to raise the taxes, but did not have the courage to go through with it.*

go together Blend satisfactorily, match † *I like your new dress. It goes (together) with your coat* (or *Your dress and coat go together*).

go under (of person, company, etc) Fail; become bankrupt † *When they lost their market abroad, the firm went under.*

go up 1 (of prices, temperature, etc) Rise. 2 (of buildings) Be erected † *New blocks of flats are going up everywhere in the city.* 3 Explode, be suddenly destroyed † *The house went up in flames.*

go with 1 Agree with † *I'm in favour of the Government's policy in general, but I can't go with them on the question of national defence.* 2 Form a legally inseparable part of † *The garden and garage go with the house.* 3 Match (*See* **go together**).

go without Miss, accept the lack of † *He was so determined to finish the job that he went without his lunch.* † *I'm sorry, Peter. There are no sweets in the cupboard. You'll have to go without.*

go it alone Follow a course, conduct business, etc without help from others † *He was in business with his brother, but his brother died, so he had to go it alone.*

GO *n.*

a go A turn † *Let me try now. It's my go* (or *Let me have a go*).

at one go At one attempt † *He knocked down all the skittles at one go.*

no go Implying that something will not work or be successful † *I've tried all the ways I know of mending it, but it's no go.*

be on the go Be active † *She's always on the go with all those children to look after.*

have a go Make an attempt, take a chance † *Why don't you have a go at the job? You will have lost nothing even if you fail.*

make a go of Make a success of † *I am pleased to hear about your new job. I'm sure you'll make a go of it.*

GOOD *adj.*

as good as Used to mean *practically*, *almost*, as well as in direct comparison † *He as good as promised me the job* (i.e. made me believe I would get it without actually making the promise). † *The matter is as good as decided.*

good for All right; valid † *There's nothing wrong with this radio. It's good for another ten years.* † *Will this ticket be good for the concert now that the date of the performance has been changed?* † *When I am short of money, I go to my uncle. He's usually good for a loan* (He may be safely approached about a loan). [ALSO: **good-for-nothing** *adj. & n.* Useless, valueless (person) † *You are a good-for-nothing (scoundrel), a disgrace to the family.*]

good for you! I congratulate you; I'm glad about your success or luck †) *I've won £10 on the football pools.*) *Good for you!*

a good many (few) (number) A considerable number † *There were a good many people at the lecture.* † *A good few of them were your students.*

make good 1 (of debt, losses, etc) Repay; recoup † *How long has the bank given you to make good what you owe?* **2** (of statement, promise, etc) Give evidence for; prove true † *You say you think you recognised the man who attacked you. But can you make that good?* **3** (of escape, etc) Effect † *He took advantage of the guard's attention being distracted to make good his escape.* **4** (of a person) Be successful (in career, etc) † *He's very intelligent. He's sure to make good sooner or later.*

GOOD *n.*

much (a lot of) good . . . Used ironically at the beginning of the sentence to imply the opposite † *Keep my money, if it makes you happy! Much good may it do you!* † ⟩ *He's going to ask his brother to help him paint the house.* ⟩ *A lot of good that will do! They're both hopeless.*

to the good Better off (usually in terms of money) † *I went to the races yesterday and by evening I was £5 to the good.*

GRADE *n.*

make the grade Succeed, reach the standard required † *He is a good actor, but I doubt if he is determined enough to make the grade.*

GRAIN *n.*

go against the grain Be contrary to one's nature or upbringing † *It goes against the grain for me to blame my own brother.*

GRANT *v.t.*

take someone for granted Assume that he is satisfied without troubling to find out † *Many women complain that their husbands take them for granted.*

take something for granted Assume it is true, will happen, without troubling to find out † *He takes it for granted that I will help him whenever he asks.*

GRAPE *n.*

sour grapes Expression used for someone saying he doesn't want something after he has failed to get it † *Peter says he would never have married her even if she hadn't met John, but that's just sour grapes.*

GRAPE-VINE *n.*

the grape-vine System for passing on information without the authorities knowing (originally used for prisoners in jail, but now applied generally) † ⟩ *I hear you're looking for another job.* ⟩ *Who told you?* ⟩ *I got it on the grape-vine.*

GREEN *adj.*

(of person) Inexperienced, naive † *You can't blame him. He's still green and doesn't know much of the world.*

GRIN *v.i. & t.*

grin and bear it Endure suffering or disappointment cheerfully † *It's no use waving your arms about. We've lost the battle and we'll just have to grin and bear it.*

GRIND *n.*

A hard, monotonous job of work † *Some people might think compiling a dictionary is an awful grind.*

GROOVE *n.*

be in (get into) a groove (rut) Be (get) stuck in a routine job, way of life † *I'm in a groove in this job and would like to find a way out.*

GROUND *n.*

break fresh (new) ground Deal with something in a new way; operate in new area, circumstances † *Previously we limited ourselves to the European market but now we are breaking fresh ground by trying to sell in America.*

common ground Shared experience or opinions † *We are on common ground as far as the project itself is concerned, but we differ over the timing.*

cut the ground from under someone's feet Anticipate his actions, plans, etc, and so make things difficult for him † *The Government cut the ground from under the Opposition's feet by doing what they were about to propose (and so taking the credit for it).*

suit someone down to the ground Be completely suitable, convenient to him †) *Will it be all right if we discuss the matter after my holiday?*) *Certainly, that suits me down to the ground.*

GROW *v.i. & t.*

grow on Gradually come to have an attraction for (someone) † *I didn't like her singing at first, but I find it grows on me.* † *The real danger of drugs is that the habit grows on people.*

grow out of Grow too big for (clothes, etc) or too mature for (childish games, adolescent habits, etc) † *Small children seem to grow out of their clothes as soon as they put them on.* † *My daughter is very shy, but she'll grow out of it.*

grow up Become adult † *What do you want to be when you grow up?*

GUARD *n.*

be on (off) one's guard Be prepared (unprepared) against attack † *Be on your guard against any suggestions he makes. He is not to be trusted.*

GUESS *n.*

your guess is as good as mine I have no more knowledge about it than you have †) *Do you think it will rain tomorrow?*) *Your guess is as good as mine.*

GUN *n.*

jump the gun Literally, start running in a race before the starting signal is given, but also act, speak, etc before the appropriate or arranged time † *The information was to be given to the newspaper tomorrow, but he has jumped the gun and told them already.*

stick to one's guns (always plural) Maintain one's position (in argument, etc) in spite of pressure † *Don't give way to him. Stick to your guns.*

GUT *n.*

guts (always plural) Courage and determination † *This is a dangerous job. We need a man with plenty of guts.*

HAIR *n.*

let one's hair down (usually of women) Behave informally † *Come to tea tomorrow and we can let our hair down and talk about all our friends.*

split hairs Make small distinctions between things † *Let's not split hairs. It doesn't matter if 84 people were killed on the roads here or 85. There were too many, whatever the figure.*

not turn a hair Show no surprise or fear † *I told him he would be sacked if he didn't work harder, but he didn't turn a hair.*

(by) a hair's breadth (By) the smallest possible margin † *He missed the target by a hair's breadth.* † *They finished the race so close together that there was only a hair's breadth between them.*

HALF *n.*

not half Very much so † ⟩ *I suppose he'll be pleased if he wins the election.* ⟩ *Not half!* † ⟩ *Was she annoyed when you told her you weren't coming?* ⟩ *Not half!*

by half By far (used critically with 'too' + adj.) † ⟩ *Of course, he's a very clever politician.* ⟩ *Too clever by half, in my opinion.*

by halves Not completely; not decisively † *It's no good doing things by halves. We must decide on the whole plan and carry it out.* [ALSO: **half-way** *adj.* (measures, etc) Incomplete; indecisive.]

HALF-BAKED *adj.*

Dull, stupid (of a person); lacking thought and originality (of ideas, proposals, etc) † *That's a half-baked suggestion. You can't have considered what would happen.*

HALT *n.*

call a halt Say that it is time to stop something; stop it † *We had to call a halt to the meeting or many of us would have missed our trains.*

HAMMER *n.*

(go at something) hammer and tongs (Do it) with great energy and noise † *They had a terrible argument. We could hear them going at it hammer and tongs.*

HAND *n.*

hand over fist (of making money) Quickly, as fast as possible † *This bad weather is good for the umbrella manufacturers. They're making money hand over fist.*

hand in glove (politics, business, etc) Closely connected with; allied with † *He has obtained some good contracts from the Government. Of course, he is hand in glove with the people at the Ministry.*

hand in hand 1 Holding hands. **2** Together † *One of the worst things about natural disasters is that disease usually goes hand in hand with death and homelessness.*

at hand Near, within easy reach (*See* **to hand**) † *She is fortunate to have so many shops close at hand.*

at first hand (of information, news, etc) From the person directly concerned, or with one's own eyes † *Did you speak to the Minister himself and get the information at first hand?* † *I cannot judge the situation without seeing it at first hand.*

at second hand From someone other than the person directly concerned. [NOTE: **first-hand, second-hand** *adjs.* (of information, etc) Obtained from the original source, or from an intermediary, respectively. **second-hand** (of goods) Used.]

by hand 1 (of things manufactured) Not by machinery † *Do they make those baskets by hand?* **2** (of letters, etc) By personal delivery, not postal service † *We haven't time to post this. It must go by hand.*

from hand to mouth (of life, financial circumstances) Using all that is earned as fast as it is earned, thus making saving impossible † *I'm tired of living from hand to mouth. I want a job where I can save money.* [ALSO: **hand-to-mouth** *adj.*]

in hand 1 In reserve † *I can afford to buy the car and still have enough money in hand for my holiday.* † ⟩ *Have you used up all your holiday?* ⟩ *No, I still have a few days in hand.* **2** Receiving attention or being planned † *We have a number of projects in hand which should be completed next year.*

off one's hands No longer one's responsibility † *He said he would be glad when his daughters were married and off his hands.*

off-hand 1 *adv.* Without previous thought or preparation † *I can't tell you the answer off-hand. I must look it up.* 2 *adj.* Casual (implying lack of interest or respect) † *I was annoyed that they dealt with my enquiry in such an off-hand way.*

on hand Available † *I shall be on hand if you need me.*

on one's hands As one's responsibility (*See* **off one's hands**) † *We must sell the apples before they go bad. We don't want them to be left on our hands.*

on the one (other) hand From one (a different) point of view † *Of course, we could sell the house now. On the other hand, it might be better to wait a little longer.*

out of hand 1 Out of control † *You must be firm with the boys or they will get out of hand.* 2 Immediately, without stopping to think † *The Union condemned the Government's intervention in the strike out of hand.*

to hand Within reach † *I'm afraid your letter is not to hand. Would you mind repeating what you said over the telephone?* [NOTE: *To hand* indicates that something is literally near to someone's hands or can easily be put into them. *At hand* implies convenience, ease of assistance, etc, but is not necessarily used of objects that can be handled.]

eat (feed) out of someone's hand (originally of animals, but also used of people) Be willing and ready to do what one is told † *The staff were suspicious of me when I first became manager but now I have them eating out of my hand.*

get the upper hand (of) Gain the advantage (over) † *The result of the argument was in doubt for a time, but eventually we got the upper hand (of them).*

give (lend) someone a hand Help him † *Give me a hand with this case, will you?*

give someone a big hand Applaud him (in theatre, meeting, etc) † *The audience gave him a big hand at the end of the performance.*

(give someone) a free hand (Give him) the opportunity to do as he thinks best, make his own decisions, etc.

have (take) a hand in Be involved in, take part in (doing something) † *He had a hand in arranging the contract, although he wasn't primarily responsible.*

have one's hands full Be very busy (*See* **handful**) † *She has her hands full, with all those children to look after.*

keep (get) one's hand in Continue to do something from time to time so as not to lose skill, ability (learn or recover such ability) † *He used to be a soldier and still keeps his hand in with a pistol by shooting at targets in his garden.*

not lift a hand Do nothing to help † *I had to carry all my luggage myself though there were several porters standing around and not lifting a hand!*

play into someone's hand(s) Make a mistake to the advantage of someone else (originally used of a hand at cards, but now applied generally with the same meaning).

put (lay) one's hand(s) on Find (*See* **to hand**) † *Your letter must be here somewhere, but I can't put my hand on it at the moment.*

show one's hand Disclose one's (real) intentions (from exposing one's hand in playing cards) † *The negotiations will not make progress as long as they refuse to show their hand.*

take in hand Take care of (someone), giving him advice based on experience, or take control of (situation) † *As you're new here, I'll ask Mr Brown to take you in hand and show you how we work.*

throw in one's hand Abandon one's attempt to do something; withdraw from participation (again, from playing cards) † *He was a candidate for the Presidency, but he threw in his hand when he realised he had no chance of success.*

try one's hand at Attempt (something) in order to see if one is capable of doing it well † *Have you ever tried your hand at interior decorating?*

wait on someone hand and foot Look after him, giving him any small service he requires † *Butter your own bread! Do you think I'm going to wait on you hand and foot?*

wash one's hands of Disclaim further responsibility or concern for † *I've been patient with you for a long time, but this behaviour is too much for me to stand. From now on, I wash my hands of you.*

win hands down Win very easily.

an old hand A very experienced person † *He's an old hand at persuading people to vote for him.*

HANDFUL *n.*
Someone who keeps one busy or is difficult to control † *My little boy is a real handful.*

HANDLE *n.*
fly off the handle Lose one's temper † *He suddenly flew off the handle and accused me of lying to him.*

HAND-OUT *n.*
1 Something given as charity to poor, etc † *He waited outside the hotel, hoping for a hand-out.* **2** Prepared statement, information, given to newspaper men in advance of speech, etc as a guide.

HANG *v.t. & i.*
hang about Wait, without doing anything † *A group of young men were hanging about on the corner of the street.*

hang back Be unwilling to act, come forward † *We invited him to join in the game but he hung back.*

hang on 1 Depend on † *His decision hangs on the special report which is being prepared for him.* 2 Refuse to give up; wait in the hope of being satisfied † *Mr Smith isn't in his office at the moment. Will you hang on while I try to find out where he is?* 3 (someone's words, expression, etc) Wait anxiously or expectantly for † *Mary hangs on every word he says.*

hang on to Keep tightly, not let go of † *Hang on to your ticket. You'll need it later.*

hang out Live (colloquial) † *Where does he hang out?*

hang together 1 (of people) Support each other in a common attitude † *We must hang together if we are to survive.* 2 (of argument, story) Be consistent.

hang up Replace telephone receiver, ending call † *Don't hang up! I have something else to tell you.*

HANG *n.*

get the hang of Understand the general idea or method † *Watch me do it two or three times. You'll soon get the hang of it.*

HANGOVER *n.*

1 Feeling of sickness, headache, etc after drinking too much alcohol † *I woke up the next morning with a terrible hangover.* [ALSO: **hung-over** *adj.* Having this feeling.] 2 A tradition or object now out of date but still in existence † *The cloths at the backs of the armchairs, called antimacassars, are a hangover from the days when men used a lot of oil on their hair.* [ALSO: **hung over** *p.p.* Remained in existence in this way.]

HARD *adj.*

hard and fast (rules, etc) Fixed and incapable of being changed † *Most people wear white sweaters at the tennis club, but there is no hard and fast rule.*

hard up Short of money † *I won't ask him to pay anything. He's very hard up.*

hard up for (ideas, staff, etc) Short of † *They must have been hard up for ideas if they gave you that excuse again.*

HARD *adv.*

hard done by Unfairly treated † *We have all had a difficult time. You have no reason to feel hard done by.*

HARP *v.i.*

harp on Continually refer to (misfortunes, trouble, etc) † *You must learn to accept his death. It does no good to harp on it.*

HAS-BEEN *n.*

Person who has lost previous ability, influence, etc.

HASH *n.*

make a hash of Do (something) badly, make a mess of it.

HAT *n.*

talk through one's hat Talk nonsense (because of ignorance of the situation, etc) † *He's talking through his hat. He doesn't know the facts of the case.*

HAVE *anom. v.*

[NOTE: Where *have* means *possess* there is a fundamental difference between British and American usage in interrogative and negative † *I haven't got a car* (Great Britain). *I don't have a car* (USA). Occasional possession, however, employs *do* in Britain also † *I haven't (got) a clean shirt. I don't have a clean shirt every day.* Where *have* relates to an experience, *do* is always used in interrogative and negative † *Did you have a good time last night?* † *Do you have breakfast in bed on Sundays?*]

HAVE TO *anom. v.*

Expressing obligation or necessity (imposed from outside) (*See* **must**) † *I have to go now. My wife is waiting for me.* [NOTE: 1 While *must* and *have to* are used interchangeably in most contexts in the affirmative, *must* in the 1st person indicates that the obligation stems from the person himself † *I must and I will become a better person* (*See* **will** as compared with **shall**). 2 In the negative, *don't have to* is used for absence of obligation in general terms (= *needn't*)† *I don't have to get up early every morning. Haven't got to* is used for absence of obligation on a particular occasion † *You haven't got to get up now if you don't feel like it.* Prohibition is not expressed through *have to – mustn't* or *isn't to* are correct. 3 In questions, *do you have to?* and *have you (got) to?* are both found – the preference usually following the lines indicated in (2) above. It should be added that the distinctions pointed out in these notes are becoming less clear among English speakers, and this, together with the growing influence of American English (*See* **have**) means that they should be adopted as guides rather than rules.

HAVE *v.t.*

have had it Be finished; incapable of going on, succeeding, etc † *He is too tired to go on. He's had it.* † *You've had it; we sold all the tickets yesterday* (You are unlucky).

let someone have it Express one's annoyance at him; hit him † *He was smiling at me so complacently that I let him have it.*

have (got) it in for Be looking for an opportunity to punish, revenge oneself on (someone) † *He's keeping out of my way. I've got it in for him because he cheated me.*

have something on Have a previous engagement † *Have you anything on this evening?*

have someone on Deceive him (usually as a joke) † *He can't have won £100,000 on the football pools. He must be having you on.*

have a thing out (with someone) Settle it by argument † *I've been meaning to have this problem out with you for a long time.*

have up Prosecute someone (often used in passive, **be had up**) † *He was had up for parking his car in a prohibited area.*

HAY *n.*

make hay while the sun shines Proverbial expression meaning 'take advantage of opportunities, favourable situations, by acting before they disappear or change'.

HEAD *n.*

above one's head Beyond one's understanding † *His argument was so complex that what he said was above my head.* [ALSO: **talk over someone's head** Fail to realise the level of intelligence, etc of audience, listeners, and therefore speak in a way they cannot understand.]

on someone's head The responsibility, blame, etc will be his † *If your plan goes wrong, it will be on your (own) head.*

bite (snap) someone's head off Speak to him sharply and aggressively † *I'm sorry I interrupted you. But you needn't have bitten my head off.*

get (take) into one's head Come to believe (usually for confused, unsatisfactory reasons) † *How did he get it into his head that we were trying to get rid of him?*

give someone his head Allow him to act freely on his own initiative † *You will never get good work from a manager unless you give him his head and don't interfere.*

go to someone's head 1 (of success, social position, etc) Spoil his judgement by making him proud, etc † *His success has gone to his head. He never listens to anyone nowadays.* [ALSO: **turn someone's head** Used in the same way, but suggesting character rather than judgement.] 2 Make him drunk † *The beer has gone to my head. I can't see straight.*

have one's head screwed on Be sensible, unlikely to do anything foolish or be deceived † *Don't worry about him. He has his head screwed on.*

keep one's head above water Avoid sinking into (financial) difficulties † *The firm is only just managing to keep its head above water.*

make head or tail of (with 'can') Understand any part of † *His writing is so bad that I can't make head or tail of his letter.*

put (our, your, etc) heads together Consult each other † *Put your heads together and see if you can work out a better plan.*

HEADACHE *n.*

Problem; worry † *She is a terrible headache to her parents.* † *The list of guests for the wedding is proving rather a headache.*

HEAR *v.t. & i.*

unheard of Extraordinary (often implying so outrageous (socially) as to be unacceptable) † *His behaviour was quite unheard of. He arrived at the party in a swimming costume.*

I've never heard of such a thing How extraordinary! (That is outrageous). [NOTE: **heard of** Often carries the meaning of *known about, discovered,* as well as literally *heard about,* especially in the negative † *Television wasn't heard of when I was a boy.*]

HEART *n.*

after one's own heart Of the kind one likes or approves of † *We got along very well. He was a man after my own heart.*

at heart (of a person) When one really knows him; in his real self † *He was a good fellow at heart.* † *At heart he knew he had lost her, though he refused to admit it.*

(learn, know) by heart (Learn) so thoroughly that one can repeat from memory † *When I was at school, I had to learn a poem by heart every week.*

in good heart In good spirits, cheerful † *In spite of their sufferings, the survivors of the shipwreck remained in good heart.*

with all one's heart Sincerely † *With all my heart I wish you every success.*

eat one's heart out Suffer severely because of frustration, inability to act, take part in events, etc † *The deposed king ate his heart out in exile.*

have the heart to (usually with 'can', 'could') Be so cruel, unfeeling as to † *I don't know how you can have the heart to say no to the poor child.*

have one's heart in one's mouth Be frightened, nervous † *I stood outside the door with my heart in my mouth, afraid to go in.*

set one's heart on Be very anxious to obtain † *We must give him a bicycle for Christmas. He has set his heart on it.*

take (lose) heart Become confident and cheerful (despondent and miserable) † *He will take heart at this encouraging news.*

take something to heart Be very much affected by it and unable to forget it † *He didn't mean to upset you. You mustn't take it to heart.*

wear one's heart on one's sleeve Show one's feelings openly, risking criticism, hurt, etc † *You shouldn't wear your heart on your sleeve. It isn't wise to let him know that you are in love with him.*

HEEL *n.*

Achilles heel Weak or vulnerable point (in a person's character) † *He is ashamed of his humble background. That is his Achilles heel.*

down at heel Untidily or poorly dressed † *The old man looked down at heel.*

cool (kick) one's heels Be kept waiting deliberately † *I'm in no hurry to see him. Let him cool his heels outside for a time.*

take to one's heels Run (away) † *I saw the bus was already at the stop, so I took to my heels.* † *They took to their heels as soon as the enemy came in sight.*

HEN *n.*

hen party Party to which only women are invited (particularly bride just before wedding and her girl-friends) (*See* **stag party**).

HEN-PECKED *adj.*

(of a husband) Ruled by his wife (implying frequently criticised for his behaviour, etc).

HERE *adv.*

here and there In various places † *The country was wild, but here and there there were signs of human life.*

here, there and everywhere In all parts, in every place imaginable † *I've been looking for you here, there and everywhere.*

neither here nor there Irrelevant † *What you're saying is neither here nor there.*

HIDE-OUT *n.*

Hiding place, particularly of criminals, guerrillas, etc.

HIGH *adj.*

high and dry Isolated, on one's own † *She got up in the middle of the meal and I was left high and dry.*

HIGH-POWERED *adj.*

Used of people to mean dynamic, forceful and influential (often critically, implying that they are unpleasant or frightening) † *He's one of the new breed of managers, very high-powered and determined to run things his way.*

HIT *v.t. & i.*

hit it off Get on well (with someone) † *I introduced them and they hit it off (together) straightaway.*

hit someone off Imitate him accurately † *That's just like him. You've hit him off exactly.*

hit on (an idea, scheme, etc) Suddenly discover; discover by accident or inspiration † *We tried several methods before we hit on this way of doing it.*

HOBSON *prop n.*

Hobson's choice No choice at all because there is only one alternative really available † ⟩ *You can either accept the rise in salary I have offered or resign.* ⟩ *I see. Hobson's choice.*

HOLD *v.t. & i.*

hold forth Speak to an audience (usually used critically) † *Your brother has been holding forth to the other guests for an hour or more.*

hold something forth Offer it (usually in order to tempt interest) † *This opportunity holds forth the promise of success.*

hold (oneself) in Check, restrain (oneself) † *I could hardly hold myself in when he accused you.*

hold off Stay away; keep at a distance † *Do you think the rain will hold off until we get home?*

hold on (imperative) Wait! † *Hold on a minute! I'm not ready.*

hold out **1** Offer (hope, possibility, etc) † *I don't hold out much hope of an improvement.* **2** Continue resistance; not give in † *They held out for three days before the enemy broke through their defence.* **3** Last; be enough † *Will the milk hold out until tomorrow?*

hold over Postpone † *There are two things to be discussed which were held over at the last meeting.*

hold to (one's word, promise, etc) Keep † *I know he said that, but can we trust him to hold to his word?* [ALSO: **hold someone to his word etc** Ensure that he keeps it.]

hold up **1** Delay † *The train was held up by fog.* [ALSO: **hold-up** *n.* Delay † *What was the reason for the hold-up?*] **2** Stop a vehicle in order to rob passengers, etc † *They held up a train and escaped with £2 million.* [ALSO: **hold-up** *n.* Robbery of this kind.] **3** Exhibit † *Don't hold him up as an example to others.* **4** (of story, argument, etc) Be consistent † *When you study his story in detail, it doesn't hold up (or hold water) (See **water**).*

hold with Agree with; approve of (an action, principle) † *I don't hold with letting children do just as they like.*

hold one's own **1** (of people who are ill) Not get worse † *He's been holding his own since last night and we hope he will soon improve.* **2** Not give ground to someone, not be defeated † *He isn't winning the game, but he's holding his own.*

HOLE *n.*

be in a hole Be in a difficult situation † *Can you help me? I'm in an awful hole.* [ALSO: **put someone in a hole.**]

pick holes in Find fault with (a plan, argument, etc) † *A clever lawyer always tries to pick holes in his opponent's case.*

HOME *n.*

be (feel) at home (in) Feel comfortable, be at ease (in) † *I speak Spanish fluently, but I don't feel at home in French.* † *He soon felt at home in his new surroundings.*

HOME *adv.*

bring (drive, etc) something home Make it clear, so that it is fully understood or appreciated † *His stay in the village brought home to him the need for better communications there.* † *I want to drive this point home, so that there will be no possibility of misunderstanding.*

get home Reach the target † *That remark was so near the truth that it got home.*

get home to Make absolutely clear to † *What I am trying to get home to you is that you must plan your future before it is too late.*

HOMEWORK *n.*

do one's homework Prepare oneself thoroughly (for discussion, meeting, task, etc) † *He gave all the necessary facts and figures in his speech. He had obviously done his homework.*

HONOUR *n.*

on one's honour On one's reputation for being honest † *I promise you, on my honour, that I will return it to you tomorrow.*

do the honours (always plural) Act as host, guide, etc † *Are you going to do the honours and pour out the tea?*

HOP *n.*

(catch someone) on the hop (Find him) unprepared † *The manager came in unexpectedly and caught us on the hop.*

HOPE *v.t. & i.*

hope against hope Hope in spite of the unfavourable signs † *He went on hoping against hope that his wallet would be found.*

HOPE *n.*

some hope(s)! Exclamation meaning 'there is no hope of that, that is most improbable' † *Your worries would be over if you won the football pools.*) *Some hope(s)!*

HORSE *n.*

dark horse Someone whose chance of success, etc has been underestimated † *Jones proved to be the dark horse of the competition by beating several better-known players.*

from the horse's mouth From the genuine source; first-hand † *You must believe the news. I got it straight from the horse's mouth.*

back the wrong horse Gamble unsuccessfully on the success of people, projects, etc, as well as race-horses † *He said Mr Wilson was sure to win the election, but he backed the wrong horse.*

flog a dead horse Waste one's energy on arguments already lost or settled † *He's flogging a dead horse in trying to persuade people to use canals instead of roads.*

look a gift horse in the mouth Proverbial expression meaning 'question the value of something received for nothing'.

HOT *adj.*

blow hot and cold Constantly change one's mind about a proposal, etc, favouring it and opposing it.

HOUSE *n.*

on the house (of drinks, food, cigarettes, etc) Free, given away by the management or hosts † *It was the publican's birthday, so all the drinks were on the house.* † *Have another drink. The Company are paying, so it's on the house.*

HOUSE-WARMING *n.*

Party given by new owner of house to celebrate moving in.

ICE *n.*

break the ice Encourage people to become friendly (at a party, etc) or take the first step in a difficult matter † *Everyone stood around in silence until he broke the ice by offering them a drink.* † *No one seems to want to talk about it, so I suppose I must break the ice.*

cut no ice Fail to persuade or attract (someone) † *His charming manner cuts no (doesn't cut any) ice with me.*

ICEBERG *n.*

the tip of the iceberg The relatively small part of the mass which shows above water and hence recognisable evidence of what is believed to be a social trend, etc on a much larger scale † *It is thought that the outbreak of violence against the Government in this city is only the tip of the iceberg. A revolution throughout the country is feared.*

IN *prep.*

1 Indicating place † *He lives in London* (*See* **at** for differences between use of the two prepositions). *He was sitting in an armchair* (but on *a chair* – *in* implies being enclosed or surrounded by a thing). † *I saw it in a shop-window* (as part of the display of objects on sale). **2** With verbs of action, movement, indicating place † *He put the money in his pocket.* † *He threw the case in the river.* [NOTE: *Into* in the last sentence would suggest interest in the action; *in* emphasises the place where the object goes.] **3** Indicating direction † *He went in that direction.* **4** Indicating time when † *He got married in the Spring.* † *It is often foggy here in November.* † *He was born in 1940.* [NOTE: *On* is used for particular days † *on Sunday, on March 1st. at* for religious festivals, etc † *at Christmas, at Easter*, but *in* is correct for all periods longer than a day.]

5 Indicating time within which something happens † *It rained a lot in the night* (last night) (*See* **at** for use of *at night*). † *In the morning, we went out shopping.* **6** Indicating time by the end of which something takes place; within † *He will be back in an hour('s time).* **7** Indicating parts of a whole † *There are seven days in a week and twelve months in a year.* **8** Indicating dress † *She was (dressed) in blue.* † *The man in the dark suit.* **9** Indicating physical surroundings † *I love to walk in the rain.* † *He is afraid to go out in the dark.* **10** Indicating physical or mental state or condition † *We are in love.* † *I am in a hurry.* † *We are all in good health.* **11** Indicating means of expression † *This book is written in English.* † *Please write your name in capital letters.* **12** Indicating form, division † *You must pay for the car in monthly instalments.* † *They were standing around in small groups.* **13** Indicating respect (in which there is a comparison) † *In some ways he is very like you.* † *I was his equal in strength but not in judgement.* † *There is nothing wrong with it in price, but it is inferior in quality.* **14** Indicating occupation, activity † *He is in the army, Civil Service, etc.* † *He is in business in the north of England.* **15** By way of † *In reply to your letter of the 4th, . . . Have you anything to say in your defence?* **16** As far as something is concerned † *There's nothing wrong with the plan in itself.* **17** (followed by gerund) While † *In trying to repair the hole in the roof, he fell off the ladder.*

IN *adv.*
1 (after 'to be') At home † *Is anyone in?* **2** (after 'to be') In the fashion † *It seems that mini skirts are in again.*
in for Likely to experience † *They say we are in for a spell of good weather.* † *You'll be in for it* (be in trouble) *if the boss catches you.*
in on Included in, informed about (colloquial) † *Only his closest friends were in on his plan to get married the next day.*
in and out Continually coming and going out † *The boss has been in and out of my office all day.* [ALSO: **ins and outs** *n.* Details (of a complicated job, story, etc) † *He seems to have been the guilty one, but we shall never know the ins and outs of it.*]
(well) in with On (very) good terms with (someone and likely to gain advantage from it) † *He is sure to be promoted. He is well in with the Managing Director.*

INSIDE *prep.*
1 Within † *Inside the box, there was a diamond ring.* **2** On the inner side of † *He was standing just inside the door.* **3** Within (a period of time) † *He returned inside an hour.*
inside out *adv. phrase* **1** With the inner side outside † *Your socks are inside out.* **2** (following 'know', 'study', etc) In every detail † *He knows the subject inside out.*

INSTEAD OF *prep.*

1 In place of † *This year we went by car instead of going by air.* **2** As a substitute for † *Do you mind having tea instead of coffee?* **3** Rather than † *You ought to do some work, instead of sitting there reading the paper.*

INTEREST

with interest With additional force (from use of *interest* as money charged for a loan) † *He hit me, so I repaid the blow with interest.*

INTO *prep.*

1 Indicating movement to or towards a point within † *We went into the house.* † *He looked into her eyes.* **2** Indicating change of state or condition † *Translate this passage into English.* † *She burst into tears.* † *The witch turned the prince into a frog.*

IRON *v.t. & i.*

iron out Smooth out, remove † *We are trying to iron out our differences and reach an agreement.*

IRON *n.*

strike while the iron is hot Act quickly while a situation is to one's advantage.

have too many irons in the fire Be concerned in too many schemes, projects, etc to pay sufficient attention to them.

JACK *n.*

jack of all trades (and master of none) Person with experience of a wide variety of jobs (who has never stayed long enough in any one of them to become proficient).

JIB *v.i.*

jib at Show unwillingness † *She didn't mind him giving her presents, but she jibbed at accepting money from him.*

JOB *n.*

a good job (too) Fortunate; (with 'too') so much the better † *It's a good job I brought my umbrella. It is starting to rain.* † *She couldn't come. A good job, too. I don't like her.*

a put-up job A scheme, arrangement made in order to give a false impression † *The house appeared to have been burgled, but the police believe it was a put-up job.*

jobs for the boys (always plural) Positions given to friends, political supporters, etc instead of thrown open to competition.

have a job to Find it difficult to † *He was a good worker and we will have a job to replace him.*

give something (someone) up as a bad job Accept that it (he) is a hopeless case † *After trying to get the car to start for half an hour, he gave it up as a bad job.* † *We did what we could to help him, but in the end we had to give him up as a bad job.*

JOKE *n.*

no joke A serious matter † *The car broke down miles from the nearest town. It was no joke, I promise you.*

JUMP *v.i. & t.*

jump at Eagerly seize (an opportunity, etc) † *He jumped at the chance of going to Canada to represent the company.*

jump on Reprimand (a person) severely; take strong action to correct a fault † *The sergeant jumped on his men at the first sign of carelessness.*

jump to (a conclusion) Reach (a conclusion) hastily, without sufficient thought † *As soon as I mentioned your name, he jumped to the conclusion that we had been talking about him.*

JUST *adv.*

just about Almost, but not quite (used for emphasis, rather than as a precise expression) † *I've just about had enough of your grumbling.*

just as well For the best, under the circumstances † *You left the key in the door when you came in. It's just as well that I saw it there.* [NOTE: In a sentence like † *You might just as well be told the news now, just* is used purely for emphasis and does not affect the meaning.]

just now 1 A short time ago † *Mr Jones came into the office just now. He is looking for you.* 2 At this moment, at present † *We haven't any red shoes in stock just now.*

just too bad Unfortunate, but cannot be altered † 〉 *It's essential that I should see Mr Brown today.* 〉 *That's just too bad. He's gone out and won't be back till tomorrow.*

KEEP *v.t. & i.*

keep (oneself) to oneself Avoid meeting people † *He's very quiet. He keeps (himself) to himself.*

keep something to oneself Not tell anyone about it † *This is a secret between the two of us. Keep it to yourself.*

keep at it Persist in working on something or make sure that someone else continues to work † *Once you start a big job like this, you must keep at it or you lose concentration.* † *He made the prisoners break up stones and kept them at it all day.*

keep back (information, etc) Withhold, not tell † *I must tell you what happened. I can't keep it back any longer.*

keep down 1 Control † *We must try to keep our expenses down.* † *He sprayed his garden with weed-killer to keep down the weeds* (prevent them from spreading). 2 (of food) Retain in the stomach † *He couldn't keep his food down and was violently sick.*

keep in with Remain on good terms with † *You will have to keep in with the boss if you want to make progress in the firm.*

keep off 1 Not touch, not go on to † *Keep off the grass.* † *Keep your hands off the cakes.* 2 (of bad weather) Not come † *It looks as if the rain will keep off, after all.*

keep on 1 Continue † *He kept on working until he was 70 years old.* 2 Do something repeatedly † *She keeps on telling me that we should buy a new car.* 3 Not dismiss someone † *This part of the factory has been closed down, but we are keeping the men on in other jobs.*

keep on at Continually worry with complaints, suggestions, etc † *Don't keep on (at me) about it! I'll mend it as soon as I have time.*

keep up 1 (of spirits, courage, etc) Prevent from failing † *Have a drink of brandy. It will keep your spirits up.* 2 (of customs, correspondence, etc) Not allow to lapse † *They kept up a lively correspondence for several years.* 3 (of aggressive action) Maintain † *They kept up the pressure on him until he gave in.* 4 (of property) Maintain in good condition † *It costs more and more to keep up the house.* 5 (of people) Prevent them from going to bed † *I won't keep you up any longer. You look tired.*

keep up with 1 (*See* **keep up** 2) Maintain contact with, interest in † *We kept up with them while they were abroad by writing to them every*

Christmas. † *Have you kept up with your English since you returned to your own country?* **2** (fashion, customs, etc) Be up to date † *It is very expensive to keep up with the fashion.* **3** Not fall behind † *He ought not to be in this class. He can't keep up with the rest.* † *Don't walk so fast. I can't keep up with you.* [ALSO: **keep up with the Joneses** Try to compete with neighbours in buying clothes, cars, etc (used to imply waste of money in an attempt to gain social position).]

KEEPING *n.*

in keeping with Consistent with † *That is not in keeping with what he told me.* † *He was told that his conduct was not in keeping with the behaviour of a gentleman.*

KEEPS *n.*

for keeps Child's phrase meaning *to keep*, used colloquially to suggest *for ever* † *Is it a present? Is it mine for keeps?*

KEY *v.t.*

key up (usually passive) Make (be) tense with excitement † *Everyone was keyed up waiting for the game to start.*

KICK *v.t. & i.*

kick off Start † *We're going to kick off with a short speech of welcome before the dinner.* [ALSO: **kick-off** *n. For a kick-off I'd like a tomato juice.*]

kick out Eject someone from a club, party, etc or dismiss from job † *He was so inefficient that they kicked him out.*

kick up (**a noise, fuss, etc**) Make a disturbance † *The children were kicking up an awful row.*

KICK *n.*

1 Thrill † *I got a kick out of steering the boat myself for the first time.*
2 (of alcohol, etc) Powerful effect † *Be careful of those cocktails. They have quite a kick.*

for kicks Just to get a thrill (implying pointless, destructive action) † *The boy said he broke the windows of the telephone kiosk for kicks.*

KID *v.t.*

you're kidding You are lying to me for a joke † ⟩ *We think you should enter for the Miss Britain contest.* ⟩ *You're kidding!*

KIND *n.*

(pay) in kind (Pay) in goods, not money † *The farmers in these small villages often pay their bills in kind.*

(repay) in kind (Repay) in the same way (of insults, etc) † *He was rude to me, so I repaid him in kind.*

nothing of the kind Not at all, nothing like that † ⟩ *I suppose you were angry*

when you heard she was going to marry him. 〉Nothing of the
kind. [ALSO: **something of the kind** Something like that (used more
precisely to refer to the subject of conversation) † 〉*I suppose you know I
am going to take up a job in Glasgow.* 〉*I heard something of the kind.*]

of a kind (implying criticism) Hardly deserving the name, some sort of † *He's
a doctor of a kind, but I wouldn't trust him to look after me.*

KING-SIZED *adj.*

American expression now widely used in Britain to mean extra-large
† *King-sized cigarettes are longer*, but so much used by advertisers that it
has come to mean big.

KISS *n.*

the kiss of death Action of betrayal (Judas Iscariot's betrayal of Jesus Christ)
but now more widely used to imply either rejection, betrayal by someone
supposed to be friendly, favourably disposed, or ironically, praise which
dooms whatever is concerned to disaster † *He submitted the plan to his
boss, who said he liked it but gave it the kiss of death.* † *Don't tell me that
he praised my play in his column. That's the kiss of death.*

the kiss of life Artificial respiration by breathing into a person's mouth.

KNIFE *n.*

have (get) one's knife in (into) Persecute † *Ever since I refused to do as he said,
he has had his knife in me.*

KNOCK *v.t. & i.*

Criticise (unfairly) † *Most authors get annoyed when critics knock their
books.*

knock about Wander from place to place; do a variety of jobs † *He's been
knocking about the Continent.* [ALSO: **knocking about** Lying around, still
in existence but not generally known about † *These cars have not been
made for forty years, but there are still a few knocking about.*]

knock back (of drink, food) Drink, eat quickly † *He knocked back a pint of
beer in a few seconds.*

knock down (of prices) Lower or cause someone else to lower † *He wanted
£5,000 for his house, but I knocked him (the price) down to £4,800.*

knock off **1** (of price) Deduct † *The article is priced at £101, but I'll knock off
the odd pound.* **2** Stop (work) † *What time do you knock off (work)?*
3 (of writing) Put together quickly † *He knocked off 1,000 words before
lunch.*

knock out Originally, knock down a boxer who cannot get up before *out* is
called, but generally used for a blow which makes someone unconscious
† *The shelf fell on his head and knocked him out.* [ALSO: **knock-out** *n.*
Such a decisive blow.]

knock together (of furniture, etc). Put together quickly, without care † *I'm not* *proud of the bookcase. It's just something I knocked together one weekend.*

knock up 1 Wake up by knocking on door or window. **2** (a meal, etc) Make quickly without much preparation † *He brought two of his friends home without warning me, so I had to knock up a meal for them.*

KNOW *v.t. & i.*

I know 1 Used to propose an idea one has just thought of † *I know. Let's go round to Mary's.* **2** (in conditional clauses) Judging from my knowledge of † *If I know him, he won't spend more than he has to.*

I don't know 1 (as exclamation) Expressing surprise † *I don't know! Fancy him not telling us he was coming!* **2** I am not sure † *I don't know that I will be able to come.*

I don't know about you Expressing one's own preference, whatever others may want † *I don't know about you, but I'm going to have another drink.*

not that I know of Not as far as I know † *He called in here yesterday, didn't he? Not that I know of.*

you know 1 Assuming knowledge on the listener's part † *You know the cinema in Broad Street. There was a fire there last night.* **2** Remember (assuming that the listener does so) † *You know the girl we saw outside your house yesterday.* **3** For emphasis, reminding listener of what he certainly knows † *I've been working here longer than you, you know.* **4** For emphasis, informing listener of something he probably does not know † *I was in the navy during the war, you know.*

what do you know? Expressing surprise † ⟩ *I'm going to get married tomorrow.* ⟩ *Well, what do you know? It's the first I've heard of it.* [NOTE: *You know* is often used with no meaning at all, to join together phrases while the speaker is thinking. **4** (above) is an example of this.]

KNOW *n.*

in the know Informed (of something secret) † *Only his brother and I were in the know.*

KNOW-ALL *n.*

Person who tries to give the impression of knowing everything.

KNOW-HOW *n.*

Practical expertise gained from experience † *They are going to make our machines abroad under licence, but they will have to rely on us for the know-how.*

L

LAND *v.t. & i.*

(job, order, etc) Obtain in spite of competition † *The firm have landed an important contract in America.*

land (up) (in) End up (in) (usually somewhere unexpected or undesirable) † *I took the wrong turning and landed up on the other side of the town.* † *If he doesn't change his ways, he will land up in prison.*

be landed with (passive only) End by having to accept (a situation) or look after (people) † *He was away ill and I was landed with all his work.* † *We were landed with our grandchildren for the Christmas holidays, while my son and his wife were in America.*

LAND *n.*

no man's land Area separating opposing armies (particularly when they have taken up fixed positions).

LAP *v.i. & t.*

lap up Take in (information, compliments, etc) greedily (like a cat drinking milk) † *The readers of that newspaper lap up scandal.*

LARGE *n.*

at large **1** (of convicts, etc) At liberty; not caught † *The murderer is still at large.* **2** (of a group) In general; on the whole † *I don't think the public at large would support such a scheme.*

LAST *n.*

the last of . . . The end of (a matter), the back of (someone) for the last time † *He is so proud of his achievement that we shall never hear the last of it.* † *I hope we have seen the last of him.*

at last Finally, after a delay † *At last he saw the opportunity he had been waiting for.* [ALSO: **at long last** After a long delay.]

LAST *adj.*

last but not least The last to arrive, be mentioned, etc, but not the least important † *Last but not least I must thank my parents, who have helped us so much.*

the last **1** The least desirable or likely † *He's the last person I would want to marry.* † *That's the last thing I would expect.* **2** The last (thing, word)

The most modern or most original (not always favourable) † *Their house is the last word in comfort.* † *She looked like the last thing* (very odd).

LATE *adj.*

late in the day Almost too late † *It's a little late in the day for me to change my plans.*

of late Recently † *He's been very bad-tempered of late.*

the (my) late The former (used when referring to a (recently) dead person) † *The late King George VI.* † *My late husband was very fond of the garden.*

the latest The most recent news, fashion, etc † *Have you heard the latest? George is going to marry Margaret.*

at the latest Preferably before but not later than † *I must have it by Monday at the latest.*

LAUGH *v.i. & t.*

laugh away Dismiss, cause to disappear by suggesting that fear, concern is laughable † *He laughed away their fears, pointing out that they could not possibly be hurt.*

laugh off Overcome painful, embarrassing situation, etc by jokes, good humour † *He made a silly remark about foreigners, not knowing my guests were from abroad, but I managed to laugh it off.*

LAUGH *n.*

have the last laugh Finally get the better (of someone) † *Columbus was considered mad by many people but he had the last laugh (on them).*

LAUNCH *v.t. & i.*

launch out into Make a start on, enter on (something new) † *Many big companies which previously depended on one product are now launching out into a variety of fields.*

LAUREL *n.*

look to one's laurels (plural only) Take note of rivals, competition, in order to maintain one's reputation † *The fast times recorded by Brown and Green suggest that White will have to look to his laurels when he defends his championship.*

LAW *n.*

be a law unto oneself (not *to oneself*) Go one's own way, taking no notice of convention, other people's example or advice † *It's no use expecting him to submit to a common plan of training. He's a law unto himself.*

lay down the law Make statements on rules as if one had the authority to enforce them † *It would do him more good to write to the bus company about the bad service instead of laying down the law to me.*

LAY *v.t. & i.*

lay about one (not *oneself*) Strike out in all directions † *He laid about him desperately as the crowd tried to stop him.*

lay aside **1** Put by † *I have laid aside some money for him, which he will have when he is 21.* **2** Stop work on something for the time being † *I have had to lay aside the novel I am writing because I have too many other things to do.*

lay by Save (similar to **lay aside 1** (above) but more general in meaning) † *I expect he has some money laid by for his old age.* [NOTE: **lay-by** *n.* Area at the side of a main road where drivers may stop vehicles and rest.]

lay down **1** Give up, surrender † *He promised that if the rebels laid down their arms they would be forgiven.* **2** (life) Sacrifice for a cause † *A service is held every year for those who laid down their lives for their country in the war.* **3** Establish regulations, price, etc order by regulation † *This is the price laid down by the manufacturers.* † *The Government have laid down that people travelling from countries where there has been an outbreak of this disease must be vaccinated.*

lay in Store in anticipation of future need † *I like to lay in sufficient coal to last through the winter.*

lay into Attack (someone) with all one's force † *I laid into him with both hands.*

lay off **1** Suspend temporarily from work because there is not enough to do † *Several car manufacturers have laid off their workers because of the shortage of parts.* **2** Stop doing (something) (usually for reasons of health) or stop attacking (someone) † *The doctor has told me to lay off smoking.* † *Lay off him! He's had enough.*

lay on **1** Supply, connect the supply of (gas, electricity, telephone, etc) † *I don't want to move into the house until they've laid on the electricity.* **2** Provide (facilities for entertainment, food) † *We have laid on a buffet for the wedding reception and a band to play later on.* **3** Apply a layer of (usually used figuratively. We say *put on a coat of paint*) † *He lays it on thick, doesn't he?* (of flattery, compliments).

lay out **1** Put ready for use † *I've laid out your clothes in the bedroom.* **2** Invest † *I have to lay out £100 straightaway, but I shall get a good return on the money.* **3** Make unconscious (*See* **knock out**) † *He laid the man out with one blow.* **4** Design, make a plan for † *He called in a professional gardener to lay out his garden.* † *This book is very well laid out.* [ALSO: **layout** *n.* Design, rough plan for book, plan of works, etc † *Can you give me a layout to work from?*]

lay up **1** Confine in bed (usually passive) † *He is laid up with a bad leg.* **2** Store up (trouble, etc) (seldom used for things) (*See* **lay aside, lay by, lay in**) † *You could be laying up trouble for yourself by not listening to their advice.* **3** Take (a ship) out of service † *The ship has been laid up for repairs.*

LAYABOUT *n.*
Idle person who does not work (and may be suspected of crime for this reason).

LEAD *v.t. & i.*
lead astray Tempt (someone) to do wrong † *He was a good boy until his companions led him astray.*
lead up to (in conversation) Prepare for by previous remarks or (of events) be the signs that something will take place † *Lead up to the question gradually.* † *This series of events led up to the revolution.*

LEAF *n.*
take a leaf out of someone's book Imitate his action † *I ought to take a leaf out of your book and buy a house in the country (as you did).*
turn over a new leaf Reform one's conduct † *He has promised to turn over a new leaf.*

LEAGUE *n.*
in league with Allied with (usually secretly) † *We believe the rebels are in league with a foreign government.*

LEAK *n.*
inspired leak (of news, information) Information supposed to be secret deliberately allowed to reach the press, etc so that public reaction may be known before the authorities commit themselves to an action.

LEAN *v.i. & t.*
lean over backwards Make every effort, be prepared to suffer inconvenience (in order to satisfy or please someone) † *We have leaned over backwards in trying to help him and understand his point of view.*

LEAP *n.*
by leaps and bounds Very quickly † *At first he spoke English very badly, but now he is progressing by leaps and bounds.*

LEAST *adj. & n.*
at least 1 At the lowest estimate † *The repairs will cost at least £100.* 2 If nothing more † *Having asked him to come, you might at least invite him into the house.* 3 Indicating a favourable action which partially disarms criticism † *He didn't give me what I wanted, but at least he explained to me why he couldn't.* 4 Anyway, at any rate (qualifying statement) † *The company my father works for are very mean – at least, that's what he says.*
(not) in the least (Not) at all † ⟩ *Do you mind if I borrow your pen?* ⟩ *Not in the least.*

LEAVE *v.t. & i.*
leave someone to himself (his own devices) Let him alone to do as he likes

without interference † *If he doesn't want to play, leave him to himself.*

leave someone to it Let him do (finish) what he has to do, alone † *They were still arguing at midnight, so I went to bed and left them to it.* † *He seemed capable of finishing the job, so I left him to it.*

leave well alone Not interfere in something that is good enough as it is † *The machine isn't running perfectly, but I prefer to leave well alone rather than risk a breakdown by trying to improve its performance.*

leave off Stop (doing something) † *I left off reading the story at the end of Chapter 1.*

leave out Omit (implying accidentally unless otherwise stated) † *You left out his name from the list of invitations.*

leave over Let (something) wait until a later date † *There is no time to discuss the remaining items, so we will leave them over until the next meeting.*

leave (someone) standing Be much better, make much more progress (than someone else) (or car, ship, etc) † *His entry for the competition was so good that he left the rest of us standing.*

LEG *n.*

on one's (its) last legs Very weak, about to collapse † *The firm is losing money so fast that it must be on its last legs.*

not have a leg to stand on Have no defence, reason for one's actions, opinions † *Once I proved his figures were all wrong, he hadn't a leg to stand on.*

pull someone's leg Tease, by making him believe something untrue † *Hey, John, your house is on fire. It's all right, I was only pulling your leg.*

LEISURE *n.*

at one's leisure When one has time without hurrying † *I'll leave the detailed report with you and you can go through it at your leisure.* [NOTE: **at leisure** Not occupied, free (of tasks). But nowadays it is more common to say *Mr Jones is free to see you now*, instead of *at leisure to see you.*]

LENGTH *n.*

at length **1** Eventually, after a long time or delay † *At length I came to the conclusion that I had been wasting my time.* **2** For a long time † *He explained the subject at (great) length.*

go to any lengths Be ready to do anything (to achieve or avoid something) † *He would go to any lengths rather than admit that he was wrong.*

LET *v.t. & i.*

let be Leave in peace † *Let him be! You won't gain anything by worrying him.*

let it go at that Agree to say (do) no more about it † *I can't remember the other thing I wanted, so we'll let it go at that.*

let oneself go Behave in a relaxed way, not hold back one's feelings, desires, etc † *Let yourself go! You're only on holiday once a year.*

let down Not fulfil one's obligation (to someone) † *You can trust me to help you. I won't let you down.*

let someone down lightly Be gentle in telling him bad news, disappointing him. [ALSO: **let-down** *n.* Disappointment.]

let someone (oneself) in for Involve him (oneself) in (difficulty, work, etc) † *When I agreed to help him clear his garden, I didn't realise how much work I was letting myself in for.*

let off 1 Excuse, pardon † *The judge let him off with a warning. I'll let you off your homework as it is the last week of term.* 2 Fire off (fireworks) or allow to fire (gun, etc).

let on Disclose † *Don't let on to Mother that I've bought her a present.*

let up Become less severe; relax and slacken effort † *I wonder if the rain will let up enough for us to go out.* † *Don't let up now! We've nearly finished the job.* [ALSO: **let-up** *n.* Rest from pressure, effort.]

LETTER *n.*

(keep) to the letter (of the law) (Follow) precisely † *I want you to obey my instructions to the letter.* † *He has no imagination. He insists on keeping to the letter of the law (and ignores the spirit).*

LEVEL *n.*

on the level Honest (colloquial), reliable (of information, etc) † *Is he on the level?*

LIE (LAY, LAIN) *v.i.*

lie in Stay in bed after the usual time when one gets up † *We like to lie in on Sunday morning.* [ALSO: **lie-in** *n.* Time spent in this way.]

take lying down Accept insult, provocative action without replying † *How dare he behave like that? I'm not going to take it lying down.*

LIE *n.*

white lie Untrue statement made with good intentions (to spare someone pain, etc) † *When she asked me if I liked her hat, I had to tell a white lie.*

LIFE *n.*

for life For the rest of one's life (or working life) † *He won't find another job at his age. It looks as if he will be there for life.*

not on your life Under no circumstances †) *Will you lend me £100?*) *Not on your life.*

to the life An exact copy of a person (either in painting, etc or because of physical similarity) † *What a perfect likeness! It's your father to the life.*

the life and soul of the party Someone in good humour who tries to make others in his company enjoy things to the same extent † *Until he arrived, it was a dull occasion, but he soon established himself as the life and soul of the party.*

have (lead someone) a dog's life Have (cause someone to have) a miserable existence (particularly through nagging, continually ordering him about) † *She never gives him a moment's peace. He has (she leads him) a dog's life.*

LIGHT *n.*

according to someone's lights (plural) According to his private standards of behaviour, moral attitude † *He was doing the right thing, according to his lights.*

in the light of In view of, considering knowledge gained from † *In the light of the employer's refusal to see our representatives, we shall consider strike action.*

come (bring) to light Become (make) known † *The situation has been altered by new facts which have come to light in the last few days.*

see the red light See danger ahead (and therefore draw back, take action avoiding it) † *He saw the red light and got out of the country just before the revolution started.* [NOTE: **red-light area (district)** Part of a town where there are brothels.]

LIGHT *adj.*

make light of Treat as unimportant (of fears, objections, etc) † *It is easy for you to make light of their complaints.*

LIKE *v.t. & i.*

I like that! Used ironically to express surprise † ⟩ *I don't think you should go to see him.* ⟩ *I like that! You were the one who suggested it.*

if you like If it suits you † ⟩ *Will you have tea or coffee?* ⟩ *Whatever is easier. Tea, if you like.* † *I'll carry the parcel for you, if you like.*

LIKELY *adj.*

as like(ly) as not The corrupt form *like* is more common in Southern England † *They'll get there before us as likely as not.*

not likely! Certainly not (*See* **not on your life**) † ⟩ *Have you invited your mother-in-law?* ⟩ *Not likely!*

LIMIT *n.*

he's (that's) the limit His (that) behaviour can hardly be tolerated † *He suddenly arrived on the door-step without any warning. Isn't he the limit?*

LINE *v.t.*

line up for Prepare (someone) to take over a job; make (things) ready for action, work, etc † *He is lined up for Smith's job when Smith retires.*

LINE *n.*

in line with **1** Following naturally from † *The Government's decision to change the law is in line with the proposals made to them by the Royal Commission.* **2** In agreement with † *His speech was not in line with party policy.* [ALSO: **be (get) in (out of) line with** Agree with (rebel against) the attitudes of other members of the group one belongs to † *The Prime Minister is alarmed because several members of the party have got out of line on this issue.*]

not in my line Not something I am familiar with † *Stamp collecting is not in my line. I prefer outdoor amusements.*

on the lines of Following the same principles as, based on † *I have planned the book on the lines suggested.* [ALSO: **on these lines, on those lines, on similar lines to, etc**]

on the right lines Going in the right general direction; generally in the right way or manner † *Your work is on the right lines, though there are some mistakes in detail.*

draw the line at Stop short of (because of moral scruple, etc) † *I have been guilty of crimes, but draw the line at murder.*

drop someone a line Write a letter to him.

read between the lines Find out the real feelings, opinions of a writer or speaker which are not directly expressed in words † *Reading between the lines, I feel sure he is not so convinced about it as he pretends.*

toe the line Obey orders † *You had better toe the line in future or you will be in trouble.*

LINEN *n.*

wash one's dirty linen in public Discuss disagreeable private matters (e.g. family quarrels) when others are present.

LIP *n.*

(keep a) stiff upper lip Used to describe very strict control of emotions (particularly in presence of danger or in reaction to personal sorrow or loss).

LIST *n.*

short list Final list of candidates for a job following earlier processes of selection which have eliminated the rest † *He didn't get the appointment, but he qualified for the short list.* [ALSO: **short-list** *v.t.* Select candidates for such a list.]

LITTLE *n.*

little by little Gradually † *Little by little he found himself depending on her more and more.*

LIVE *v.i. & t.*

live down Overcome past disgrace by one's way of life † *It was a terrible scandal. I don't believe the family will ever live it down.*

live for Live with a certain end in view † *Since her husband died, she has had nothing to live for* (i.e. no reason to encourage her to go on living). † *Ever since I told my little boy that we are going to the circus next week, he has been living for the day.*

live off Take advantage of in order to live † *You can't expect to live off your parents* (rely on their resources so as not to work).

live on 1 Continue to live † *Her brother died in 1924 but she lived on until a few years ago.* 2 (of money, income) Spend on things one needs for living † *How much have you got to live on?* 3 Have as food † *He lives on fruit and nuts.*

live up to 1 Fulfil (promise) † *He did not live up to the great expectations everyone once had of him.* 2 Reach the standard expected of † *The hotel did not live up to its reputation.*

LOCAL *adj.*

the local *n.* The local public-house (used particularly when it has a central position in the community, is a meeting-place, etc).

LOCK *n.*

lock, stock and barrel The whole thing † *I've given all the papers to the lawyers so they can sort out the affair lock, stock and barrel.*

LOGGERHEAD *n.*

at loggerheads (with) In dispute (with) † *The Government and the Trade Unions are at loggerheads (with each other) over strike legislation.*

LONG *n.*

the long and the short of it The main thing to be said (avoiding further discussion in detail) † *Whatever the detailed points of criticism may be, the long and the short of it is that they will not agree to our proposal.*

LONG *adv.*

as (so) long as Provided that † *As long as we agree, it doesn't matter what they think.*

LONG-WINDED *adj.*

(of speech, explanation, etc) Unnecessarily slow in reaching the point † *He was so long-winded in his introductory remarks that I lost interest.*

LOOK *v.i. & t.*

look after Take care of † *Will you look after the children for me while I go out shopping?* † *Look after your own affairs and don't interfere in mine.*

look at 1 Examine † *Would you mind looking at the television? There is something wrong with it.* 2 (in negative, with 'will' or 'would') Consider; have anything to do with † *I suggested a way of resolving the problem, but they wouldn't look at it.*

look down on Despise † *She looks down on us because she is better educated.*

look for 1 Try to find † *What are you looking for? Have you lost something?* 2 Expect (results, performance) † *I shall be looking for an improvement in your work this year.* [NOTE: **unlooked for** Only used with the second meaning to mean unexpected.]

look forward to Anticipate with pleasure † *I look forward to seeing you again.*

look in (on) Pay a brief visit (to) † *Since I was passing her house, I looked in (on her) to see how she was getting on.* [NOTE: **look-in** *n.* Colloquially used to mean chance (of winning), share of gain † *The other candidates were so good that I didn't get a look-in.*]

look into Investigate † *I'll look into your complaint, Madam, and find out who was to blame.*

look on 1 Regard, consider † *We look on this invention as one of the most important in modern times.* 2 Take no active part, be only a spectator † *I couldn't stand there looking on when I saw him attacking the girl.* [ALSO: **onlooker** (more common) and **looker-on** *ns.* Person who does this.]

look out 1 (usually imperative) Take care (of yourself) † *Look out! There's a car coming towards us.* 2 Select by making an inspection † *Go through the books in my library and look out any that you would like to borrow.*

look out for Be on the watch for; be prepared for † *Look out for trouble once he finds out that we haven't sent him the order we promised.* [ALSO: **look-out** *n.* Person on the watch. **that's your look-out** A colloquial expression meaning: That's your responsibility, not mine. **a poor look-out** Also colloquial, means small prospect of success † *It will be a poor look-out for him if the police catch him* (i.e. the future for him will be bad).]

look over 1 (house) View, to see if it is worth buying † *I must stay in tomorrow. Some people are coming to look over our house.* 2 Examine papers, letters, etc to make sure they are all right.

look round 1 Examine before deciding (more general than **look over**) † *I'm just looking round (the shop) (to see if there is anything I would like).* 2 Go sight-seeing † *We only had an hour to look round the town.* [ALSO: **have a look round** *n.* Same meanings as 1 and 2 (above).]

look to Rely on † *Don't look to him for help.*

look up 1 Improve † *Business is looking up.* 2 (in a book) Find a reference † *Look up his number in the telephone book.* [ALSO: **look someone up** Visit him (unexpectedly) (used particularly when in a strange place where it might be necessary to look up his address, etc) † *Look me up if you are ever in London.*]

look up to Respect, admire † *I have looked up to him since I was a small boy.*

look here! (as exclamation) Introducing 1 a suggestion 2 a protest or complaint † *Look here, let us wait until we know all the facts before we start arguing.* † *Look here! I've stood enough nonsense from you!*

look like (as if) Seem likely to (that) † *It looks like rain.* † *It looks as if we have taken the wrong turning.*

LOSE *v.t. & i.*

lose out New expression, meaning be at a disadvantage and therefore lose † *A majority of the men in Britain voted Labour at the last election, but the Labour party lost out because of the women's vote.*

LOSS *n.*

be at a loss (for words) Not know (what to do or say) † *What an extraordinary thing! I'm at a loss for words.* † *I can't help you, I'm afraid. I'm completely at a loss.*

cut one's losses Withdraw from business, relationship, etc after suffering a loss, in order to avoid a greater loss † *I decided to cut my losses before all my money was swallowed up.*

LOVE *n.*

for love or money At any price † *Servants are so scarce in this area that they can't be found for love or money.*

there's no love lost between them They dislike one another.

LOW-DOWN *n.*

Inside information † *Can you give me the low-down on the negotiations?*

LUCK *n.*

down on one's luck Suffering a run of bad luck.

worse luck Unfortunately (used in parenthesis) † *It started to rain, worse luck, so we went home.*

LUMP *v.t.*

(only in) **if you don't like it, you can (will have to) lump it** You must put up with it, even if you don't like it.

LURCH *n.*

(only in **leave someone in the lurch** Abandon him when he is in need of help.

MAD *adj.*

mad about 1 (on) Very enthusiastic about † *They're mad about opera.* 2 (at) Very angry about (towards).

like mad Furiously, very energetically † *They were all at the station to meet us, waving like mad.*

MADAM *n.*

a (little) madam A woman who treats others as if they were inferior (a girl with precocious airs) † *She spoke to me as if I was her maid. She's a real madam, I assure you.* † *You can see from the way she orders her brother about that she's a little madam.*

MAIN *n.*

in the main In the majority of cases, for the most part † *There will be showers in all parts of England today, but in the main they will be light.*

MAKE *v.t. & i.*

make (it) 1 Keep an appointment † *I'm sorry I won't be able to make the meeting tomorrow.* 2 Be at a place in time (to catch) † *The letters won't make the last post.*

make do (with) Manage (with something) because nothing better can be obtained † *We haven't time to cook a proper meal. We'll have to make do with sandwiches.*

make for 1 Go in the direction of † *The escaped prisoners are believed to be making for London.* 2 Contribute towards, promote † *This discussion will make for a better understanding between us.*

make of Understand to be the meaning of, character of † *I don't know what to make of it. What do you make of him?*

make off (with) Run away (with), especially after doing wrong, stealing, etc † *When he saw the farmer coming, the tramp made off (with the chicken) as fast as he could.*

make out 1 Write out, fill in (bill, form, etc) † *Shall I make the cheque out in your name?* 2 (a case) Formulate or prove † *The Government are trying to make out a case for simplifying taxation.* 3 Distinguish (in seeing, reading, etc) (usually in spite of difficulty) † *Through the fog he could just make out the shape of the church in front of him.* † *I can't make out his writing.* 4 Arrive at a conclusion †) *When you have paid me for the apples, you will still owe me £3.*) *How do you make that out?* 5 Claim, pretend † *He's not as honest as he makes out.* 6 Understand (usually with 'can') † *I can't make out why she was so rude.* † *She's a strange person. I've never been able to make her out.* 7 Get on, succeed † *How are you making out in your new job?*

make over Transfer (money, property, etc) † *He made over all his property to his son.*

make up 1 Complete, supply a deficiency † *How many stamps do you need to make up the set?* † *I can only let you have half your order now. I'll make it up next week.* 2 Invent (a story, excuse, etc) † *He made up stories for* *his children.* **3** Put together (a page of type, suit of clothes, doctor's prescription, etc) † *Will you make up a suit for me from this material?* [ALSO: **make-up** *n*. Arrangement of type on a page.] **4** Use paint, cosmetics † *The actor had to make (himself) up before going on the stage.* † *Wait a minute while I make up my face.* [ALSO: **make-up** *n*. Actors' paint, powder, etc or cosmetics.] **5** (a quarrel) Become friends, lovers again † *My husband and I have some terrible rows, but we always kiss and make up afterwards.*

make up for Compensate for † *He was too ill to go to the children's party, so we bought him a toy to make up for it.*

make up to **1** Be pleasant to (someone) in the hope of gain † *The young actress made up to the producer hoping that he would give her a part.*
2 Compensate (someone) for † *Do you mind working late, Miss Smith? I'll make up the extra hours to you next week.*

MAKE *n*.

be on the make Be intent on one's own profit † *It was clear to me that the girl wasn't in love with him. She was on the make.*

MAKING *n*.

have the makings of (always plural) Have the necessary qualities to become † *He is a very promising player. I think he has the makings of a champion.*

MAN *n*.

man to man Openly, without fear or deception † *It's time we had a talk about this, man to man.*

to a man Without exception † *To a man they approved his action.*

MAP *n*.

off the map Away from the main centres of population, lines of communication † *We live in a little village. It's a bit off the map.*

(put) on the map (Make) (a place, company name, etc) well-known † *Shakespeare put Stratford-on-Avon on the map.*

MARCH *n*.

steal a march on Gain an advantage over (a competitor, etc) by doing something before he expects it † *A rival publisher stole a march on them by bringing out a book on the same subject the week before theirs was ready.*

MARK *v.t.*

mark someone out for Recognise his ability as exceptional and expect to promote him in the future † *He was marked out for a high place in the Government as soon as he entered Parliament.*

MARK *n.*

up to the mark As good as normal (particularly of health) † *I haven't been feeling up to the mark recently.*

wide of the mark Wrong, incorrect † *I'm afraid you are (your guess is) well wide of the mark.* [ALSO: **off the mark** The same meaning.]

MASTER *n.*

a past master Someone with a great deal of practice in doing something (and therefore an expert in it) † *He is a past master at twisting his opponent's argument to prove his own point.*

MATTER *n.*

a matter of course Something which is part of the normal procedure † *There's no need to write 'airmail' on letters to Europe. They go by air as a matter of course.*

as a matter of fact In fact (although you may not know it and may be surprised to hear it) † ⟩ *Did you have any difficulty in finding this restaurant* ⟩ *As a matter of fact, I had been here before.*

for that matter As far as that is concerned † *He isn't sure if he will be able to come. For that matter, neither am I.*

the matter (with) The thing that is wrong (with) † *What's the matter with him? Is he ill?* † *The television set has broken down. See if you can find out what is the matter with it.* [NOTE: In the indirect question, verb comes before subject – not *What the matter is.*]

MAY (MIGHT) *anom. fin.*

1 Indicating possibility † *It may rain later today.* † *Ask John. He may know the answer.* [NOTE: 'Might' in the place of 'may' in these sentences suggests the possibility is less likely † *Nobody seems to know where Mary is. Perhaps John might know.* In the past, the same distinction applies † *It is surprising that Frank hasn't arrived yet. Of course, he may have missed the train.* † *Of course, he might have missed his train, but he has never done so before.*] **2** Asking for permission or indicating permission † *May I borrow your pen?* † *You may go as soon as you have finished your work.* [NOTE: 'Might' is used in the question form only as a sign of politeness or to indicate fear of refusal † *Might I have another cake, please?*] **3** Used as the equivalent to a subjunctive in clauses expressing purpose † *I have lent him some old papers so that he may have a better idea of what the examination requires* (i.e. in the hope that they will give him a better idea.) † *In order that he might improve his knowledge of French, he was sent to Paris for a year.* (**may** only) Indicating a concessive effect † *He may have a lot of worries at present, but that's no excuse for his bad manners* (i.e. Even if (though) he has . . .).

may (might) as well **1** It would be (as) sensible to . . . (as) † *You may as well* *take what is offered now, rather than wait for something better.* **2** It would be reasonable, sensible (without comparison) † *There is nothing for us to do here, so we may as well go home.* [NOTE: Again, 'might' in this sentence does not change the meaning, but includes a greater element of doubt.] (**might** only) **1** Making a suggestion which amounts to a request † *If you're going to the post office, you might buy me some stamps.* **2** Expressing reproach or criticism † *You might have* (ought to have) *told me that you were bringing your friends home to dinner.*

MEAN *n.*

by all means Certainly † ⟩ *Would it be all right if my brother came with me?* ⟩ *Yes. By all means.*

by no means **1** Certainly not (to express polite agreement with a request etc, not refusal) † ⟩ *Would it be too much trouble for you to look after the children?* ⟩ *By no means.* **2** Certainly not (in clause) (stressing negative) † *I know that I am by no means the first person to complain about it.*

MEASURE *n.*

for good measure In addition (to ensure that the quantity is enough or that it is a fair price, etc) † *The curtains cost £1 a yard, but for good measure I'll give you the rings and hooks for nothing.*

made to measure Literally, of a suit cut by a tailor to fit someone's measurements, but used more widely to mean 'perfectly suited for' † *The new law contains so many omissions that it seems made to measure for people to evade it.*

MEET *v.t. & i.*

meet someone half-way Reach a compromise with him, give way in order to do so † *I'll meet him half-way. I'll give him half my commission if he leaves me free to negotiate the deal.*

MENTION *v.t.*

don't mention it Phrase suggesting that thanks are unnecessary † ⟩ *Thank you so much for your help.* ⟩ *Don't mention it.*

not to mention Apart from; as well as (the most important item of all or less important ones) † *We had all those cases to carry, not to mention the children's push-chair.* † *The whole family will be there, father, mother and grandparents, not to mention all the uncles and aunts.*

MESS *v.t. & i.*

mess about **1** (**with**) Work (on) without apparent purpose or result. † *He's been messing about (with the car) all morning.* **2** Cause inconvenience to (someone) by inefficiency or lack of consideration † *They messed us about at the airport. We had to get on and off the 'plane three times.*

mess up Spoil † *He was called back to his office in the middle of his holiday* *and that messed it up completely.* [ALSO: **mess-up** *n.* Confusion, muddle resulting from inefficiency, misunderstanding, etc † *There's been a mess-up over the delivery of the goods.*]

MIDDLE-OF-THE-ROAD *adj.*
(policies, attitudes, etc) Moderate, avoiding extremes.

MIGHT *anom. fin.*
(*See* **may**).

MILL *n.*
go (put someone) through the mill Undergo hard training or experience (subject someone to it) † *There is no easy way to success in this firm. We all have to go through the mill.*

MINCE *v.t. & i.*
not mince matters (words) Speak plainly, avoiding polite phrases † *I'm not going to mince words. Your work is very bad.*

MIND *v.t. & i.*
mind you Take note of this † *I shan't invite him. It's not that I don't like him, mind you. It's simply that we can't put him up for the night.*

never mind 1 It doesn't matter † *Never mind what he told you. Listen to me!* 2 Don't worry about it † *⟩ I'm sorry I forgot to bring that book back. ⟩ Never mind.*

MIND *n.*
have in mind Plan, think of † *⟩ What are you going to do this evening? ⟩ Have you anything particular in mind?* † *My secretary will be retiring soon. Have you anyone in mind as a replacement?*

on one's mind In one's thoughts (causing worry, etc) † *He looks as if he has something on his mind.*

out of mind (only in proverbial expression 'out of sight, out of mind' and in expression 'time out of mind' (*See* **time**)) Not thought about † *Once people retire from public affairs, they are soon forgotten. Out of sight, out of mind.*

out of one's mind Mad † *If they show that advertisement on television again tonight, I'll go out of my mind!*

to my mind In my opinion † *He is determined to get married in the spring, but to my mind he would be wiser to wait.*

be in two minds about Be unable to decide between † *I'm in two minds about what I should wear.*

be of one (the same) mind (of two or more people) Be in agreement † *I am glad we are of one mind on the question.*

cross one's mind Come into one's head † *It never crossed my mind that the girl was your sister.*

have a good (half a) mind to Be almost convinced that one will (think one might) do something † *I've a good mind to take this dress back to the shop. There's a mark on the sleeve.*

make up one's mind Decide † *Make up your mind! Do you want it or don't you?*

put one in mind of Make one remember † *That puts me in mind of the time I was staying in Brighton.*

absence of mind Inability to concentrate on what one is doing. [ALSO: **absent-minded** *adj.* Having a tendency to forget, not concentrate on what one is doing (because one is thinking of something else) † *He is so absent-minded that he often gets out of the train at the wrong station.*]

presence of mind Ability to act calmly and quickly to avoid anger, confusion, etc † *If it had not been for his presence of mind, there would have been a serious accident.*

one-track mind Mind obsessed by one thing † *He has a one-track mind. The only thing that interests him is golf.*

MISS *n.*

a miss is as good as a mile Proverbial expression meaning that one is as safe after a narrow escape as after an escape by a wide margin † *That car came very close. Still, a miss is as good as a mile.*

MISTAKE *n.*

and no mistake! Without a doubt (used for emphasis) † *It is going to be a hot afternoon, and no mistake!*

make no mistake about it Do not deceive yourself (used for emphasis as a warning) † *Make no mistake about it, the Government will put up the taxes, whatever they say.*

MIXER *n.*

a good (bad) mixer Person who gets on well (badly) with people of all kinds.

MIXTURE *n.*

the mixture as before Literally, the same prescription authorised by the doctor as on previous occasions, but used to mean the same remedies for problems in general † *The new Government say they are going to adopt a new approach to taxation, but no doubt it will be the mixture as before.*

MOCK-UP *n.*

Rough model made to indicate how proposed machine or part of it would work; design done in rough to indicate layout of type, etc.

MOMENT *n.*

at the moment At this present moment, now † *Mr Jones is out at the moment, but he will be back soon.*

not for a moment Never † *I would not suggest for a moment that you should do it all alone* (more common than *Not for a moment would I suggest . . .*).

MOON *n.*

once in a blue moon Very rarely *The Austin 7 car was very common before the War but now they are seen only once in a blue moon.*

MOST *adj. & n.*

at (the) (very) most At the highest limit or estimate † *At most there were only 50 people at the meeting.*

make the most of Use to the best advantage † *She is rather plain, but she makes the most of herself (her looks).* † *We have only two weeks' holiday a year, so we must make the most of it.*

MOTION *n.*

go through the motions Do one's work or carry out one's social duties without care or enthusiasm † *They shook hands with the guests when they arrived, but it was clear that they were just going through the motions.*

MOUTH *n.*

down in the mouth Depressed; sad † *Why is he so down in the mouth this morning?*

MOVE *n.*

get a move on Hurry up † *Get a move on! We can't wait here all day.*

MUCH *adj. n.*

make much of 1 (used in negative) Understand (something) † *It is supposed to be a very good book, but I couldn't make much of it* (implying this was the author's fault). 2 (usually with 'too') Give importance to † *Newspapers make too much of such incidents.* 3 Show (too much) kindness, attention to someone † *They make much of her when she was staying with her grandparents.*

not think much of Not have a good opinion of † *I don't think much of that suggestion.*

not up to much Not very good † *His first book was good, but the latest one wasn't up to much.*

MUG *n.*

Someone easily deceived (colloquial).

no mug A shrewd person † *If he believes the story, there must be some truth in it. He is no mug.*

a mug's game Something with no sure profit in it, which attracts fools (e.g. gambling).

MUSIC *n.*

face the music Stand up to punishment, one's critics † *There's no point in making excuses now. The only thing to do is to face the music.*

MUST *anom. fin.*

1 Expressing obligation or necessity felt by person himself (*See* **have to**)

† *I must remember to post this letter.* † *I must have a new dress for the party.* **2** Expressing obligation imposed on someone else † *You must remind me of it.* **3** Expressing prohibition (negative) [NOTE: Absence of obligation is expressed by **needn't**] † *Passengers must not get off the bus before it stops.* [NOTE: The past tense in these cases is expressed by 'had to' † *I'm sorry I'm late. I had to go to the bank.*] **4** Expressing logical probability † *You must be John's sister. You look just like him.* † *If you didn't have any lunch, you must be hungry.* [NOTE: 1 The opposite of these examples is expressed by **can't be** † *You can't be hungry. You've only just had dinner.* 2 The past tense here is expressed by 'must have' † *You must have been hungry when you got home last night if you hadn't eaten anything all day.*]

MUST *n.*

a must An essential object, requirement, etc † *This new refrigerator is a must for your kitchen, Madam* (i.e. you will feel that you must have one).

NAIL *n.*

hit the nail on the head Say or do something which is exactly right; provide a true explanation † *You've hit the nail on the head. That is just what is needed.*

pay on the nail Pay what one owes immediately † *I have no complaints about my customers. They all pay on the nail.*

NAME *n.*

call someone names Insult him † ⟩ *You stupid idiot!* ⟩ *Calling me names won't help you.*

NEAR *prep.*

1 Indicating proximity of place † *He lives near the station.* **2** Indicating approach to, in time or age † *He must be near retiring age.* † *It is getting near the time to go home.* **3** (negative) In sentences emphasising a determination to keep away † *He hasn't been near his father since they quarrelled* (He has kept away from him deliberately). † *They never go near a church.*

nowhere (not anywhere) near Very far from (not only in place) † *What he told you was nowhere near the truth.*

126

NECK *n.*

neck and neck (of competitors in race, etc) Running even † *The horses were neck and neck as they passed the winning post.*

neck or nothing Taking great risks in race, competition † *We must go neck or nothing if we are to get there ahead of them.*

stick one's neck out Risk criticism by saying or doing something † *I'm not going to stick my neck out and make a decision with no one to back me up.*

NEED *anom. fin.*

Indicating lack of obligation or necessity (*See* **must**) † ⟩ *Need I go with you?* ⟩ *You needn't if you don't want to.* [NOTE: 1 *Need* is not used in positive statements except in subordinate clauses where the main verb is negative or interrogative † *I don't think we need go over that again.* 2 In the past tense, *didn't need to* indicates that the person was aware that there was no obligation or necessary for him to do something and he therefore did nothing. *Needn't have* means he was not aware, and therefore did something unnecessarily † *John called in unexpectedly last night, so I didn't need to ring him up about the invitation.* † ⟩ *You needn't have written to him. He is coming here this evening.* ⟩ *Yes, but I didn't know that until just now.* 3 It is important not to confuse the anomalous finite form with the transitive verb *need*, meaning require, be necessary to. This is followed by a noun, gerund or infinitive (with *to*) † *I need some money.* † *I need to know how many of you will be staying for dinner.* The gerund type cannot be used in the passive, but the others can † *He needs to be taught a lesson. All that is needed is a little common sense.* However, the gerund type implies a passive meaning † *Your hair needs cutting* (ought to be cut).]

NERVE *n.*

get on someone's nerves Irritate him † *He sings out of tune and it gets on my nerves.*

have (got) a nerve Have a cheek; be audacious † *I don't know how you have the nerve to ask to borrow the car again after crashing it the last time.*

have the nerve (to do something) Be sufficiently cool and brave (to do it) † *I wouldn't have the nerve to drive a racing car.*

NEST-EGG *n.*

Money saved for the future.

NEVER *adv.*

I never (said, did, etc) Used for emphasis instead of *not* † *That's a lie! I never said anything of the kind.*

well, I never! Expressing disbelief, surprise † *Well, I never! Who would have thought that he would marry a woman ten years older than himself?*

the never-never *n*. The hire purchase system (because the payments never seem to end) † *I bought a television on the never-never.*

NEXT *adj*.

the next man Anyone else † *In normal circumstances I'm as honest as the next man, but I avoid paying taxes if I can.*

what next? What will happen next? (in a context where one is surprised, or annoyed by what has happened already) † *He expects to be paid in full for the job before he has started on it. What next?*

NEXT TO *prep*.

next to no time Almost immediately † *You won't have to wait long. I'll be back in next to no time.*

next to nothing Almost nothing † *She was wearing next to nothing.*

NICK *n*.

in the nick of time At the last possible moment in order to succeed, avoid a disaster, etc † *The hero arrived in the nick of time, just as the villain was about to kill the girl.*

NINETEEN *n*.

talk nineteen to the dozen Talk rapidly and continuously (thereby preventing others from speaking).

NOBODY *n*.

a nobody A person without influence or importance † *I hoped to speak to the Head of the Department, but I was left to explain my case to a nobody.*

NOSE *n*.

under one's nose Directly in front of one, where it should be easily seen † *I spent ten minutes looking for the letter and in the end found it under my nose.* † *Why do they want to import coal into Wales, when they have so much under their (very) noses?*

cut off one's nose to spite one's face Harm one's own interest in a vain attempt to cause trouble for someone else † *If you go on strike and the firm collapses as a result, you will have cut off your nose to spite your face.*

have (keep) one's nose to the grindstone Be (keep) working hard without stopping to rest † *The boss comes round the office from time to time to make sure that we keep our noses to the grindstone.*

look down one's nose at Despise, disdain † *She looked down her nose at me because I have a cockney (London) accent.* [NOTE: The difference between this and *turn up one's nose at* is basically the physical difference between the two actions. *Look down one's nose at* is most often used, therefore, to show a sense of social superiority, *turn up one's nose at* to indicate taking offence at goods of inferior quality being offered.]

pay through the nose Pay much more than something is worth.

put someone's nose out of joint Spoil his plans † *The Council have refused permission for him to build a factory there. That will put his nose out of joint.*

turn one's nose up at Disdain † *Eat your dinner. It's good food and there is no reason for you to turn your nose up at it* (*See* NOTE *above*).

NOTHING *n.*

nothing doing (as reply to suggestion) No, certainly not † *He wants a rise in pay but I've told him there's nothing doing.*

nothing to write home about Not very interesting or exciting † 〉 *Is she very pretty?* 〉 *Nothing to write home about.*

be nothing to 1 (of people) Used to disclaim feeling, affection for † *I went out with her a few times last year, but she's nothing to me.* **2** Be as nothing in comparison with † *We are a successful company, but our profits are nothing to yours.*

NOW *adv.*

now and then (again) From time to time, occasionally † *He comes in to see us now and then although he doesn't work here any more.*

now then (at the beginning of sentence) Used either to attract attention or as a warning † *Now then. What have we got to do this morning?* † *Now then! Behave yourself!*

NUMBER *n.*

back number Literally, past issue of newspaper, magazine, etc, but extended to person or thing now out of date (particularly person who no longer has influence) † *Since his son took over from him as managing director, he has become a back number.*

one's opposite number Person holding post with similar duties, of similar responsibility in another organisation, country † *The Foreign Secretary has been having talks with his opposite number in France* (i.e. the French Foreign Minister).

look after (take care of) number one Look after one's own interests, be selfish † *He won't help you. He's too busy looking after number one.*

NUTSHELL *n.*

in a nutshell Accurately expressed in very few words † *That's the situation in a nutshell. No further details are necessary.*

OAR *n.*

put one's oar in Intervene in a discussion; interfere † *I thought she wouldn't be able to resist putting her oar in.*

OAT *n.*

sow one's wild oats Lead a gay life while young before settling down.

OCCASION *n.*

rise to the occasion Show that one is equal to a test, emergency † *When the captain fell ill he rose to the occasion and brought the ship back safely.*

ODD *adj.*

odd man out 1 Person left when others have been arranged in groups † *We made up two equal teams and John was the odd man out.* **2** Person who does not fit into society, group, etc to which he belongs † *We encourage everyone to take part in our activities, but there is always someone who proves to be an odd man out.*

ODDS *n.*

(always plural) **be at odds (with)** Disagree † *She is at odds with her mother about what she should wear at the wedding.*

it makes no odds It doesn't matter (which alternative is chosen) † *It makes no odds (to me) whether he goes or stays.*

what's the odds? (with singular verb) What is the difference? What does it matter?

odds and ends Small articles of no great importance or value, bits and pieces † *I have to call at my flat to pick up a few odds and ends.*

OF *prep.*

1 Indicating possession or origin † *The works of Shakespeare.* † *This watch was the property of his father.* [NOTE: In these cases the apostrophe form – *Shakespeare's works* – is almost always used to indicate ownership † *This watch was his father's.* The *of* form in example **1** suggests that the author, artist, etc is important – compare *John Smith's recent novel*] **2** Indicating social origin or place of birth, etc † *He came of poor parents.* † *He is a native of Glasgow.* [NOTE: *He is* of *Glasgow* is wrong, however. *He is (comes) from Glasgow* is correct.] **3** Indicating association with, authority over, responsibility for † *the University of Cambridge, the Queen of England, the manager of the factory.* **4** In cases where two nouns are in opposition: *the City of London, the history of England.* **5** Indicating materials from which things are made, constructed, etc † *This chair is made of wood.* † *The house was built of stone (See* **from** for difference between *made of* and *made from*). **6** Indicating measure, what something consists of † *a pint of milk, a glass of wine, a piece of meat.* **7** Indicating personal characteristics † *a man of great intelligence, a girl of gentle nature.* **8** Indicating cause † *It could not have broken of itself* (i.e. because of some internal defect). † *She died of a rare disease.* **9** Indicating freedom from (irritation, disease, etc) † *I wish I could cure her of that habit.* † *Books are free of customs duty.* **10** About, concerning † *He spoke of you when we met.* [NOTE: **speak of** Mention in the course of conversation, a speech etc (*See* **on 11** for **speak on**) †)*Have you any corrections to make?*) *None to speak of* (worth mentioning).] **11** In a partitive sense † *three of them, a number of us.* **12** To express a subjective relationship between the noun following *of* and a noun before it † *He is upset because of the death of his father* (his father's death). [NOTE: The apostrophe form is correct here, as in **1** above.] **13** To express an objective relationship between the noun following *of* and a noun before it † *The murder of Becket.* † *The thief went in fear of capture.* † *This gives us proof of his innocence.* **14** In constructions of the type adj. + *of* + (pro)noun. These are almost always used to associate actions with people † *How kind of you to let me come.* † *It was silly of you to leave the door open.* **15** With superlative adjectives † *He was the best of men.* † *I'm afraid that's not the worst of it.* [NOTE: A superlative idea can also be expressed by repetition of the noun after *of* † *King of Kings and Lord of Lords.* Here *of* resembles *among*, as in the following sentence † *You, of all people, should have known better* (You, among all the people I know, are the one who should have known).] **16** Indicating regular practice (before nouns denoting particular times) † *What do you do of an evening?* (i.e. in the evening as a general rule). **17** Indicating distance or time from a given point (after *within*) † *We climbed to within a hundred feet of the top of the hill.* † *They were born within ten minutes of each other.* **18** Indicating direction (after direction and before particular places) † *His house is south of here.* **19** Implying an analogy (after a noun) † *He was in the devil of a temper* (i.e. a temper like the devil's).

OFF *prep.*
1 Indicating separation from, not being in contact with (where *on* is the opposite) † *He fell off his horse.* † *The stamp has come off the envelope.*

† *Keep off the grass.* † *Those remarks are off the point.* **2** Indicating removal from † *She took off her clothes.* † *There is ½ p off soap today* (i.e. the price has been cut by ½ p). **3** Indicating free from (work, duty) † *He is off work because he has hurt his hand.* **4** Indicating a short distance out to sea in relation to land, shore, etc † *Lundy is a small island off the coast of England* [ALSO: **off-shore** *adj.* A short distance out to sea (of islands, etc); blowing from land to sea (of winds).] [NOTE: *Off the main road*: here *off* is used in the sense of **1** (above), but can also convey nearness, as in **4**. *Just off the main road* here *off* is used to mean not on, but close to.]

OFF *adv.*

1 Cancelled or postponed † *The marriage is off (for the time being).* **2** Disconnected † *Is the gas off?* **3** (of food) Bad, rotten † *I think this milk is (has gone) off.* [NOTE: Food may be *off* a menu in a restaurant in the sense of **1**, not **3**! † *I'm afraid the steak Diane is off, Sir* (i.e. no longer available).] **4** Going; on one's way † *Are you off already? Wait a little longer.*

OFF-BEAT *adj.*

Unconventional, unfashionable (not necessarily critical) † *They took us to an off-beat restaurant near the harbour.*

OFF-HAND *adj.*

1 Casual, showing little concern or respect † *The assistants in that shop are so off-hand that one wonders if they are interested in selling things.* **2** (of remarks, etc) Without previous thought † *It is unwise for politicians to make off-hand statements when newspapermen are present.* [ALSO: **off-hand** *adv.* Without thinking about, checking something † *I can't tell you the answer off-hand.*]

OFF-PUTTING *adj.*

Used for manner, action, etc making one doubt the wisdom of one's own plan or action, or upsetting one by spoiling one's concentration † *When we mentioned that hotel the travel agent's expression was so off-putting that we decided not to go there.* † *He found the continual interruptions to his speech very off-putting.*

OFFICE *n.*

in (out of) office Holding (being without) an official post † *When my party was in office we governed the country better.*

OIL *n.*

burn the midnight oil Stay up late in order to work.

pour oil on troubled waters Try to end a quarrel between people by speaking calmly, gently, etc.

OKAY (OK) *adj.*

All right. [ALSO: **give someone the okay** *n*. Give him permission to go ahead with an action, plan, etc.]

OLD-FASHIONED *adj.*

1 Out of date † *Her clothes are very old-fashioned.* 2 (of looks, expressions) Reproving, critical † *She gave me a very old-fashioned look when I invited her up to my flat.*

ON *prep.*

1 Touching or covering the outer surface of (not always with the sense of *on top of*) † *There is a cloth on the table.* † *There are two pictures on the wall.* † *There is a stamp on the envelope.* 2 Indicating that the outer surface is touched as a result of activity † *He knocked on the door.* † *He was sitting on a chair* (but in *an armchair*). † *He was hit on the head* (*arm, leg*) (but *He was hit* in *the chest*, in *the stomach*, etc). 3 Indicating that one is mounted on or being carried by a form of transport † *He was riding on a bicycle.* † *We had lunch on the train.* † *He went on board the ship* (*aeroplane*). [NOTE: As in 2 (above), where the emphasis is placed on being inside, *in* is used † *It is in the car.* † *The captain (pilot) is in his cabin.*] 4 Indicating a means of support † *He is not strong enough to stand on his legs.* † *The flats are built on pillars.* 5 Indicating locality, particularly to describe relationship of towns, houses, to rivers, sea, roads, etc † *Newcastle-(up)on-Tyne. Southend-on-Sea.* † *He has a house on the main road.* † *It was built on the site of an old farmhouse.* 6 Indicating physical relation to or (with verb of movement) direction † *You'll find it on the left-hand side of the road.* † *The army marched on London* (i.e. towards it, in order to capture it). 7 Indicating means of supporting life, business, etc, or enabling businesses, machines, etc to run † *He hasn't much (money) to live on.* † *He lives on vegetable foods.* † *The bus runs on diesel oil.* 8 Indicating day (but not hour or religious festival) (*See* **at**) † *I'll see you on Sunday (on the 5th of August).* † *I am paid on the last day of the month.* [NOTE: *On occasion* (from time to time) is also correct.] 9 Indicating membership of a group or official body † *He is on the committee (the board of directors).* [NOTE: *He is* in *the army*, where profession is the determining factor.] 10 Indicating reasons, basis, conditions for actions † *I did it on the advice of my lawyer.* † *I have it on good authority.* † *He bought his car on hire-purchase.* 11 About, concerning (referring to subject of talk, article, etc) † *Have you read his new book on Shakespeare?* † *I would like to have your views on the subject.* [NOTE: **speak on** Mention as main subject of speech (*See* **of** 10 for **speak of**).] 12 Indicating that one is engaged in, occupied by something † *He is away on business.* † *I don't want to be bothered by that while I'm on holiday.* 13 Followed by gerund or verbal noun to suggest 'as soon

133

as' † *On arriving at the station, he immediately looked for a taxi* (as soon as he arrived). † *On hearing the news, he shouted with joy.* **14** With a verbal noun, to express a passive idea for a transitive verb or active idea for intransitive verb † *Goods are on sale here at reduced prices* (being sold). † *The soldiers are on parade* (parading). **15** With *the* + a verb used as a noun, the meaning being close to that expressed by the present participle † *We are on the look-out for a stolen car* (looking out for). † *We must be on the move soon* (moving). **16** With *the* + an adjective, having an adverbial sense † *Can you let me have some cigarettes on the quiet?* (quietly, secretly). † *She bought those curtains on the cheap* (cheaply). [NOTE: This construction always implies that the action is not to be approved of, e.g. *on the cheap* suggests looking out for ways of avoiding paying the market price.]

ON *adv. part.*

1 Going on, arranged or on the programme † *Is there (have you) anything on this evening?* (Is anything arranged for this evening?) † *What's on this week at the local cinema?* **2** In use; functioning † *Put the light on.* † *Is the water on?* **3** Being worn; (with 'put', etc) wear † *He had nothing on* (He was naked). † *Put your coat on.*

on and on Without stopping (of place or time) † *The road went on and on for miles ahead of us.*

ONCE *adv.*

once and for all Now and finally † *I am going to settle the matter once and for all.*

once in a while Very occasionally (not as often as *now and then*) † *We have very few visitors from abroad. Once in a while, a group of Americans come for the fishing.*

once upon a time Once (traditional opening for a fairy story).

at once **1** Immediately † *Come here at once.* **2** At the same time † *We can't do everything at once.*

all at once Suddenly † *All at once I grew frightened and ran away.*

for once On this occasion (as a change from usual practice) † *Everyone we have invited has accepted, for once.*

just (for) this once As **for once**, but implying an exception being made because of special circumstances † *Please let me stay up late. Just this once.*

ONE *pron.*

at one In agreement † *I'm glad we are all at one on this point.*

it's all one (to me) It makes no difference (to me) † *I don't mind what you do. It's all one to me.*

one up (on) Having an advantage (over); being better informed (than) † *If you know who the next managing director is going to be you're one up on me.*

ONE-EYED *adj.*

(of places) With poor facilities † *I don't want to spend my holiday in a one-eyed place like that.* [ALSO: **one-horse town** This sort of town.]

ONESELF *reflex pron.*

beside oneself Mad (with grief, rage, etc) † *Don't take any notice of what she says. She is beside herself with grief.*

by oneself 1 Alone † *Don't sit by yourself. Come and join us.* 2 Without help † *I can't carry all the cases by myself.* [ALSO: (for emphasis) **all by oneself.**]

ONE-UPMANSHIP *n.*

Ability to show superiority towards other people by means of an action, comment, etc which suggests to them that one is more knowledgeable or more experienced than they are (implying use of trick to reverse a real disadvantage, inferiority) † *He doesn't really know much about wine. He sent the bottle back just to impress us. It's a crude form of one-upmanship.*

ONION *n.*

know one's onions (always plural) Be shrewd, worldly † *You can rely on his advice. He knows his onions.*

OPEN *v.t. & i.*

open out (of people) Be frank, not hold back feelings † *At first he was very shy, but then he opened out (to us) and told us about his experiences.* [ALSO: **come out into the open** *n.* Explain one's ideas, plans, etc clearly, after keeping them secret.]

open up (land, territory) Make it possible to develop.

ORDER *n.*

in order to (that) With the purpose of (so that) † *In order to understand the problem, we must first consider the following points.* † *I have told you this in order that you might understand what is involved.*

on order Ordered, but not yet delivered † *That book is not in stock, but we have it on order.*

out of order Not functioning (properly) † *The lift is out of order.* † *I have eaten something that did not suit me and my stomach is out of order.*

to order In response to directions † *They no longer make cars on a large scale, but are still prepared to construct one to order.*

in (holy) orders (plural) Ordained as a priest or clergyman.

a tall order A difficult task to carry out or unreasonable request † *) The goods must be delivered before the end of the year.) That's a tall order, in view of the Christmas holidays.*

OUGHT *anom. fin.*

1 Expressing (moral) obligation, but different from *must* because the idea

135

of compulsion is absent † *You ought to go and see your aunt* (implying 'she would be happy if you went, though I cannot force you to go'), but *You must pay the rent* (because the landlord will throw you out if you do not). † *Ought I to go to the station with him, in case he loses his way?* (Should I go?) **2** Indicating what is advisable or desirable † *You ought to read that book. You'd enjoy it.* **3** Indicating what is logically probable (compare **must**, where something is logically almost certain) † *If the train left London an hour ago, it ought to have been here by now.* † *He has travelled all over the world, so his conversation ought to be interesting.* **4** (in past) Implying an unfulfilled condition † *She bandaged my leg so well that I told her she ought to have been a nurse* (i.e. If she had been a nurse, she would have been a good one). † *You ought to have heard the way they spoke to one another* (i.e. If you had heard it, you would have been shocked, surprised, pleased, etc depending on context).

OUT *adv. part.*

1 Away from a place (*See* **out of** *prep.* 1) † *Mr Jones is out, I'm afraid.* **2** Not available (*See* **out of** *prep.* 10) † *I went to the library to borrow the book, but it was out.* **3** At a distance from (*See* **out of** *prep.* 4) † *When we were three days out from Southampton, the ship ran into a storm.* **4** Indicating that something has appeared, become known or visible † *His new book is out.* † *His secret is out.* † *It's warm, now the sun is out.* **5** (of light, fire, etc) No longer alight † *The lights were out all over the town.* **6** Completely † *I'm tired out.* † *He is worn out after working all day* (completely exhausted). [ALSO: (with expressions of time) Over, finished † *Before the year is out, prices will have risen sharply.*] **7** Wrong, incorrect † *When we added up the figures, we found we were a few pounds out* (a few pounds were not accounted for or were missing). † *Your guess is not far out* (almost correct). **8** (with certain verbs) (*See* **out of** *prep.* 3) Implying that something is made clearer, or is more easily seen or recognised † *Don't be afraid to speak out.* † *He brings out the real meaning of the book in his commentary on it.* † *The church stood out from the surrounding country.*

out and away By far † *He was out and away the most brilliant student in the class.*

out-and-out (usually *adj.*) Thorough; absolute † *He was an out-and-out villain.*

all out At full speed, with all one's energy † *He was going all out for the winning post.*

be out for Be interested in getting † *He's out for all he can get.*

be out to Try to, intend to † *I'm out to show them who is best qualified to do it.*

OUT OF *prep.*

1 Away from † *He's out of his office at the moment.* **2** Indicating

136

movement from inside to outside † *Take the money out of the drawer.*
† *He fell out of a window.* 3 Indicating protrusion from (e.g. *standing out, sticking out*) † *The nail stuck out of the wall.* 4 Indicating a certain distance from † *We live a few miles out of London.* 5 Beyond † *The book was on the top shelf, out of reach.* 6 In proportion to † *We have found that two out of ten people cannot tell the difference between butter and margarine.* 7 Indicating reason, motive † *She took him in out of pity.* † *I only asked out of curiosity.* 8 Indicating source, origin † *He copied a poem out of the book.* 9 Indicating materials from which things are made † *I made a bookcase out of some old planks of wood.* [NOTE: But, *The table is made* of *wood. Out of* suggests that the condition of the materials has changed. It may be used in place of *from*, but implies more individual effort and ingenuity. Compare the example above with *Wine is made from grapes* (an accepted, even if not simple, process).]
10 Indicating that one no longer has something or that it is not available † *He is out of work* (unemployed). † *We seem to be out of matches* (We have used them all). † *That size is out of stock* (We have sold them all). 11 Indicating a change from previous or normal conditions † *Her clothes are out of fashion.* † *The lift is out of order.*

out of it 1 Not part of a group, celebration, etc and thus lonely † *Everyone here is so much younger than I am that I feel out of it.* 2 Not involved in a scheme, etc † *It seems a crazy plan and I am glad to be out of it.*

OUTSIDE *prep.*

1 On the outer side of † *I waited for her outside her office.* 2 Beyond † *You must not let this be known outside the family.* 3 Apart from, except for (particularly of work, interests) † *He has no interests outside gardening.*

at the (very) outside At the most, at the maximum possible † *There were very few people present. Twenty, at the outside.*

OVER *prep.*

1 Covering, above or in front of † *Her hair came down over her ears.* † *She laid the cloth over the table.* † *Put the picture over the hole in the wall.* 2 Directly above † *The sky is over our heads.* † *Hold the umbrella over me.* 3 From one side to another of † *He climbed over the fence.* † *The bridge runs over the river.* 4 On the other side of † *The people who live over the road have a new car.* † *Over the border in Scotland.* 5 (with 'all') In or across all parts of (country, world) † *His books are sold all over the world.* 6 Indicating downward movement from a high point (cliff, etc) or as the result of hitting an obstacle, with the meaning of 3 (above) † *He fell over the cliff into the sea.* † *I tripped over a toy my little boy had left on the floor.* 7 Indicating superiority in rank, authority, etc † *Who is over you at your office?* (i.e. Who is your boss?). 8 More than

† *He was over seventy when he retired.* † *It is over a hundred miles from here to London.* **9** *(of time) During* † *Did you see him over the weekend?* **10** (of time) For † *The population has been rising over a long period.* **11** Concerning † *He worries over any small mistake he makes.* † *Two dogs were fighting over a bone.* † *We'll talk over your suggestion when we meet again.* [NOTE: The distinction between *over* and *about* is slight, but *over* indicates more continuous activity. *Talk over* implies thorough discussion, where *talk about* could mean *refer to.* *Worry over* suggests continual return to the subject.] **12** While engaged in (eating, etc); in doing † *We'll talk about it over lunch.* † *He's taking a long time over the job.*

over and above In addition to † *Three more letters have arrived, over and above those that came yesterday.*

OVER *adv. part.*

1 Left, remaining † *Would you like another piece of cake? There is still some over.* **2** More † *He has jumped twenty feet and over.* **3** Finished † *Come round for a drink when the game is over.* † *When we arrived at the hospital, they told us it was (all) over (with him)* (i.e. He was dead). [ALSO: **over and done with** Used with the same meaning, but implying *and nothing further can be done.*]

all over 1 As in **3** (above). **2** In all parts † *I am aching all over.* **3** (of people) Through and through † *He forgot he had the appointment, did he? Well, that's Peter all over* (i.e. That is typical of Peter).

over and over again Repeatedly, time after time † *I've told you over and over again to be more careful.*

OWING TO *prep.*

Because of † *Mr Smith regrets that he cannot accept your invitation, owing to a previous engagement.*

OWN *v.i.*

own up Confess (usually for children) † *If no one owns up to having thrown a stone through my window, I will punish you all.*

OWN *n.*

on one's own 1 Alone, by oneself † *I'm on my own now that my children have left home.* **2** Independently; not employed by someone else † *I prefer to work on my own.* [NOTE: As in the case of *by oneself,* all on one's own suggests lonely, as well as alone † *They've left the poor child all on his own.*]

come into one's own Receive what one rightly inherits, deserves, but now used frequently to mean display one's real or inherent ability in appropriate circumstances † *The horses were all together as they came round the bend, but then Nijinsky came into his own.*

hold one's own (in a fight, argument or against illness) Maintain one's ground or progress † *He can hold his own in a debate with anyone.*

PACK *v.t. & i.*

pack in Give up   † *I no longer enjoy playing tennis, so I'm going to pack it in.*

pack off Send (someone) away quickly   † *I just had time to pack the children off to school before going to work.* [ALSO: **send someone packing** Same meaning as **pack off** but indicating that the person has been unnecessarily troublesome (trying to borrow money, sell goods at the door, for example).]

pack up Stop (working), put one's tools away   † *It's getting dark. Let's pack up and go home.*

PALE *n.*

beyond the pale Outside the limits of acceptable social behaviour (or, because of this, unacceptable on a social occasion)   † *He put himself beyond the pale by insulting his host.*

PALM *v.t.*

palm off (on someone) Get rid of something not wanted (by convincing someone else that it has value)   † *Now he's hoping to palm this stuff off on some tourists.*

PAN *v.t. & i.*

pan out Turn out, result   † *We were afraid that something would go wrong, but in the end the party panned out well.*

PART *n.*

for my part As far as I am concerned   † *For my part, I would be happy to forget about the matter.*

on someone's (the) part (of) By or from (whoever is mentioned) (often in legal context where a lawyer is acting for the person)   † *There was no complaint on his part, but several were made on the part of his wife.*

take in good part Accept what is said (about one) in an amiable spirit   † *We made several jokes at his expense, but he took them all in good part.*

take part in Have a share in   † *Are you going to take part in the ceremony?*

take someone's part Take his side in an argument (particularly in defending him against accusations)   † *Has none of you the courage to take my part?*

PASS *v.i. & t.*

pass away A euphemism for 'die' † *I was sorry to hear your husband had passed away.*

pass for Be thought to be † *He speaks Spanish so well that he could pass for a Spaniard.*

pass off 1 Slowly go away (of pain, tiredness) † *I have a bad headache, but it will pass off when I have taken some aspirin.* 2 Proceed to an end (of an event, meeting, etc) (used when there is a possibility of its being broken up) † *At first he was frequently interrupted, but once the police arrived, the rest of his speech passed off without incident.* 3 Pass (false articles) to people, pretending they are genuine † *He was arrested for passing off forged notes as real money.* [ALSO: **pass oneself off** as Pretend to be (someone else) for one's own advantage † *The confidence man passed himself off as a rich business man.*] 4 Cover up (something embarrassing) † *He asked the customs officer to carry his case and tried to pass it off by saying the man's uniform was like a porter's.*

pass over 1 Overlook † *He was passed over for the job in favour of a younger man.* † *I'm prepared to pass over your other mistakes, but I can't ignore this one.* 2 Not discuss (of subjects at meeting, etc) † *We'll pass over the first three points of the agenda and begin with number 4.*

PASS *n.*

come to a fine (pretty) pass Reach an awkward situation, bad position (used ironically) † *Things have come to a pretty pass if one can't get a cup of tea while one is waiting for a train.*

come to pass Happen (no longer common).

make a pass at (a woman) Try to kiss, make love to (her) (used when she has no reason to expect it) † *My wife said he made a pass at her.*

PAST *prep.*

1 (of time) After; beyond † *It is ten past three.* † *It is past your bedtime.* 2 (of place) Beyond; from one side to the other of and beyond † *You have gone past my (bus) stop.* † *I saw him go past the window.* 3 Beyond the limits of, no longer capable of † *I am past caring whether you repair it or not.* [NOTE: **I wouldn't put it past him (to)** My opinion of him is not so high that I would believe him incapable of (doing something dishonest or unfair † *The next time he rings up, ask him if he has paid for the call. I wouldn't put it past him to charge it to us.*]

past it No longer capable of doing something † *He was a good worker once, but now he's past it.*

PATCH *n.*

not a patch on Not nearly as good as † *He is a good player, but not a patch on his elder brother.*

PAY *v.t. & i.*

pay off **1** Make a final payment (to someone), settle (debt, etc) † *We hope to pay off what we owe next month.* **2** Prove a successful investment, risk † *We have spent a lot of money (time) on building the hotel, but I'm sure it will pay off when it is finished.*

put paid to Finish, so that it gives no more trouble † *That has put paid to his scheme. We won't hear from him again.*

PEG *v.t. & i.*

peg away at Keep working on (something) with determination; keep trying † *I haven't found a job yet, but if I peg away at it, something will turn up.*

peg down Limit (someone) to a course of action † *I'm willing to help, but I don't want to be pegged down to any specific task.*

PEG *n.*

a square peg in a round hole Someone in a job he is not suited for.

off the peg (of clothes) Ready-made (so that they can be taken from the peg in the shop).

take down a peg Humble (someone) (by reproving him in front of others, for example) † *He's too pleased with himself. It's time someone took him down a peg.*

PENNY *n.*

a pretty penny A lot of money (implying more than it was worth) † *Did you see her new coat? That must have cost her husband a pretty penny.*

in for a penny, in for a pound Once one has started on something, one should go on with it, whatever the cost.

PEOPLE *n.*

a man of the people Someone who has come from an ordinary background and remains faithful to it, or who tries to identify himself with the common people.

PEP *n.*

pep talk Speech intended to encourage listeners and give them energy and spirit for the task in front of them.

PERSON *n.*

in person Oneself (as against being represented by someone else) † *The opening of the concert hall will be a great occasion. The Queen will be there in person.*

PICK *v.t. & i.*

pick on **1** Single out (a person) (for a difficult or unpleasant task) or point to in an argument, etc (for criticism, discussion) † *I don't see why he picked on me to do it.* † *This was the sentence in the contract that the lawyer picked*

141

on as unacceptable. **2** Single out (a person) for unfair treatment; blame † *Johnny says the teacher keeps picking on him.*

pick out **1** Distinguish from surroundings † *In the distance, I saw three people climbing the mountain and picked out my father in front.* **2** Choose from a group † *He picked out Smith from the younger men around him as the one most likely to succeed him.*

pick up **1** Acquire; get to know (articles, information, languages) without conscious effort † *I picked up this copy of 'Hamlet' on a second-hand bookstall.* † *I was never taught German, but I have picked up a working knowledge of it on my visits to Germany.* **2** Increase (of trade, business, speed) † *Business has picked up now that Christmas is near* (implying that it was not good before that). † *The train picked up speed as we left the city.* **3** Improve (of health) † *She has picked up gradually since the doctor came.* **4** Call for (in a car); give a lift to † *I'll pick you up at your house at 7 o'clock.* † *We picked up two people whose car had broken down.* **5** Meet (someone of the opposite sex) by chance and go with him or her † *Who's that girl with him? Someone he picked up at the party last night.* [ALSO: **pick-up** *n.* **1** Someone (usually girl) met in this way. **2** The part of a record-player that holds the needle. **3** A small truck used by builders, etc.]

pick up with Make acquaintance with (as **5** (above), but without any sexual implications).

PICK-ME-UP *n.*
Drink of spirits to revive strength, energy, etc.

PICNIC *n.*
no picnic Not an easy job or situation † *We had to rescue the people from the burning house. It was no picnic.*

PICTURE *n.*
the pictures The cinema † *I'm taking my girl friend to the pictures to-night.*
put (keep) someone in the picture Inform him (keep him informed) of what has happened or is planned † *You don't know about the changes that have taken place recently, so I'll put you in the picture.*

PIECE *n.*
go to pieces **1** (of a person(Suffer a nervous collapse † *He went to pieces when his mother died.* **2** (of groups) Collapse, losing sense of teamwork, unity † *The home team went to pieces when the visiting team scored a goal.* † *The firm has gone to pieces since the old manager retired.*

PIG-HEADED *adj.* Stupidly obstinate, unwilling to listen to sensible advice † *I told him it would be a disaster, but he is so pig-headed that he took no notice.*

PIGEON *n.*
one's pigeon One's responsibility † *Let Jack look after it. It's his pigeon.*

PIGEON-HOLE *n. & v.t.*
Open box in office (usually arranged in series) for papers. The verb means file for future reference in such a box and implies put away and forget † *I wrote to the Ministry about this matter a year ago, but no doubt my letter has been pigeon-holed.*

PILLAR *n.*
driven from pillar to post Driven from one place to another (implying cruel or unfeeling treatment) † *The poor woman is being driven from pillar to post. No one is prepared to listen to her case.*

PIN *v.t.*
pin down Make (someone) do what he has promised or firmly commit himself to something † *He agreed to lecture here next year, but I couldn't pin him down to a firm date.*

pin up Fix (a picture, notice) to wall. [ALSO: **pin up** *n.* Picture (usually of film star, etc) pinned to wall in this way, and also the star himself † *Marlene Dietrich was my pin-up when I was young.*]

PINCH *n.*
at a pinch In an emergency; if absolutely necessary † *Normally we need six men to operate the plant, but at a pinch we could manage with four.*

PINK *n.*
in the pink In very good health † *You look in the pink (of health).*

PIPE *v.i. & t.*
pipe down Shut up; talk less † *He was just about to give away the secret, so I told him to pipe down.*

pipe up Speak (usually of children, interrupting suddenly) † *I was just going to dismiss the class when a little voice piped up from the back of the room.*

PIPER *n.*
he who pays the piper, calls the tune The person who is paying the bill is the one who can decide how the money should be spent.

PIPELINE *n.*
in the pipeline (of goods ordered, letters, forms, etc) Already on the way, receiving attention as part of the administrative procedure, etc † *We have dealt with fifty requests for the book today and no doubt there are plenty more in the pipeline.*

PITCH *n.*
queer someone's pitch Upset his plans † *I came into the room when he was*

trying to persuade her to go out with him instead of with me, and that queered his pitch.

PLACE *n.*

in (out of) place 1 In (out of) the proper place, (un)tidy † *When I go away on holiday, I like to leave everything in the house in place.* 2 Socially (not) appropriate † *His jokes were out of place on such a serious occasion.*

in place of Instead of, substituting for † *I am here in place of Mr Brown, who is not well.*

in the first place Indicating the first of a series of reasons, conditions, etc † *There are several reasons why she should not marry him. In the first place, he is much too old for her.*

all over the place Everywhere † *I've been looking for you all over the place.*

PLANT *v.t.*

plant on someone Hide (stolen goods) in his clothes, property, etc to make him seem guilty.

PLATE *n.*

on one's plate (of work, tasks) One's responsibility to do or complete † *I've had a lot more on my plate since Jones left the firm.*

PLAY *v.i. & t.*

play at Do (something) in a half-hearted way † *He doesn't really run the firm. He just plays at it* (i.e. He has the title of managing director, but the decisions are made by others).

play down Minimise the importance of (something) † *The newspapers are asking questions about our new invention but we are playing it down until we are sure it will work.*

play off (one person against another) Use their mutual dislike, rivalry, etc to one's own advantage † *The King managed to keep his throne by playing off the barons against the common people.*

play out Play to a finish † *The chess champion expected his opponent to give up the game, but he preferred to play it out.*

be played out (passive only) Be exhausted, no longer popular † *The old music-halls (vaudeville theatres (USA)) are played out and the performers have gone into television.*

play up Cause trouble (of children, machines, recurrent pains, etc) † *They always play up when it is bedtime.* † *My backache has been playing me up this winter.*

play upon (on) Make use of (others' fears, weakness) † *He played upon her fear of a scandal to persuade her to give up her lover.*

play up to Flatter † *She's playing up to the boss in the hope that he will give her a rise.*

PLAY *n.*

child's play Something very easy † *My brother is a skilled decorator. Painting your kitchen will be child's play to him.*

fair play Justice, equal conditions for both sides † *He has been appointed as an impartial chairman to see that there is fair play between the two sides in the dispute.* [NOTE: The traditional references to *fair play* in British sport really imply impartial refereeing, not that the competitors never break the rules. However, **play fair** Play fairly, do not break the rules (*See* **foul play**).]

foul play Violent crime † *The police are convinced that he committed suicide and do not suspect foul play.* [NOTE: *Foul play* is sometimes used in a sporting context but it is more common to refer to *a foul* or *fouling* an opponent where bodily contact is possible, or *cheating*, where it is not. But the phrase is found in sentences like † *The Football Association have accused the managers of some teams of deliberately encouraging foul play* (i.e. telling the players to commit fouls, foul opponents).]

POCKET *n.*

in (out of) pocket Better (worse) off † *He was considerably out of pocket after his visit to the racecourse.*

POINT *v.t. & i.*

point out 1 (something) Show, indicate position of, draw attention to † *He pointed out the most interesting features of the landscape.* 2 (a fact) Draw attention to † *He pointed out that we could not go ahead with the plan without the Council's approval.*

POINT *n.*

beside the point Irrelevant † *Your reasons for going there are beside the point. We are only interested in what you did there.*

in point of fact As a matter of fact. [ALSO: **a case in point** A relevant example † *If we are talking about cities that have benefited from destruction by having to rebuild, Coventry may be a case in point.*]

off the point Not relevant to the subject † *His remarks were off the point.*

to the point Relevant to the subject.

carry (gain) one's point Convince people of the rightness of one's argument † *You've gained your point. We'll do as you say.*

come (keep) to the point Reach (not wander away from) the essential idea or fact in one's argument † *He took so long to come to the point that people were too bored to understand it when it arrived.*

have a point Have a valid argument † 〉 *You ought not to buy the house until it has been surveyed professionally.* 〉 *Yes, you have a point there.*

make a point Put forward an idea in an argument.

make a point of Be especially concerned to † *He made a point of thanking his parents for having helped him so much before the wedding.*

POLISH *v.t. & i.*

polish off 1 Finish (a job of work, a meal) very quickly † *The children polished off all the cakes in no time.*

polish up Revise and improve (one's knowledge of something) † *I shall have to polish up my Spanish if we are going to Madrid for a holiday.*

POP *v.t. & i.*

(with various prepositions) Go, come quickly or for a short time † *I popped in to see her for five minutes.* † *Pop round the corner and buy me some cigarettes, will you?*

pop on Put on quickly or for a short time † *Pop the kettle on the stove and we'll have a cup of tea.*

pop up Appear (unexpectedly) † *Five years ago, there wasn't a night club in town, but now they're popping up all over the place.*

POP *n.*

Until recently, popular music, but now also used as an adjective.

pop art Art using popular motifs, such as strip cartoons, news photographs.

pop culture Culture of people belonging to the world of pop entertainment or influenced by its standards, etc.

POT *n.*

Drugs, particularly marijuana and so-called 'soft' drugs.

POT-BOILER *n.*

Work of art, particularly book, produced merely to gain money.

POWER *n.*

the powers that be Those in authority † *The powers that be say it must be done that way, and so it must.*

PRACTICE *n.*

in practice 1 When carried out in a real situation, as opposed to **in theory** † *It's all very well as an idea, but will it work in practice?* [ALSO: **put into practice** Carry out in real surroundings.] 2 Having done something (particularly played a game) regularly, not long before. [ALSO: **out of practice** Not having done something regularly, for a long time † *I'm not going to take part in the competition. I'm out of practice.* 3 Practising as a doctor, lawyer † *He is in practice in the London area.*

PRESENT *n.*

at present Now, at this time † *He lives in London, but at present he is on holiday abroad.* [NOTE: **presently** *adv.* Soon (Britain); now (USA) † *I'll change my clothes and be with you presently* (Britain). † *Mr Jones is presently American Ambassador to France* (USA) (British speakers would use *at present* here).]

for the present For the time being † *We have enough butter for the present, though we may have to buy some more next week.*

PRESS *v.t. & i.*

press for Urge, demand repeatedly † *The newspapers are pressing the Government for action on the pollution of rivers.*

be (hard) pressed for (time, money) Be (very) short of † *I can't stop to talk to you now. I'm pressed for time.*

press on Go on in a determined way in spite of obstacles, tiredness, etc † *The climbers were almost exhausted, but they pressed on to the summit.*

PRETTY *adv.*

Fairly † *He is pretty tall. We are pretty near home now.*

sitting pretty In a very comfortable situation † *He won a lot of money on the football pools and now he is sitting pretty.*

PRINCIPLE *n.*

in principle Regarding the validity of the idea, proposal in general † *In principle I have nothing against the plan, but I would like to see it in detail before giving my approval.*

on principle Because of one's (moral) convictions † *He is against divorce on principle.*

PRINT *n.*

in (out of) print (of books) Available (no longer) from booksellers † *They told me the novel was now out of print.*

PRO *n.*

pros and cons (plural only) Arguments for and against † *We went over the pros and cons of the proposal.*

PROUD *adj.*

do someone proud (only used as adv. in this phrase) Treat him very well (particularly in entertaining or honouring him) † *What an excellent dinner! You have done me proud.*

PUDDING *n.*

the proof of the pudding (is in the eating) Proverbial expression meaning that the proof of something's being good can only be determined in practice.

PULL *v.t. & i.*

pull off Succeed in (a plan, action) (in spite of competition, obstacles) † *The thieves have pulled off one of the most daring robberies of the century.*

pull out of 1 (of trains) Move away from a station. 2 Withdraw from (negotiations, a team, etc) † *The Communist delegation have pulled out of the peace talks.*

pull over (of cars, ships, etc) Move to one side. [NOTE: **pullover** *n*. A sweater, pulled on over the head.]

pull round Recover from illness, or (of firms) from bad period of business or help someone recover † *She has had a bad shock, but I think she will pull round.* † *Give her some brandy to pull her round.*

pull through Withstand and recover from illness, difficult economic or political situation, etc, or nurse, so that person recovers (similar to **pull round** (above) but more gradual).

pull together Make a co-operative effort † *If we all pull together, we can put the country on its feet again.*

pull oneself together Recover one's self-control † *Pull yourself together. It's no use crying any more.*

pull up 1 (of cars, trains, etc) Stop † *He pulled up at the traffic lights.*
2 Reprimand, check (someone) † *The police pulled him up for parking on the wrong side of the road.*

PUNCH *n*.

pull one's punches Not hit or criticise as hard as one could † *When he asked me what I thought of his book I pulled my punches because I like him.*

PUSH *v.t. & i.*

push on Go on, with determination (*See* **press on**).

push off Leave (colloquial) † *Do you mind if I push off? I'm meeting Jane at 7 o'clock.*

be pushed for (time, money) Be short of (*See* **be pressed for**).

PUSH *n*.

at a push In an emergency, if it were absolutely necessary (*See* **at a pinch**).

if (when) it comes to the push If we are faced with an emergency, when a decisive moment arrives † *We are not prepared for war, but if it comes to the push we will defend ourselves.*

PUSHOVER *n*.

A task or opponent that proves very easy to overcome † *The examination was a pushover, I'm glad to say.*

PUT *v.t. & i.*

put about Spread (story, rumour, etc) † *I would like to know who put it about that I am going to resign.*

put across (over) 1 Convey (ideas) successfully † *The speaker put across to the audience his conviction that the growth of world population should be restricted.*

put it across (over) Deceive (someone) by a trick † *The salesman put it across the housewife by pretending the washing machine was the best she could buy.*

148

put by (aside) Save money for some future need † *He puts by five pounds a week for his summer holiday.*

put down Write down † *Put down your expenses on this form and the company accountant will give you the money.*

put down as Judge (someone) to be † *All his friends put him down as a failure, but he was happy, none the less.*

put down to Consider to be the result of † *I put his enthusiasm down to his youth.* † *The air crash was put down to engine failure.*

put forward Express, propose (ideas, plans, etc) † *He put forward the view that more money should be spent on primary education than on universities.*

put in 1 Install † *The firm have put in six new machines this year.* 2 (with expression of time) Do (work) † *He always puts in a good day's work.* † *I put in an hour's training in preparation for the game.*

put in for Apply for, enter one's name for (a job, examination) † *Did you get the job you put in for?*

put off 1 Postpone † *The meeting has been put off for a week because the boss is away.* † *We shall have to put him off until a more convenient time* (postpone our meeting with him). 2 Delay (with gerund) † *You should not put off going to the dentist.* (Different from 1 because the person is not postponing an arranged visit, but holding back from going at all.) 3 Switch off (light, radio, etc). [NOTE: *Put off (on)* are used when a mechanical means (switch, plug, etc) is being used. *Put out* is correct for extinguish (candle, etc).] 4 Deter, prevent from doing something † *We are not going to be put off by threats.* 5 Keep (someone) from reacting against (by excuses, lies, etc) † *You are not going to put me off with that story.* 6 Cause (someone) to lose concentration † *His opponent's remarks put him off (his game)* † *Will it put you off if I have the television on while you're writing your letter?*

put on 1 Switch on (*See* **put off** 3). 2 Adopt, assume (an expression, attitude) † *When I accused him, he put on an innocent face (look).* 3 Increase (speed, weight) † *You must have put on a stone (about 6 kg) since I saw you last.*

put it on Pretend, exaggerate (an emotion, reaction, etc) † *The fall can't have hurt him as much as all that. He's putting it on* (his expression, cries of pain, etc).

put out 1 Extinguish (*See* **put off** 3). 2 (generally passive) Annoy; upset † *He was put out when he heard that they had changed their plans without consulting him.*

put oneself out Do something inconvenient to oneself; take more trouble than usual † *Please don't put yourself out on my account* † *She put herself out to make everyone feel at home.*

put through 1 Pass through (established procedures) † *We have put your* *application for a driving test through (to the regional office).* † *The government hope to put their bill on industrial relations through in this session of Parliament.* **2** Connect (on the telephone) † *Would you put me through to your sales office, please?* **3** (usually **put through it**) Make (someone) submit to (questioning, torture, etc) † *The customs men put him through it for several hours until he told them where he had got the drugs.*

put to Convey (suggestion, etc) to † *I will put your proposal to the members of the Committee.*

put up 1 Stay (at hotel, etc) † *I put up for the night at the local inn.* **2** Provide accommodation for † *My brother arrived unexpectedly, so we had to put him up for the night.* **3** Offer (oneself) for election or propose (someone else) for election † *He is putting up (as a party candidate) for Parliament.* † *The other party are putting up a man called Smith.* **4** Offer (for sale) † *He has put his house up for sale.* † *The losing boxer put up a good fight.*

put up to Encourage (someone) to (do something wrong) † *He was arrested for the crime, but it was found that his brother had put him up to it.*

put up with Tolerate, endure (unpleasantness, inconvenience, etc) † *I won't put up with your insults any longer.* † *People nowadays would not put up with the working conditions my father was used to* (implying that they would refuse to accept them, not that they would be too weak to stand them).

a put up job (*See* **job**).

QUESTION *n.*

beyond question Undoubtedly † *He was beyond question the greatest leader this country has ever had.*

in question Being spoken about † *Has the man in question ever been employed in a similar position?*

out of the question Impossible (in the circumstances) † ⟩ *Can't we go by sea?* ⟩ *No, that's out of the question. It would take far too long.*

without question Without asking for proof (of what is said) or doubting it † *He was so well-dressed that the shop accepted a cheque from him without question.*

beg the question Speak in the course of discussion as if the matter were indisputable (therefore implying that the discussion itself is meaningless)

150

e.g. saying 'All modern art is rubbish' in the course of a serious discussion about its value.

QUIET *adj.*
on the quiet *n.* Secretly (*See* **on** *prep.* **16**).

QUITE *adv.*
1 Completely † *You are quite right.* † *I don't quite understand your problem.* **2** Fairly † *He is quite tall for his age.* [NOTE: 'Quite' before a verb means 'completely'. Before an adjective it means 'fairly' unless the adjective itself is absolute in its implications. In such cases, of course, 'quite' is really redundant † *The play was quite good* (fairly good). † *The play was (quite) wonderful.* If the adjective is critical in implication, it is more common to use 'rather' for 'comparatively bad' † *The play was rather poor.* However, there are some cases where 'quite' would be used † *He is quite poor* (implying no criticism to him on this account).] **3** (used alone to express agreement with what has been said) Exactly † 〉 *The point I am making is that we must act together.* 〉 *Quite.*

RABBIT *n.*
A poor player at a game, especially tennis and golf.

RACKET *n.*
1 Loud noise † *I can't hear what you're saying. The children are making such a racket.* **2** Illegal way of getting money (especially organised by a gang – for example, **protection racket** System in which shopkeepers are forced to pay money to a gang to prevent their shops' being attacked (in theory by anyone but in fact by the gang itself)).

RAGE *n.*
all the rage Very much in fashion, very popular † *Not long ago, their songs were all the rage.*

RAIL *n.*
off the rails Away from the proper course of action † *He used to be a very sensible fellow, but he's gone off the rails recently.*

RAIN *n.*
it never rains but it pours Proverbial expression meaning that things do not

come singly but in numbers † *I've had nothing to do for days, and now three jobs have arrived at the same time. It never rains but it pours.*

RAKE-OFF *n.*

Share of profits (implying that it is not deserved or not honestly obtained) † *The Mayor was accused of having given the contract to his friends and got a rake-off for himself.*

RAT *n.*

the rat race The competitive struggle for success in society (implying attitude of distaste towards it because of unscrupulous or undignified actions necessary in order to win).

smell a rat Suspect that something is wrong † *When he refused to answer my question, I smelt a rat.*

RATE *n.*

at any rate At least † *We are all going to get a rise at Christmas. At any rate, that's what I've been told.*

at that rate 1 If things go on in this way † *John telephoned to say he had arrived at the airport. At that rate, he will be here soon.* 2 If that is (were) so † *The teachers here would like to abolish examinations, but at that rate it would be difficult to assess the students' ability.*

at this rate If things go on as they are at present † *We are already spending more than we earn. At this rate we shall have nothing left by the end of the week.*

RATHER *adv.*

1 (with adj.) To some extent, comparatively (*See* **quite**). [NOTE: 1 While *quite* is used in contexts where the speaker means comparatively good, *rather* is more common for comparatively bad † *She is rather ugly* (but, *quite pretty*). Depending on the implications, of course, either may be used with the same adjective † *Your son is getting quite tall.* † *We cannot give her the part of the heroine. She is rather tall, you know* (i.e. too tall to be suitable, taller than the leading actor, etc). 2 *Rather* is used to mean comparatively good, however, with comparative adjectives. *Quite* and *fairly* are not used in this construction † *He made a rather better attempt at the examination this time than last.* It is also found with a favourable implication where the speaker is disagreeing with or anticipating a critical judgement † ⟩ *She is so dull.* ⟩ *I don't think so. I think she is rather sweet.*] **2** (with noun) Comparatively. [NOTE: The same general rule applies to *quite* and *rather* as in NOTE 1 (above) † *He earns quite a lot of money.* † *He's drunk rather a lot.* † *I don't think he ought to drive the car.*] **3** (with adverb) Comparatively (frequently implying more than expected) *Don't you think you're behaving rather childishly?* † *He did rather well in the examination* (implying greater approval than *quite well,* because the success was not expected).   **4** (used alone as answer) Yes, indeed (indicating enthusiasm for what has been suggested)   † 〉 *Would you like to earn a lot of money?* 〉 *Rather!*

would rather   (+ verb) Choose or would prefer   † *Would you rather have coffee or tea?* (offering the choice; *Do you prefer . . .* implies 'in general'). † *I would rather be happy than rich* (I would prefer to be happy, if I had the choice).

READ *v.t. & i.* (ri:d)

read into   Interpret from (actions, speech, etc)   † *You are reading into what he wrote a meaning that he never intended.*

take as read   (red) Assume as agreed (and therefore not devote time, attention) † *You can take it as read that he is in favour of the arrangement.*

REASON *n.*

it stands to reason (that)   It is obvious to anyone reasonable (that)   † *It stands to reason that they will not give you a driving licence until you have proved you can drive safely.*

RECKON *v.t. & i.*

reckon on   Count on, rely on   † *Can I reckon on his support for my proposal?*

reckon with   Take into account   † *They have made themselves a firm to be reckoned with in the field of aircraft design.*   † *You'll have to reckon with a body of opinion already prejudiced against your ideas.*

RECORD *n.*

for the record   (of spoken statements) So that it may be put down (recorded) for use in the future   † *John Smith already knows how much we appreciate his work, but for the record I would like to express our thanks to him.*

off the record   (of spoken statements) Unofficially and not to be quoted in newspapers, etc   † *The Minister emphasised that what he had said was off the record.*

on record   Recorded in print, on television recording, etc   † *He is on record as saying that he would never work with the present Prime Minister again.*

RED *adj.*

(be) in the red   (Be) in debt (because debts are entered in red ink in accounting) (*See* **black**).

see red   Become very angry   † *When he started criticising my father, I saw red.*

catch someone red-handed   Catch him immediately after he has committed a crime (when the evidence (e.g. blood on his hands) makes him obviously guilty)   † *They came out of the bank carrying the money and the police caught them red-handed.*

REFLECT *v.t. & i.*

reflect upon Harm the reputation of; discredit † *The mistake he made reflects upon the company as a whole.*

REFLEX *n.*

conditioned reflex Automatic response by reflex action to a stimulus (from Pavlov's experiments whereby dogs learned to associate a bell ringing with feeding and therefore salivated on hearing a bell), now used more generally † *They shouted him down from a conditioned reflex although what he had to say really supported their case.*

RESORT *n.*

as a last resort As a final attempt (at overcoming a difficulty) when all other methods have failed † *No one will lend me the money. I suppose, as a last resort, I could steal it.*

in the last resort All else having failed † *It may be too late to get in touch with him personally. In the last resort, we could leave a message at his office and hope he telephones.*

REST *v.i.*

rest on Depend on, be based on † *The case for the prosecution rests on the fact that the accused man was seen coming out of the house.*

rest with Be the responsibility of † *It rests with the Government to decide what should be done.*

at rest Not in movement (also used of a person to mean 'dead') † *The machines of the great factory were at rest, and there was no sign of life.*

set someone's mind at rest Give him reassurance to stop his worrying † *I can set your mind at rest. Your son has been found.*

RIDE *n.*

take someone for a ride Trick him (by promises, etc) † *Don't give them any money until you have seen the goods. They may be taking you for a ride.*

RIG *v.t. & i.*

rig out 1 Dress † *The children at the wedding were rigged out in eighteenth-century clothes.* 2 Provide clothes for period of time, special purpose † *Great care was taken in rigging out the expedition to climb Mount Everest.* [ALSO: **rig-out** *n.* Clothes (suggesting that they are unusual) † *Did you see the rig-out she turned up in?*]

rig up Put together, construct something from available materials (on a temporary basis) † *We have rigged up this rough model to show you how the machine will work when it is installed.*

RIGHT *n.*

by rights If justice were (had been) done † *By rights, I should have been promoted instead of him.*

in the right (Morally) correct † *You are in the right in refusing to give in to them.*

in one's own right (of reputation, title) Not depending on anyone else's reputation, etc † *Apart from the assistance he gave Professor Jones in his research, he is a distinguished scientist in his own right.*

RIGHT *adv.*

right away Immediately † *I'll deal with your request right away.*

RING *n.*

make rings round Prove totally superior to (an opponent, etc) in technical skill † *The home team made rings round the other side.*

RING *v.t. & i.*

ring (up) Make a telephone call (to someone) † *John rang (you) (up) while you were out.*

ring off End a telephone call.

RIOT *n.*

read the Riot Act Warn someone that he will be punished if he does not behave better † *The boys were making such a noise in class that I had to read the Riot Act to them.*

RISE *n.*

give rise to Be the cause of, promote † *His strange behaviour is giving rise to unpleasant gossip.*

take a rise out of Make fun of (someone) in a good-natured way (without his realising it) † *He was so full of his own importance that he didn't realise that we were taking a rise out of him.*

ROBBERY *n.*

daylight robbery An exorbitant price (which must be paid) † *How can you charge £35 for a television licence? It's daylight robbery.*

ROCK *n.*

on the rocks **1** In a very bad financial situation † *John's firm is on the rocks.* **2** (of a drink) Served with ice (originally American).

ROLL *v.t. & i.*

be rolling in (money) Be surrounded by (implying that there is so much that he doesn't notice or value it) † *I let him pay the bill. He's rolling in money.*

roll up Arrive (casually or late) † *I was wondering when you would roll up. I've been here half-an-hour.*

ROPE *n.*

give someone some rope Allow him freedom of action † *If you give him some* *rope, you will see if he's capable of looking after himself.* [ALSO: **give someone enough rope to hang himself** Allow a suspected criminal, rival, etc freedom so that he can make mistakes.]

know (learn) (teach someone) the ropes (always plural) Be (become) (make him) experienced in a craft, procedure † *Don't try to do everything yourself. Wait until you know the ropes.*

ROUGH *v.t.*

rough it Do without comfort † *He was sent out to Australia as a young man and learned to rough it on a sheep station.*

ROUGH *adj.*

(on someone) Hard (luck), unfair †) *They say they won't pay me for the extra work I did.*) *That's rough (on you).*

rough and ready Adequate, but not precise or carefully prepared † *An exact estimate of the cost would take hours, but I can let you have a rough and ready calculation now.*

ROUND *v.t. & i.*

round off Complete neatly, satisfactorily † *We rounded off our visit to the works by inspecting the most modern machine they had.*

round on Turn on (someone) to attack him (usually verbally) † *As soon as I mentioned her, he rounded on me and called me names.*

round up Collect, drive together † *Round up the members of your party and get them into the coach.* [ALSO: **round-up** *n.* (of suspected criminals, cattle) Collecting together.]

ROUND *prep.*

1 Indicating movement in a circular direction, encircling † *The first men to sail round the world were the crew of Magellan's expedition.* † *She wore a string of pearls round her neck.* **2** Indicating movement in different directions, but returning to starting point † *We had very little time to go round the town before we had to rejoin our party.* **3** Indicating change of direction towards place nearby but out of sight † *The town hall is just round the corner.* **4** In or to different places in (making a circuit) † *He goes round the country selling brushes and things like that.* † *I looked round the house for your book, but I couldn't find it.* **5** On all sides of, surrounding † *They were sitting round the table, playing cards* (not necessarily a round table). † *Gather round me and listen to what I have to say.* **6** Enveloping † *He wrapped a sheet of paper round the parcel.*

round and round Indicating repeated movements round (*See* **1**, **2** and **4** above) † *The astronauts went round and round the earth.* † *The tiger went round and round its cage.* [ALSO: **taking it all round** *adv.* Considering it from all points of view † *Taking it all round, I think this is the best performance of 'Hamlet' I have seen.*]

round about **1** In the neighbourhood of, near † *There are some pleasant old pubs round about London.* **2** (At) approximately † *I'll see you round about 6 o'clock.* † *He must be round about fifty.* [ALSO: **round-about** *n.* **1** Island at a road junction causing traffic to go round. **2** Circular amusement at fairground with horses, cars, etc mechanically operated to give rides to children. [NOTE: **swings and roundabouts** refers to proverbial saying 'What you lose on the swings you make up on the roundabouts', meaning that in business the profits and losses of different investments, etc balance each other.] **roundabout** *adj.* Indirect (implying needlessly so) † *Why can't he say what he wants, instead of approaching the subject in such a roundabout way?*]

ROUND *n.*

in the round Taking everything into consideration (to produce a balanced view) † *The approach the Government have adopted must be seen in the round before one can judge it.*

RUB *v.t. & i.*

rub in Emphasise (a lesson, unpleasant fact) † *I know I made a mistake, but you needn't rub it in.*

RULE *v.i. & t.*

rule out State or think of as out of the question, exclude † *The union promised to discuss the employers' offer, but said that they could not rule out the possibility of a strike.*

RULE *n.*

as a rule Usually † *As a rule I catch an earlier train, but I got up late this morning.*

work to rule Slow down production, etc as alternative to strike, by paying exaggerated attention to work regulations.

RUN *v.i. & t.*

run away with **1** (an idea, etc) Accept hurriedly without further thought † *Don't run away with the idea that I'm going to help you* (Don't assume that I will). **2** (of emotions) Get out of control † *He didn't mean what he said. His temper ran away with him.*

run down Criticise, attack in words † *I won't listen to you running down my mother.*

be run down Be overtired, suffer from mental exhaustion † *There's nothing seriously wrong with me. I'm just run down and need a rest.* [NOTE: **run-down** *n.* Brief summary of main points in plan, programme, etc † *Can you give me a run-down on the Queen's visit?*]

run into **1** Meet (someone) by chance † *I ran into your brother in Oxford Street yesterday.* [NOTE: **run across** is also used here, but more commonly employed for finding things by chance (*See* **come across**).] **2** Reach (a figure) † *His book has run into several editions.* † *His collection of books runs into thousands.*

run out 1 Expire, be due for renewal (of leases, licences, etc) † *My television licence runs out this week.* **2** Be used up (of supplies) † *We must order some more before our stock runs out.* [ALSO: **run out of** Use up † *We have run out of butter.*]

run over 1 Read quickly or repeat main points of (article, plan, etc) † *He ran over the main points of his speech* (either to make sure he himself was satisfied or to help the audience understand it better). **2** Knock down (in car) † *He was run over by a bus.*

run to 1 Afford † *We can't run to holidays abroad.* **2** (Reach a specific figure) (*See* **run into 2**) † *I doubt if the expenses will run to £100.*

run up 1 Make or construct quickly † *My mother ran this dress up for me over the week-end.* **2** Cause to rise quickly (of amounts of money) † *She ran up an enormous bill at a dress shop.*

run up against Meet, encounter † *I've never run up against that expression before.*

RUN *n.*

a run on something A great demand for it † *That's a very popular make. There's been a run on it lately.*

in the long run In the end † *It is more expensive, but in the long run you will save money, because it will last longer.*

on the run Being pursued † *He escaped from prison and was on the run for several weeks.*

give someone a run for his money Provide him with enjoyment (or frequently with competition) in return for his efforts † *They realised they would be caught but were determined to give the police a run for their money* (i.e. to make the pursuit as long as possible).

RUNNER-UP *n.*

Second in a race, competition.

RUNNING *n.*

in (out of) the running Competing (no longer) † *He is in the running for the post of Managing Director.* † *Three of his rivals are now out of the running.*

RUNNING *adv.*

(following expressions of time) In succession † *He won the prize three years running.*

RUSH *n.*

rush hour Time of day when people go to work or return and traffic is greatest.

RUT *n.*

be in a rut Be in a way of life, job, which offers no prospect of change, new interest † *I'm going to change my job. I'm in a rut here.*

SACK *n.*

get (give someone) the sack Be dismissed (dismiss) † *Her boss gave her the sack because she was always late for work.*

SAILING *n.*

plain sailing Course of action which is free from difficulties † *We had no difficulty in finding your house. It was plain sailing with the map you gave me.*

SAKE *n.*

for the sake of 1 For the benefit of; in the interests of; out of consideration for (used with possessive adjective or genitive for people) † *I did it for your sake.* † *I let him have what he wanted for the sake of peace and quiet.* † *He did not like his sister, but was kind to her for his parents' sake.* 2 As a basis for † *For the sake of argument, let us suppose that a law was passed prohibiting people from having more than two children. . .* 3 For no good reason (but simply because a person wants to do something or enjoys it) † *You are arguing for the sake of it.*

SAY *v.t. & i.*

1 Supposing † *Say you found out that your wife had a lover, what would you do?* 2 Let us say, shall we say? (suggesting an idea, quantity, etc) † *We can't supply all the cars you want immediately, but we could let you have − say six or seven.*

I say 1 To attract someone's attention † *I say, Charles, there's a report of your sister's wedding in this paper.* 2 To express surprise, admiration † *I say! What a beautiful view!*

you don't say Really? Is that true? (sometimes used ironically in answer to an obvious comment) † ⟩ *I'm getting married again.* ⟩ *You don't say.* † ⟩ *Of course, it often rains in England.* ⟩ *You don't say.*

SCARCE *adj.*

make oneself scarce Get or keep out of the way † *Father and Mother started quarrelling so I made myself scarce.*

SCENE *n.*

behind the scenes In the background; secretly † *I would like to thank all those who have worked behind the scenes to make this occasion a success.*
† *Although nothing has been said in the papers, the politicians are negotiating behind the scenes.*

make a scene Cause a row, unpleasant situation by violent display of emotion † *He found a hair in his soup, so he called the head waiter and made a scene (about it).*

SCHOOL *n.*

at school 1 Attending school (as against working) † *I learnt Latin at school.*
2 Attending school (as against being at home, on holiday) † *The children are all at school.* **3** Inside the school building † *He couldn't play football, because he had left his boots at school.*

in school 1 Inside the school building (as against the playground) † *What are you doing out here? You ought to be in school.* **2** During school hours
† *You can start the composition in school and finish it for homework.*
[NOTE: Pupils *go to school* and *come home from school*, but anyone going to the building for a different purpose would *go to* the *school*.]

SCORE *n.*

on that score As far as that (point) is concerned † *The children will be safe with me. You need not worry on that score.*

SCORE *v.t. & i.*

score off someone Make a remark at his expense (usually in answer).

SCRATCH *n.*

come (be) up to scratch Reach (be at) the standard expected † *We cannot renew your contract. Your work has not come up to scratch.*

start from scratch Start from the very beginning † *He threw away everything he had written and started the novel again from scratch.*

SEA *n.*

(all) at sea Confused, not knowing how to handle a situation, work, etc † *I was all at sea until he explained the job to me.*

SEAT *n.*

take a back seat Assume an unimportant role † *He is a member of the Committee, but he generally takes a back seat.* [NOTE: **back-seat driver** Someone who insists on advising person with responsibility on how he should do his work (for example, drive the car).]

SEE *v.i. & t.*

let's see Let us think or consider (before discussing a problem or making a calculation) † *Let's see, what would be the best way of doing it?* † *Let's see, John is two or three years older than James, so James must be about 30.*

you see Used parenthetically in an explanation to mean 'You will understand' † *You see, I saw nothing wrong in telling him. You didn't say it was a secret.*

see about 1 Do something about, make arrangements for † *It's 6 o'clock. I must see about (making the) dinner.* 2 Do something about (an action) contrary to what has gone before † *He says he won't pay me, does he? We'll soon see about that* (i.e. take action to make sure that he pays).

see off Accompany (someone going on a journey) to station, airport, etc † *We saw her off at the airport last night.*

see out 1 Accompany (someone) to the door. 2 (**through**) Endure (something) to the end † *He refused to abandon his ship in the storm, saying he would see it out (through) or die in the attempt.* 3 Outlast (someone) † *He's been working here for twenty years and he'll see me out* (i.e. still be here when I leave). † *It's an enormous task, enough to see me out* (i.e. enough to occupy me until I leave or retire).

see through 1 Not be deceived by † *He pretended to be a rich businessman, but we saw through him (his disguise).* 2 Guide or keep watch on (something) until it reaches a (successful) conclusion † *Mr Jones will be seeing your book through the press.* 3 Guide (someone) safely through difficulty † *Don't be afraid of the examination. Your own good sense will see you through.* 4 Endure to the end (*See* **see out 2**).

see to 1 Attend to, deal with † *Will you see to this customer (letter), Miss Jones?* 2 Attend to (something) so as to ensure (that it is done) † *Everything you want will be provided. I'll see to that.* † *I'll see to it that you're not troubled any further.*

SEED *n.*

go to seed Become shabby in appearance (of property, people's dress) † *He used to be very smart, but he's gone to seed recently.* [ALSO: **seedy** *adj.* Shabby in appearance † *He is living in a seedy boarding house.*]

SEIZE *v.t. & i.*

seize up Become stuck (of machinery) or knotted (of muscles) † *A muscle in my leg seized up while I was playing tennis and I could hardly move.*

SELL *v.t. & i.*

sell off Sell cheaply in order to get rid of † *We are selling off last year's models to make room for the new fashions.*

be sold on Be convinced of the value of (an idea, etc) † *I'm sure it will be a success. I'm completely sold on it.*

sell out Sell one's share (in a business) † *My partner has sold out and retired to the Bahamas.*

be sold out (of) Have sold the stock (of) † *There are no more (cheap) tickets for the concert. We are sold out (of all but the dearest ones).* [ALSO: **sell-out** *n.* Betrayal † *The Union must not accept the employers' offer. It would be a sell-out (of the workers' interests).*]

sell up Sell one's possessions (to pay debts) or sell one's business (under pressure) † *The new supermarket has been so successful that some small shopkeepers have had to sell up.*

SET *v.t. & i.*

set about 1 Hit, strike at † *The two men set about each other.* 2 (+ gerund) Make a start on † *I must set about getting the dinner.*

set aside (apart) (by) (of money) Save for some purpose in the future † *Every month I set aside £100 for the rent.*

set back 1 Reverse (of progress, etc) † *Some teachers say the Government's proposals will set education back thirty years.* 2 Cost (someone) † *The repairs to my house have set me back £100.*

set the clock back Revert to the situation before more recent progress or development. [ALSO: **set-back** *n.* Check, hindrance (to progress, development) † *The project has been delayed by a number of unexpected set-backs.*]

set in Start and establish itself for a time (of weather, etc) † *Winter is setting in.* [ALSO: **inset** *n.* Extra page inserted in a book or a small map attached to a larger one (to bring out detail, etc).]

set off 1 Start (a journey) † *The party set off (for the country) at 8 o'clock.* 2 Cause explosion of (bomb, firework, etc) or cause (gun) to fire, (alarm) to ring † *The burglar passed through an electric circuit and set off the alarm.* 3 Make more attractive (by means of contrast) † *I like the bright wallpaper. It sets off the pale carpet.* 4 Balance † *The profit we have made on selling the house must be set off against the legal fees and agent's expenses.* [ALSO: **off-set** *v.t.* Balance, compensate for † *He managed to off-set his losses on some stocks and shares by making a profit on others.* **offset** *n.* Method of printing.]

set on Attack † *He was set on by a gang of youths.* [ALSO: **onset** *n.* First attack (of bad weather, disease, etc).]

set out 1 Start (a journey) (*See* **set off** 1). 2 (with 'to' + infinitive) Attempt to † *He set out to prove that he was a good workman.* 3 Display (goods, etc); present in sequence (of arguments, ideas) † *The rings were set out in the jeweller's window.* † *I have set out all the arguments in favour of the plan in my article.* [ALSO: **outset** *n.* Beginning, not necessarily of a journey † *The negotiations were ruined at the outset by the uncompromising attitude of the other party.*]

set to Start working on something vigorously (*to* is stressed) † *The workmen set to and installed the new machines very quickly.* [ALSO: **set-to** *n.* Violent argument or quarrel.]

set up 1 Establish † *The Government have set up a special department to deal with the problem.* † *When you set up house together, you will have a lot of bills to pay* (i.e. when you establish yourselves in your own house). **2** Establish (someone) (in a business) by providing capital, etc.

set oneself up as Profess to be † *He sets himself up as an expert on Shakespeare.*

set oneself up (for) Provide oneself (with) † *I have set myself up very well for home comforts.*

be well set up (for) Be well provided for. [ALSO: **set-up** *n.* Established arrangement, position (with regard to an organisation, situation) † *I spent the first two weeks in my new job studying the set-up.* **upset** *v.t. & i.* Overturn (an object) or spoil, disturb (plans). **be upset** Indicates emotional shock. **upset** *n.* Change of plan, emotional disturbance, or reverse of expected result in sport.]

SET *n.*

make a dead set at Make a determined direct attack on (sometimes used of a girl trying to attract a man by getting close to him and making her intentions plain) † *She obviously liked the look of him. She made a dead set at him as soon as he came in.*

SETTLE *v.t. & i.*

settle down 1 Become accustomed to routine, not be distracted † *He found his new surroundings strange at first, but now he's settling down.* **2** Establish oneself in social routine (implying by marriage) † *You've lived a gay bachelor life long enough. It's time you settled down.*

settle down (to) Begin (to do something) with full concentration † *After lunch, I settled down (to work) and wrote the article in a few hours.*

settle for Agree to accept † *It was clear that he could not pay me all he owed, so I settled for half.*

settle on Reach a decision, choose † *She looked at all the hats in the shop and finally settled on this one.*

SHAKE *v.t. & i.*

shake off Get rid of, separate oneself from, escape from † *I've had this cold for a week and can't shake it off. He insisted on going with me although I tried to shake him off.* † *He managed to shake off the man who was pursuing him.*

shake up Make (an organisation, group of people) more active † *The whole system here is inefficient and needs shaking up.* [ALSO: **shake-up** *n.* Change of positions, etc in organisation to produce action, greater efficiency † *He lost his post as Minister of Health in the recent Government shake-up* (*reshuffle* is the official word).

SHALL *anom. fin.*
(*See* **will**).

SHAPE *n.*
in good shape **1** In good physical condition † *I don't think I could play tennis for more than an hour. I'm not in very good shape.* **2** Satisfactory; well-ordered † *The company's affairs are in good shape.*
in the shape of In the form of † *I received an appreciation of my long service in the shape of a gold watch.*

SHARE *n.*
the lion's share The greater portion † *He received the lion's share of the credit for the firm's achievement.*

SHAVE *n.*
a close (near) shave A narrow escape (from capture, an accident, etc) † *That was a close shave. That car missed me by inches.*

SHEEP *n.*
the black sheep (of the family) A useless person (who will bring discredit on the family) (from the biblical idea that there is one such in every family or group).
tell the sheep from the goats Distinguish which people are good, which are bad (often used humorously to mean those who are welcome, socially acceptable, etc and those who are not) † *You mustn't waste the company's hospitality on everyone indiscriminately. Learn to tell the sheep from the goats.*

SHELF *n.*
on the shelf No longer required, wanted (of people) † *It is upsetting to be put on the shelf at 60 as if one could no longer do useful work.* † *Years ago they used to say a girl was on the shelf if she passed 25 without getting married.*

SHIFT *v.t. & i.*
shift for oneself Manage without help † *I can give three of you a lift, but the rest will have to shift for themselves.*

SHIPSHAPE *adj.*
(originally, **all shipshape and Bristol fashion**) In good order † *It takes time to get everything shipshape when one moves house.*

SHIRT *n.*
keep one's shirt on Not lose one's temper (colloquial).

put one's shirt on Gamble all one has on † *I am fairly sure the horse will win, but I wouldn't put my shirt on it.*

SHOE *n.*

be in someone's shoes Be in the situation he is in † *I wouldn't like to be in your shoes when he finds out that you have deceived him.*

step into someone's shoes Succeed him (in a job, etc) † *He will retire soon and there are several people hoping to step into his shoes.*

SHOESTRING *n.*

on a shoestring On a very small amount of money † *He doesn't earn much and the family live on a shoestring.*

SHOP *n.*

all over the shop Everywhere † *I've been looking for you all over the shop.* † *His papers were scattered all over the shop.*

closed shop **1** Works where only trade union members may be employed, or system of agreement between employers and unions ensuring this practice. **2** Situation existing in organisation or trading market where outsiders are not allowed to take a share, apply for jobs, etc † *The market in that country is a closed shop. It is impossible for foreign firms to compete on equal terms.*

talk shop Talk about one's profession, business affairs † *When a lot of teachers get together, they almost always talk shop.*

SHORT *n.*

a short Drink such as whisky, gin, in contrast to **long drinks**, like beer.

SHORT *adj.*

for short For the sake of brevity (particularly of names) † *Her name is Jacqueline – Jackie, for short.*

in short In a few words (summarising previous explanation, etc) † *Everything you have heard indicates that the situation is serious. In short, we are facing a crisis.*

be short of Not have much † *Will it be all right if I pay you next week? I'm rather short of money.* [ALSO: (where 'short' is adv.) **go short (of)** Do without. **run short (of)** Allow supplies to become insufficient. **fall short (of)** Not reach (level expected).]

be nothing (little) short of Amount (almost) to being † *What they offered me for the house was nothing short of laughable.*

short of Except (do something unreasonable) † *There were far too many people for me to find beds for them. There was nothing I could do, short of putting up tents in the garden.*

SHOT *n.*

a shot in the arm Injection (originally of drug, but also used for development

165

or action reviving an organisation, business) † *The reduction of purchase tax will be a shot in the arm to many companies.*

a shot in the dark Wild guess not inspired by real knowledge or information.

SHOULD *anom. fin.*

1 Ought to (*See* **ought to 1–4**). 2 Used as equivalent to subjunctive in clauses expressing purpose (*See* **may 3**). 3 Used as equivalent to subjunctive following an adjective † *I'm anxious that the affair should be settled as soon as possible.* † *It is important that they should not find out.* [NOTE: While *might* is probably more common than *should* for clauses expressing purpose, it cannot be used in place of *should* in 3 (above).] 4 After question words (implying surprise at what one has heard) † *How should I know where your husband is?* (i.e. How can you expect me to know?) † *Why should you worry? It's not your business.* (i.e. What reason have you to worry?) 5 Indicating conditional tense or future in the past (in reported speech) in 1st person † *I should help her if I were in your position.* † *I said that I should meet him at the office.* [NOTE: It is becoming increasingly common for *would* to be used in such sentences in the 1st person as well as in the 2nd and 3rd (*See* **will**).]

SHOULDER *n.*

give someone the cold shoulder Discourage him by showing no interest, disdaining him. [ALSO: **cold-shoulder** *v.t.*]

have broad shoulders Be able to take blame, accept criticism, without becoming upset † *He won't mind what they say about him. He has broad shoulders.*

rub shoulders with Come into contact with, have to do with (people) † *I've rubbed shoulders with all kinds of people on my journeys round the world.*

SHOUTING *n.*

all over bar the shouting (of a fight, game, etc) Decided and only waiting for the official ending and celebration, etc that follows † *Arsenal are leading 3–0 with one minute to go. It's all over bar the shouting.*

SHOW *v.t. & i.*

show off 1 Display to advantage † *She wore a bikini to show off her figure.* † *My husband likes to show off his garden to visitors* (take them round proudly and show it to them). 2 Make a display in order to attract people's attention † *Don't take any notice of my little boy. He's just showing off* (by being precocious, crying, etc). [ALSO: **show-off** *n.* Someone who does this.]

SHOW *n.*

give the show away Allow a secret to become known † ⟩ *Is that what* *you've bought Mother for her birthday?* ⟩ *Yes, but don't give the show away.*

SHOW-DOWN *n.*

An open declaration of intentions on both sides (implying final argument) † *If it comes to a show-down, we will support you.*

SHRIFT *n.*

give someone short shrift Spare him very little time, attention (from original meaning of priest confessing someone hurriedly) † *He went to the boss with his complaint, but the boss gave him short shrift.*

SHUT *v.t. & i.*

shut up! Be quiet! (not polite).

shut someone up Cause him to be silent.

SHY *adj.*

fight shy of Avoid (becoming involved in) † *He was willing to listen, but fought shy of giving a decision on the matter.*

SICK *adj.*

Common in recent years to describe humour, jokes, etc which are morbid or thought to appeal to a perverted sense of humour.

sick (of) Tired (of); disgusted (with) † *I'm sick of hearing about his troubles.* † *Her attitude makes me sick.* [ALSO: **sick and tired of, sick to death of** Stronger forms of expressing the same thing.]

SIDE *n.*

by the side of Compared to (not necessarily by direct visual comparison) † *It is a fine novel, but it seems limited by the side of 'War and Peace'.*

on the side (of money) From sources other than the main one (not necessarily dishonestly) † *He works as an accountant in London, but he also makes some money on the side by advising people on their taxes.*

on the (adj.) side Rather † *These shoes are on the dear (small) side.*

on the right (wrong) side of Favourably (unfavourably) close to (a figure, estimate) † *He's still on the right side of 50* (i.e. a little younger than).

put on one side Lay aside † *I will have to put these papers on one side while I deal with more urgent work.*

(put on) side (Display) self-importance, self-satisfaction † *He puts on so much side that he makes himself ridiculous.*

SIGHT *n.*

a sight An odd or ridiculous spectacle † *She looks a sight since she dyed her hair.* [NOTE: **see the sights** Visit places of interest. One of these, however, could not be praised without a qualifying adjective † *It was a lovely (beautiful) sight.*]

a sight for sore eyes Person or thing welcomed (after long absence, anxious waiting, etc).

know by sight Recognise but not be acquainted, familiar with † *I know him by sight but I have never spoken to him.*

SIN *n.*

live in sin Live with someone as if married to him, her.

SINK *v.i. & t.*

sink or swim Phrase used to indicate that a situation is so serious that there is no alternative to a desperate remedy † *We must cut our prices or be forced out of the market. It's a matter of sink or swim.*

SIT *v.i. & t.*

sit back Relax; take no action † *This is no time for sitting back. There is work to be done.*

sit for 1 (an examination) Take. 2 (a portrait, artist) Pose for.

sit on 1 (a committee, board) Be a member of. 2 (work, papers, etc) Take no action on (and therefore prevent its progress) † *I applied for a licence three months ago and the Ministry have been sitting on the application ever since.* 3 Suppress (someone) (by making him seem foolish) † *He is too full of his own importance. It's time someone sat on him.*

sit out 1 (a play, film, lecture, etc) Watch or listen to it until the end, although bored. 2 (a dance) Not take part in (a particular dance) † *I'd rather sit this one out.*

sit up (for someone) Not go to bed (because one is waiting for him) † *We have let the children sit up to watch this programme.* † *He always sits up for his daughter.*

make someone sit up Make him take notice, shock him † *I told him he would be sacked if his work did not improve. That made him sit up.*

SIT-IN *n.*

Demonstration against authority in which people occupy a building and refuse to move (*See* **teach-in**). [ALSO: **sit-down strike** Strike in which people sit down at their place of work instead of going home, etc.]

SIX *n.*

six of one and half a dozen of the other Indicating no noticeable difference † *They each say the other was to blame but I think it was six of one and half a dozen of the other* (i.e. they are equally to blame).

at sixes and sevens In confusion † *We have been (the factory has been) at sixes and sevens since the manager left.*

SIZE *v.t.*

size up Assess, estimate the nature, possible development of † *It will be impossible for us to size up the situation until we have the latest figures.*

SIZE *n.*

that's the size of it That's a fair general account (of the situation, etc) † ⟩ *I understand you have a sum of money to invest.* ⟩ *That's the size of it.*

SKELETON *n.*

a skeleton in the cupboard Something of which a family is ashamed and which it tries to hide.

skeleton key Key that will open a variety of locks.

skeleton staff The minimum staff necessary to keep machinery, office, etc running † *We are working with a skeleton staff over the Christmas holidays.*

SKIN *v.t. & i.*

keep one's eyes skinned Be alert and watchful † *A dangerous criminal has escaped from prison. Warn all policemen to keep their eyes skinned for car number ABC 123.*

SKIN *n.*

by the skin of one's teeth (Only) just † *I ran all the way to the station and caught the train by the skin of my teeth.*

have a thin (thick) skin Be sensitive (insensitive) to criticism. [ALSO: **be thin-(thick-) skinned** The same meaning † *He's so thick-skinned that you would have to tell him to his face that you disliked him for him to understand.*]

SKIN-DEEP *adj.*

Superficial (of physical attraction, characteristics, etc) † *Beauty is only skin-deep* (proverbial saying). † *He seems to be a patient man, but his patience is only skin-deep.*

SLATE *n.*

on the slate On credit or on a bill (for drinks, etc) to be added up later † *Put it on the slate, please, and I'll pay you at the end of the week (evening).*

SLEEP *v.i. & t.*

sleep on Leave taking a decision on (something) until the next day † *I'll sleep on it and let you know in the morning.*

sleep with Go to bed with (both euphemisms for *have sexual intercourse with*, unless the context obviously implies a literal meaning). [NOTE: **sleeping partner** Someone who contributes capital to a business but does not help to run it. The term is not used in the euphemistic sense of *sleep with*.]

SLEEVE *n.*

have something up one's sleeve Have an idea, plan, etc which one will not disclose until a suitable moment † *I am surprised he gave in to your demands. I wonder if he has something up his sleeve.*

SLIDE v.t. & i.

slide over Pass over (an unpleasant or awkward subject in conversation) † *He slid over the question of my rise in salary and talked about something else.*

let things slide Neglect them, do nothing about them † *The farm is not what it was in old Jack's time. His sons have let things slide.*

SLIP v.i. & t.

slip up Make an error, small mistake † *My secretary slipped up in forgetting to post the letter.* [ALSO: **slip-up** *n*. Error.]

SLIP n.

give someone the slip Escape from him (by confusing or misleading him) † *He managed to give his pursuers the slip in the narrow, crowded streets.*

SLOW adv.

go slow Work slowly as a form of protest (*See* **rule**).

SNAP v.t. & i.

snap up **1** Buy eagerly † *His house was snapped up as soon as he put it on the market.* **2** Interrupt (someone) impatiently or angrily † *I snapped him up as soon as he mentioned your name.*

snap out of it Throw off a bad mood etc † *Snap out of it! Things are not as bad as you seem to think.*

SNEEZE v.i.

not to be sneezed at Not to be despised † *They offered him £500 a year more if he would work for them. That's not a figure to be sneezed at.*

SNOB n.

Someone who values people by their social position or thinks by the impression they make in society and who despises people of lower social position. It is not used favourably to mean 'belonging to good society' though it is sometimes loosely used as an adjective with the meaning of 'fashionable', 'exclusive'. Even here, the use ought to be critical, unless the writer is a snob! [ALSO: **inverted snob** Someone who affects to despise people of his own or a higher social position and deliberately adopts the accent, behaviour, etc of a lower class.]

SNOW v.i. & t.

be snowed under (with) Be overwhelmed (by work, letters, etc) † *Since we advertised our new product on television we have been snowed under with orders.*

SO-AND-SO n.

Person or thing not named, explaining a general principle, etc † *This is a guide to the telephone numbers in the office. If you want to speak to Mr So-and-so, you'll find his name here.* [NOTE: It is not the expression used if the speaker has forgotten the name. He would then say *Mr What's-'is-name* or *Thingummybob*.]

a so-and-so Euphemism for swear-word, describing someone one does not like † *He failed everyone who took the examination. What a so-and-so!*

SO-SO *adj. & adv.*

Not bad; only moderate or fairly well †) *Is his work good?*) *So-so.* †) *Did he do the job well?*) *So-so.*

SOCK *n.*

pull one's socks up Become more alert; show greater application to one's work † *You must pull your socks up. You're falling behind the rest of the class.*

SOFT *adj.*

soft about (Sentimentally) silly about † *He's too soft about the girl to see her faults.*

soft on Lenient towards † *Many people think our courts are too soft on violent criminals.* [NOTE: In the USA, the phrase implies that the speaker distrusts the motives for leniency † *The Senator was accused of being soft on communism*, implies he is a secret admirer of it.]

SOFT-PEDAL *v.i. & t.*

Play down, avoid emphasising † *We must soft-pedal the part of our electoral programme that deals with taxation, because that will not be popular.*

SOFT-SOAP *v.t.*

Flatter, get round † *Don't try to soft-soap me. I know you only want my money.*

SOMEBODY *n.*

(a) somebody A person of importance † *I want to be somebody when I grow up.* † *He thinks himself somebody, but he is the only person who does.*

SOMETHING *n.*

something like 1 Rather like † *She is something like her mother.* 2 About, approximately † *He paid something like £10,000 for the house.* 3 (as expression of approval) Really something good, something one likes † *Now that's something like it! I didn't think home-made cakes like this could still be found.*

SONG *n.*

going (buy) for a song On sale (buy) at a very low price † *This district isn't fashionable any more. Some of the houses are going for a song.*

make a song (and dance) about Get excited about † *Have you never seen a girl in a bikini before? Why are you making such a song and dance about it?*

SORT *n.*

(a) sort of Used when person is vague about what he is describing or simply cannot express himself clearly † *There was a sort of a platform at the end of the room.* † *I (sort of) felt that it was (sort of) impolite.* [NOTE: Americans, when trying to find the right word, tend to use *kind of* rather than *sort of.*]

of a sort (*See* **of a kind; nothing of the kind.**)

a good sort A pleasant or reliable person † *She'll help you. She's a good sort.*

out of sorts Not feeling well † *I'm sorry I'm so bad-tempered. I'm out of sorts today.*

SORT *v.t. & i.*

sort out 1 (things) Separate them into groups. 2 Revise in order to clarify (a situation, organisation) † *The whole system of work here needs sorting out.* 3 (a person) Find out what is wrong with him (in attitude, temperament, etc) † *I'll try to sort him out. It's time he decided what he wants to do with his life.*

SOUP *n.*

in the soup In trouble † *If I don't finish this job to-day, I shall be in the soup.*

SPADE *n.*

call a spade a spade Speak plainly (without trying to be polite).

SPEAK *v.i. & t.*

speak for itself Be evidence enough, without the need for words † *You can see what a terrible accident it was. This photograph speaks for itself.*

so to speak In a manner of speaking, one might say (before using an unusual expression, making an unusual comparison) † *My relationship with the Spanish language is, so to speak, like my relationship with my wife. I love it but I do not dominate it.*

nothing (not) to speak of Nothing (not enough to be) worth mentioning †) *Has this tooth given you much pain?*) *Not to speak of.*

SPIN *v.t. & i.*

spin out Make (something) last as long as possible † *She hasn't very much work to do, but she tries to spin it out till the office closes.*

SPLIT *v.t. & i.*

split on Betray, give away information about (a colleague, schoolfellow, etc) † *Mr Smith would not have known who hid the chalk if you hadn't split on me* (i.e. told him I did).

SPONGE *n.*

throw in the sponge Admit that one is beaten (originally used in boxing, but now employed generally).

SPONGE *v.t. & i.*

sponge on Get money from (someone) (to avoid working oneself); live off
† *You ought to get a job instead of sponging on your friends.*

SPOON-FEED *v.t.*

Pamper, look after too carefully, too kindly † *Some people feel that the younger generation have been spoon-fed and expect everything for nothing.*

SPOT *n.*

a spot of A little † *I've been having a spot of trouble with my car.*

in a spot In a difficult situation † *I'm in a spot at the moment. My secretary is ill and I can't get anyone to type my letters.*

on the spot 1 At the place (where one is needed) † *The accident happened at 9 o'clock, and the ambulance arrived on the spot two minutes later.*
2 Immediately; without moving from the place † *A car hit him as he was crossing the road, and he was killed on the spot.*

the man on the spot The man in the place concerned (who has first-hand knowledge of conditions, the situation) † *We now have a report on the political situation in Russia from our man on the spot (in Moscow).*

SPUR *n.*

on the spur of the moment Impulsively, without thinking for very long † *On the spur of the moment, he packed a suitcase and caught the first train to London.*

SQUARE *n.*

Commonly used nowadays to mean a person of traditional tastes or what are thought to be outdated values.

SQUARE *v.t. & i.*

square a person Pay him to keep back information that might harm one's interests † *He is the only one who knows about your plan and we can square him.*

square (up) Pay what one owes † *I'd like to square up (square with you) for last night* (for what I owe you from last night's bill, etc). [ALSO: **call it square** Agree that no debt exists † *I know I paid for the train tickets, but you paid for the taxi, so we'll call it square* (even).]

square up to Prepare to fight (of two people or small groups, face to face)
† *He squared up to me and said, 'Come on, then, if you're looking for trouble.'*

square with Be consistent with (of facts, stories, etc) † *His account of his movements last night does not square with what his wife told us.*

square (it) with someone Obtain his approval † *Have you squared this plan with your boss?*

STAG *n.*

stag party Party which only men may attend (particularly party held for bridegroom just before marriage) (*See* **hen party**).

STAGE *n.*

stage whisper Whisper (deliberately) loud enough for others to hear (not necessarily, although originally, used in the context of the stage of a theatre).

STAND *v.i. & t.*

stand aside 1 Take no part, do nothing † *Do you expect me to stand aside when a friend of mine is being attacked?* 2 Withdraw (as a candidate, etc) in favour of someone else.

stand by 1 Support, take the side of † *Don't be afraid. I'll stand by you if you need help.* [ALSO: **stand-by** *n.* Person or thing one can rely on † *Shaw's plays are a good old stand-by* (One can rely on them to attract an audience).] 2 Stick to (one's promise, word) † *I will stand by the agreement.* 3 Be ready (to act, move) † *The police are standing by in case the demonstration becomes violent.* [ALSO: **on stand-by** *n.* In readiness (of troops, police, etc).] 4 Look on, do nothing (*See* **stand aside** 1 above).

stand down 1 Withdraw (as a candidate) (*See* **stand aside** 2 above). [NOTE: The difference here is very slight. *Stand down* usually implies that one is already a candidate, *stand aside* that one intends to be.]

stand for 1 Represent; symbolise † *The letters UNO stand for the United Nations Organisation.* † *The stars on the flag of the United States stand for the states of the Union.* 2 Speak in favour of (ideas, convictions, etc) † *We stand for a fair day's pay for a fair day's work.* 3 Be a candidate for † *Three people are standing for the office of President.* 4 Put up with, tolerate † *I won't stand for any more insults.*

stand in for Deputise for, temporarily take the place of † *I am standing in for the Chairman, who is unable to be at the meeting.* [ALSO: **stand-in** *n,* Actor who takes the place of a film star before filming begins or for certain shots at long distance. The correct term for someone employed to undertake dangerous feats in place of a leading actor is **stunt man**. An actor who learns the leading actor's lines in a play so that he can deputise for him when he is ill is called an **understudy**.]

stand off Stand away (from). [ALSO: **stand-offish** *adj.* Cold and reserved towards others (because one believes them to be inferior).]

stand out 1 (of people) Be easily seen in relation to others, physically or mentally; (of a feature of the landscape) be easily seen in relation to its surroundings † *His painting is so good that it stands out from the rest.* † *The castle stands out on top of the hill, dominating the countryside round about.* [ALSO: **outstanding** *adj.* Exceptional, attracting notice (of ability), easily noticeable (of a landmark). It could be used in the first example above, but not in the second.] **2** Hold out, continue to resist † *The soldiers stood out (against the attack) until the relief force arrived.*

stand over Watch closely, supervise (by standing next to, leaning over) † *I can't bear my boss to stand over me while I am working.*

stand up for Defend, work for, speak in favour of (*See* **stand for 2** above) † *If you are not prepared to stand up for yourself, how can we help you?*

stand up to 1 Continue to function, work (in spite of) (wear, hard usage, etc) † *My leg is better, but I doubt if it would stand up to a lot of exercise.* † *These components are required to stand up to great pressure.* **2** Be prepared to resist attack from (someone bigger or stronger) † *Their army is much bigger than ours, but we will stand up to them.*

START *v.i. & t.*

to start with 1 In the first place † *There are several reasons why we should refuse. To start with, we would lose money . . .* [ALSO: **for a start** *n.* Same meaning.] **2** At the beginning † *They only had one small shop to start with, but now they have hundreds of branches.*

STATE *n.*

be in (get into) a state 1 Be (get) upset † *What's the matter? Why is she in a state?* **2** Be in (get into) a condition (mental or physical) † *He came home in an awful state* (He was very worried). † *His clothes were in a bad state* (all torn).

STATUS *n.*

status symbol Something acquired for snobbish reasons because the possession of it implies that the owner is rich or important (e.g. an additional car, a coloured telephone in an office indicating that the person is the manager, etc) (*See* **snob**).

STAY *v.i. & t.*

stay put Remain in the same place; remain where one is † *I have been trying to get in touch with him all day, but he never seems to stay put.* † *Stay put and don't move until I tell you.*

STEAD *n.*

stand someone in good stead (of experience, knowledge, etc) Be useful to him † *The years he had spent abroad stood him in good stead when he opened a language school.*

STEADY *adj.*

steady (on)! Careful! (That's enough!) † *Steady (on) (with the paint)! You'll spill it.*

go steady (with) Have as a regular boy, girl-friend (used of adolescents).

STEAM *n.*

under one's own steam Without help † *They offered us a lift in their car, but we said we could get home under our own steam.*

let off steam Relax by using up one's energy; relieve one's feelings by making them plain (in both cases as a reaction to being restricted) † *It's natural that children want to let off steam after being shut up in school all day.* † *His boss irritates him so much that he likes to come down to my office and let off steam.*

STEEP *adj.*

(a bit) steep (Rather) unreasonable (as a demand, in price, etc) † *He wants me to write the article by the weekend. I think that's a bit steep.*

STEP *v.i. & t.*

step up Increase (production, etc) † *We must step up production to meet the growing demand.*

STEP *n.*

in (out of) step (with) In (not in) harmony (with); (not) moving in the same direction, at the same speed (of attitudes, developments) † *He is a misfit, out of step with the rest of society.* † *It is important that all our allies should be in step over the negotiations.*

STICK *v.t. & i.*

stick at **1** Keep on working at (a job) † *When he has a job to do, he sticks at it in spite of interruptions.* **2** (usually with negative) Draw the line at, refuse to go further than † *He will stick at nothing to get what he wants* (i.e. He will have no scruples about doing anything).

stick by (*See* **stand by 1** and **2**).

stick out Protrude, project from or cause to protrude † *I tore my coat on a nail which was sticking out of the wall.* † *He stuck his head out of the window.*

stick it out Endure (to the end); put up with † *I can't take your tooth out at this time of night. You'll have to stick it out* (endure the pain) *till the morning.*

stick out for Stay firm, in order to get † *He refused to accept a lower price, and stuck out for what he had asked for.*

stick to **1** Stay faithful to (a person); stay working at (a job) † *She stuck to him in spite of all his faults.* **2** Not digress, go away from (the subject) † *Stick to the point. What you're saying is irrelevant.*

stick together Keep together (implying loyalty, mutual help) † *Providing we stick together, we will get through the fog safely.*

stick up Rob (a bank, etc) when armed. [ALSO: **a stick-up** *n.* Robbery of this kind. **stick up for** (*See* **stand up for**). **stuck for, stuck with** (*See* **stuck**).]

STICK *n.*

get the wrong end of the stick Misunderstand an instruction, argument, etc
† *You've got the wrong end of the stick. You were supposed to be responsible for sending the letters, not I.*

STICKY *adj.*

Unpleasant; difficult (especially in set phrases) † *He'll come to a sticky end if he goes on treating people so badly* (suffer an unpleasant fate). † *We are going through a sticky patch at the office* (a difficult period). † *The banks are getting very sticky about lending money* (making borrowing difficult, being awkward).

STING *v.t. & i.*

Charge (someone) a lot of money (which he considers too much) † *When the bill came, I realised I had been stung.*

STITCH *n.*

not have a stitch on Be naked † *She walked into my room, without knocking, when I hadn't a stitch on.*

in stitches Laughing uncontrollably † *The comedian had us in stitches.*

STOCK *n.*

take stock (of) Assess (a situation, work, etc) † *We must take stock (of the situation) and decide what to do.*

STOOL *n.*

fall between two stools Fail, lose an opportunity through trying to take account of two different possibilities, courses of action † *He has been offered two jobs but if he doesn't decide quickly, he could fall between two stools* (i.e. lose both).

STORE *n.*

in store (for) Kept ready (for) † *I think he has a surprise in store for you.* † *Who knows what the future has in store for us?* (implying that our fate is predetermined).

set (great, little, no, not much) store by Consider of (adj.) value or importance, rely (adv.) on † *I don't set much store by what pupils tell me of their teachers.* † *My father set great store by this cure for backache.*

STORM *n.*

a storm in a teacup Unnecessarily excited reaction to an unimportant matter † *What was the row about? Nothing much. Just a storm in a teacup.*

STORY *n.*

a tall story One that sounds too improbable to be believed (especially when it includes examples of wild exaggeration).

STRAW *n.*

the last straw The final burden, irritation, etc, which causes collapse or
provokes a violent reaction † *That's the last straw. I've put up with his
rudeness for a long time, but this letter is unforgivable.* [ALSO: **the straw
that broke the camel's back** Same meaning.]

STREET *n.*

not in the same street (as) Not nearly as good (as) † *He is a good footballer,
but not in the same street as Pele.* [ALSO: **streets ahead (of)** Far better
(than).]

(right) (just) up one's street (Exactly) the kind of job one specialises in, or
which requires particular knowledge one has † *I'll ask Robinson to write
this article. It's right up his street.*

the man in the street The typical citizen † *Economists will understand the
reasons for raising the taxes, but how will the man in the street react to it?*

(go) on the streets (Become) a prostitute.

STRENGTH *n.*

on the strength of **1** On the basis of, relying on † *On the strength of the
Committee's report, we have decided to carry out the changes proposed.*
2 Belonging to (a group, organisation, particularly police, armed forces,
etc) † *He has been transferred from London and is now on the strength of
the Manchester police.* [ALSO: **bring up to strength** Recruit men in order
to reach the number established or required.]

at full strength Having the number of men required † *The staff is now at full
strength.*

STRETCH *n.*

at a stretch **1** Continuously, without stopping † *He often writes for several
hours at a stretch.* **2** By stretching resources to the limit † *We normally
produce 1,000 cars a week, but at a stretch we could make 1,200.* [ALSO:
at full stretch Fully occupied, using resources to the limit † *The factory is
(working) at full stretch.*]

STRIDE *n.*

get into one's stride Get accustomed to an activity and the speed of work, etc
required † *He found the job very demanding at first, but soon got into his
stride.*

take in one's stride (do (something), overcome (a problem, etc) without
making a special effort † *He is already capable of passing the examination
and when it comes, he should take it in his stride.*

STRIKE *v.i. & t.*

it strikes me It occurs to me † *It strikes me that we ought to reserve a seat on
the train or else we may have to stand.* † *It struck him that he had seen the
girl before somewhere.*

strike up **1** (an acquaintance, friendship) Make casually, by chance † *On the journey I struck up an acquaintance with an American family.* **2** (a tune, melody) Begin to play † *The band struck up a military march.*

STRING *n.*

(no) strings (attached) (of loans, contracts, etc) (Without) conditions about how the loan is to be used or contract fulfilled † *We are prepared to lend the money with no strings attached.* † *If he is offering us a contract, there must be some strings attached to it.*

pull strings Use influence (on friends, acquaintances) to obtain something † *He pulled some strings at the Ministry in order to get permission to build a new factory here.*

STRING *v.t. & i.*

strung up Tense and nervous (before an important engagement, performance, etc) † *I always get strung up before going on stage.* [ALSO: **highly-strung** *adj.* Very sensitive, liable to nervous excitement.]

STRONG *adj.*

going strong Making good progress † 〉 *How is your business?* 〉 *Still going strong, I am glad to say.*

STUCK *p.p.* of **stick**

stuck for (an answer, money) Unable to provide, obtain † *I don't know what to say. I'm stuck for an answer.*

stuck with Unable to get rid of † *Aunt Jane gave us that horrible picture so we're stuck with it.*

STUCK-UP *adj.*

Having an exaggerated idea of one's social position and therefore affecting to disdain others of one's own class † *She thinks herself refined, but I would call her stuck-up.*

STUFF *n.*

Used colloquially as a general term for material, medicine, contents of a book, etc when speaker does not know the exact word or is too casual to use it † *Have you got any more of that stuff you sold me for my backache?*

do one's stuff Show one's ability in doing something (speaking, acting, making something, etc) † *When I have finished speaking, the best man (at the wedding) will get up and do his stuff.*

know one's stuff Be an expert in the subject † *I like listening to his lectures. He knows his stuff.*

that's the stuff That's the way to do it, the way to treat people † *That's the stuff! Now you are acting the play as if you believed in it.*

STUMBLE *v.i.*

stumble across (on) Find by accident, unexpectedly (*See* **come across**).

STUNT *n.*

stunt man (*See* **stand-in**).

STYLE *n.*

do things (live) in style Do things (live) well or expensively in an original way
† *Their parties are magnificent. They always do things in style.*

SUBJECT *n.*

subject to *adj. & adv.* Conditional(ly) upon † *Subject to your approval, we will carry out the work as indicated here.*

SUCH *adj.*

as such 1 Being (whatever is stated) † *Dr Johnson's dictionary was the first in English and as such must have represented an enormous task for one man.* 2 In himself, itself, etc (and for no other reason) † *I don't object to taxation as such. I object to taxation on essential things like food.*

such as it is (they are, etc) In the state it is (they are, etc) in (implying an apology for poor quality) † *You are welcome to use any notes on the lecture, such as they are.*

SUMMER *n.*

Indian summer Period of fine weather occurring in late autumn. It is occasionally referred to as a **St Martin's summer**, because of St Martin's day (November 11th).

SUNDRY *adj.*

all and sundry *n.* Strictly speaking, *each and all*, but commonly used to mean *everyone* (without distinction) † *This club is reserved for members. It is not open to all and sundry.*

SUPPOSE *v.t.*

I don't suppose Polite way of asking for a favour, loan, etc † *I don't suppose you could look after the children for half an hour while I go out, could you?*

be supposed to 1 Be required or expected to; (neg.) be allowed to † *I am supposed to be at the office by 9.30.* † *I am not supposed to be home after midnight.* 2 Be said to (as popular belief or commercial claim, etc) † *The ghost of Anne Boleyn is supposed to haunt the Tower of London.* † *This machine is supposed to wash all the dishes in five minutes.* 3 Indicating or asking about what is thought to be a fact † *I ought not to have come out. I'm supposed to be in bed* (i.e. I was told to stay in bed and everyone thinks I am there). † *Who is supposed to be in charge here?*

SUPPOSE, SUPPOSING *conj.*
   If † *Suppose he doesn't agree to the idea, what are we going to do?*

SURE *adj.*
be sure to (in imperative) Make sure that you † *Be sure to write to us, won't you?*
to be sure Admittedly, I admit † *It's cold outside, to be sure, but you'll be warm enough if you put your coat on.*

SURE *adv.*
   (as reply, in USA) Certainly, yes † 〉 *May I borrow your newspaper?* 〉 *Sure.*
sure enough In fact (implying as expected or predicted) † *They said it would rain today and sure enough, here it comes.*

SURELY *adv.*
   Expressing confidence or disbelief, based on probability (placed next to the subject or at the end) † *Surely he doesn't want me to do the job all over again!* (It seems impossible that he wants me to). † *I've seen you before, surely* (I believe I have). [NOTE: *I have certainly seen you before* means the speaker is in no doubt about it.]

SWAN *n.*
swan song Strictly speaking, last work produced by poet, artist, etc, but used generally for last performance or final achievement in a (creative) career.

SWEAR *v.t. & i.*
swear by Take an oath (on Bible in court of law, etc) but also have absolute confidence in (a cure, medicine) † *I swear by all that I hold sacred that I will never desert you.* † *It is a good cure for colds; I swear by it.*
swear to something Take an oath that it is true (a statement made to the police, etc) but also be absolutely sure of it † *I thought I saw him in the street yesterday, but I couldn't swear to it* (swear that it was he).

SWIM *n.*
in the swim Involved in the sphere of activity referred to, in touch with important people in that sphere † *He should know who is to be invited to the dinner at the Town Hall. He's in the swim.*

SWING *n.*
go with a swing (of public events, parties, etc) Proceed without delays, difficulties.
in full swing Proceeding in a lively manner † *We arrived when the party was in full swing.*

SYMPATHY *n.*
in sympathy with **1** In agreement with, up to a point or in principle † *I am in*

sympathy with your proposals, but I don't see how they would work in practice. **2** Out of fellow-feeling for † *The London dockers have decided to strike in sympathy with the Liverpool dockers (who are already on strike).*

T *n.*

to a T Exactly (after 'fit', 'suit', 'cook', etc) † *That dress is perfect for you, madam. It fits you to a T.*

TAB *n.*

keep tabs on (usually plural) Keep under observation, keep a record of † *He was released from prison yesterday, but the police are keeping tabs on him.* † *If I didn't keep tabs on all the enquiries I answer, I would be lost.*

TABLE *n.*

turn the tables on (an opponent) Reverse the position in one's favour, revenge a defeat † *He beat me the last time we played but today I hope to turn the tables on him.*

TAIL *v.t. & i.*

tail off **1** Become smaller in size or quantity † *Demand for the book has tailed off recently.* **2** Deteriorate in quality (particularly towards the end) † *The article begins well, but tails off in the final paragraphs.*

TAKE *v.t. & i.*

take it (with 'can', 'be able to') Endure suffering, hardship, etc and not weaken or complain † *A good boxer must be able to take it.*

I take it I assume † *You'll be coming with us, I take it. (I take it that you will . . .).*

take it from me Believe me, you can be sure † *Take it from me, if the Government don't act now, we shall be in serious trouble.*

take after Look or act like (a parent or relation) † *You can see from his nose that he takes after his father.*

take back **1** Withdraw (something one has said) or agree to accept the return (of goods) † *Take that back! You know it's not true.* † *The manager of the shop said he would take the shoes back if I bought another pair for the same price.* **2** Cause (one) to remember or return to an earlier point in discussion † *Seeing the old man took me back to my childhood, when I* *used to buy sweets in his shop.* † *That remark takes us back to the first point of his argument.*

take in 1 Admit as a guest (often when taking pity on people or animals with nowhere else to go) † *She takes in lodgers in the holiday season.* † *The poor dog looked so lonely that I had to take it in.* 2 Include † *The tour of Paris by night takes in a visit to the Folies Bergères.* 3 Understand and think about † *A language teacher must speak slowly and clearly so that the students can take in everything he says.* 4 Listen to with excitement or credulously † *When he told the other children about his adventure, they took it all in open-mouthed.* 5 Deceive, trick † *I'm afraid you've been taken in. These pearls are not genuine.*

take off 1 (of an aeroplane) Leave the ground † *Flight 123 to Paris will take off in five minutes.* [ALSO: **take-off** *n.* The action of doing this † *We had a very smooth take-off.*] 2 (someone's voice, manner, etc) Imitate humorously. [ALSO: **take-off** *n.* Such an imitation † *He did a very good take-off of the Prime Minister.*]

take on 1 Undertake † *I'm too busy to take on any more work.* 2 Engage (employees) † *We have taken on more staff.* 3 Become fashionable, catch on † *The romantic look has taken on more quickly than the manufacturers expected.* [NOTE: 'Take' is sometimes used alone with this meaning † *It's a good record, but do you think it will take with the public?*] 4 Accept as an opponent † ⟩ *Does anyone want to play billiards with me?* ⟩ *Yes, I'll take you on.* 5 Assume, adopt (the appearance of) † *When she was asleep, her face took on an expression of childlike innocence.* **take out** Obtain (an official document – licence, patent, etc.) † *Have you taken out a patent for your invention?*

take it out of Exhaust, weaken † *He needs rest. The excitement of the past few days has taken it out of him.*

take it out on Relieve one's own irritation, frustration by attacking, blaming (someone else, who is innocent) † *I know you're upset at missing the train, but that's no reason to take it out on the porter.*

take over 1 Take control of † *When my boss retires, his son will take over the firm.* [ALSO: **take-over bid** *adj.* Attempt by one firm to gain control of another (by buying shares).] 2 Take control, responsibility (intransitive) † *When the pilot left the controls, the co-pilot took over.* † *Who will take over while you are away?* [ALSO: **take-over** *n.* Action, procedure of control passing from one to another † *Civil servants try to ensure a smooth take-over when a new Government comes into power.*]

take to 1 Start on (a course of action which continues) (particularly in set phrases 'take to crime, drink, etc') † *She had an unhappy childhood. Her mother left home and her father took to drink* (i.e. started drinking alcohol heavily). 2 (with gerund) Get into the habit of † *Recently he has taken to having a drink at the pub on the way home from work.* 3 Develop a liking for † *The children have taken to their new teacher.* † *He was afraid of the sea at first, but he has taken to it since he learned to swim.*

take up **1** Occupy (time, space) † *I won't take up any more of your time.* † *That bookcase takes up a lot of room.* **2** Adopt (as a profession, business, hobby, etc) † *He worked in an office for some years, and then took up teaching.* † *I think I will take up golf.* **3** Move into, start (a job, house, etc) † *I take up my new post on the 1st of October.* † *When do you expect to take up residence in college?* [NOTE: 'Take up residence' is a set phrase. One does not 'take up house'.] **4** Deal with (a matter) (particularly by official action, investigation) † *The Minister was surprised to hear complaints about his staff and promised to take up the matter.* [ALSO: **take up with** Raise (a matter) officially with † *I have received your report on the affair and will take it up with the Department concerned.*]

TALE *n.*

tell tales Tell someone (in authority) what another person has said or done in order to get him into trouble or gain favour for oneself † *I don't care what Johnny did. You shouldn't tell tales.*

TALK *v.i. & t.*

talk down to Speak to in a way that suggests the listeners are intellectually inferior † *You should avoid unfamiliar words when lecturing to foreign students, but you must not talk down to them.*

talk into Persuade (by speaking cleverly) † *I couldn't really afford the car, but my wife talked me into it.*

talk to (in some cases) Reprimand, tell off † *I must talk to my secretary about these letters. They are very badly typed.* [ALSO: **give someone a (good) talking-to** *n.* Reprimand him.]

TAP *n.*

on tap Easily reached when needed † *The Personnel Department have a card index of all the employees, so any information they need is on tap.*

TAPE *n.*

red tape Bureaucratic procedure (filling in forms, etc) (used in connection with the delays, frustrations which result from insisting on its being followed) † *Surely there is a quicker way of doing things. Do I have to put up with all this red tape?*

TAPE *v.t.*

have someone taped Know his personality, attitudes, etc (particularly his weaknesses) and be able to predict his actions † *His behaviour confused me at first, but now I've got him taped.*

TASK *n.*

take to task Reprimand (particularly about bad work) (*See* **talk to, tell off**).

TEACH-IN *n.*
Seminar specially arranged to instruct people (on subject of public interest) † *The Government should hold teach-ins on the Common Market to help people understand the issues.* [NOTE: The technique of adding 'in' to a verb to create a new noun comes from the USA. At the time of writing, 'teach-in' and 'sit-in' are the only examples which have become widely used.]

TELL *v.t. & i.*
I can tell you (at the end of a statement) I assure you (used for emphasis) † *It's not the first time your little boy has been rude to me, I can tell you.*

(I'll) tell you what Used to introduce a suggestion † *Tell you what. How about going to see if Jack is back from his holiday?*

there's no telling There is no way of knowing † *There's no telling what I should have done if you hadn't lent me the money.*

all told In total (from old use of *tell* = count) † *There were ten of us there, all told.*

tell off Reprimand † *I'd tell her off if she spoke to me like that.* [ALSO: **give someone a telling-off** *n.* Reprimand him.] [NOTE: There is little difference in meaning between 'tell off' and 'talk to' but 'tell off' implies stronger, more direct language.]

tell on 1 Have an (exhausting) effect on † *The effort he had made early in the race told on him and he was forced to retire.* **2** Give (someone) away in order to get him into trouble (*See* **tell tales**) (mainly used of children) † *Father wouldn't have known that I smoked his cigar if you hadn't told on me.*

TENTERHOOKS *n.*
(only in) **on tenterhooks** In a nervous state, anxiously waiting for something † *I was on tenterhooks until the examination results were announced.*

TERM *n.*
on good (bad) terms (with) Having good (bad) relations (with) † *We seldom see each other nowadays. We are not on good terms. (I am not on good terms with him).*

come to terms (with) Reach agreement (with) † *We haven't agreed a price yet, but we'll come to terms before long.*

come to terms with oneself Reach an understanding of one's own attitudes, behaviour, intentions, etc (and act more sensibly, logically) † *I have had to come to terms with myself and accept that I cannot make my dream come true.*

TERRIBLE *adj.*
Widely used to mean 'bad' (*See* **awful**) † *We had terrible weather on holiday.*

185

THAT *adj. & pron.*

that's that Used to indicate finality, the end of something † *Well, that's that! I'm not doing any more work today.* † *I've made up my mind and that's that* (i.e. that is my last word on the subject).

not all that Not as (used for emphasis) † *It wasn't a good programme, but it wasn't all that bad* (not as bad as you suggest). [ALSO: **not as . . . as all that** Not as . . . as you say.]

THEORY *n.*

in theory (*See* **practice**).

THICK *adj.*

a bit thick (**on**) Hard (on), unfair (to) † *It was a bit thick (on his wife) for him to leave her alone while he went to the races.*

thick with Involved with, friendly with † *He gets a lot of contracts from the Town Council, perhaps because he's so thick with the Mayor.* [NOTE: 'Thick' used alone to describe someone, means stupid † *He is so thick that he doesn't understand the simplest explanation.*]

in the thick of In the part of (a fight, situation) where there is most activity † *John was in the thick of the fight, hitting out to left and right.*

through thick and thin In all kinds of conditions (bad as well as good) (implying loyalty, courage, etc) † *During the war he stood by me through thick and thin.*

THING *n.*

the thing is The question to be decided, reason for my speaking is † *Are you going out? The thing is, I'm expecting a 'phone call and I wonder if you could take it for me.*

just the thing Exactly what one wants, needs † ⟩ *Would this be suitable, madam?* ⟩ *Yes, it's just the thing.*

quite the thing Very much in fashion † *High boots are quite the thing these days.* [NOTE: 'Not quite the thing' would mean 'not really acceptable socially'.]

(just) one of those things The kind of thing that cannot be helped (because it is inevitable) † *It wasn't your fault. It was just one of those things.*

do one's (own) thing Recent expression meaning 'do what one finds most natural or what one wishes to do'. Originally used by hippies and still used by them or in imitation of them.

THINK *v.t. & i.*

think about 1 Reflect on, study † *She spends too much time thinking about her problems* (She worries). (*See* **think of** 7). **2** Give consideration to † *I'll think about your proposal and give you my decision tomorrow.* **3** Occupy one's mind with † *All he ever thinks about is football.* **4** Turn one's mind to the consideration of † *It's time you thought about a career.*

think of 1 Have an idea, conception of † *I didn't know how to mend it until I thought of putting these wires together.* † *When I first met your mother, you weren't even thought of.* 2 Recall, call to mind † *Now that I think of it, aren't you the young man who gave me a lift home last Sunday?* [ALSO: **come to think of it** Now that I recall it.] 3 Entertain as an idea † *It was an awful place. I wouldn't think of going there for a holiday.* 4 Consider the idea of; have as a half-formed intention † *We are thinking of going to live at the seaside.* [ALSO: **think better of** Reconsider, change one's mind about † *I was going to buy a house at the seaside, but I thought better of it when I saw the prices.*] 5 To indicate an opinion † *What do you think of our new wallpaper?* [ALSO: **think nothing of** Consider not worth mentioning (of habits, etc others would think unusual) † *He is very fond of golf. He thinks nothing of playing a round before breakfast.*] 6 Imagine † *Think of what would happen if the level of the Thames rose ten metres without warning.* 7 Be interested in † *She thinks of no one but herself* (i.e. she is selfish). (*See* **think about** 1). [NOTE: 'Think about' and 'think of' are seldom interchangeable. 'Think of' could be substituted for 'think about' 3 and 4; 'think about' could be used in place of 'think of' 1.]

think out Think about (*See* 1 and 2 above) until one arrives at a solution † *I have thought out the theory I told you about and I believe it will stand up to any test.*

think over Think about (*See* 2 above) at length (before giving a decision, opinion) † *I can't say 'Yes' or 'No' to the plan now. I must have time to think it over.*

think up Devise, invent (a theory, story, plan, etc) † *I have thought up a game we could play to pass the time.* † *I shall have to think up an excuse for not meeting him.*

THRASH *v.t. & i.*

thrash out Reach a solution by frank, open discussion † *We will thrash the matter out when the Committee meets.*

THROUGH *prep.*

1 From one end or side to another, or entering at one end or side and coming out at the other (whether or not there is an obstacle) † *The road runs through the village.* † *The nail went through the wall.* † *The train went through the tunnel.* † *He put the letter through the letter-box.* † *He saw her coming towards him through the mist.* † *The noise of the traffic came through the open window.* 2 Indicating an intermediate point on a journey † *The Thames flows through Oxford on its way to London.* † *The train to Leicester goes through Luton and Bedford.* 3 Indicating medium employed (particularly in order to see, look at) † *He looked through the telescope at the stars.* 4 Indicating agency or cause † *I heard about the house being for sale through a friend who lives nearby.* † *He*

lost the money through carelessness. **5** Indicating thoroughness, leaving nothing out † *I have looked through my papers but cannot find the letter you mentioned.* **6** With certain verbs, indicating undergo or subject to test, examination, ordeal † *He went through a great deal during the war* (experienced, suffered). † *The new machine is to be put through a series of tests.* **7** From beginning to end of a period of time † *He worked through the night to repair the machine.* [NOTE: In the USA, *through* is used with a similar meaning, naming the beginning and end points of the period † *I shall be staying at the hotel from Tuesday through Saturday* (meaning 'I shall be there until Sunday morning'). In Great Britain, this sentence would be written † *I shall be staying from Tuesday to Saturday inclusive.*]

THROUGH *adv.*

Connected (on telephone) † *You're through to Paris now.*
through and through Completely, in every respect † *He is a soldier through and through.*
be through (with) 1 Have finished (with) † *I'm through (with my work) for the day.* **2** Be finished (with) (a person, job), have had enough (of) † *We're through. I never want to see you again.* † *I'm through (with this job).*

THROUGHOUT *prep.*

1 All through, at all times in † *Throughout his life, he worked to improve conditions in the industry.* † *He was abroad throughout the last war.*
2 All over, in all parts of (place) † *This product is sold throughout the country.*

THROW *v.t. & i.*

throw oneself into Begin to engage in with keenness, enthusiasm † *As soon as he returned from his holiday, he threw himself into the task in front of him.*
throw off Manage to get rid of, escape from † *I have had this cold for a fortnight. I can't throw it off.* † *He threw off his pursuers by joining the crowd coming out of the football match.*
throw out 1 Cause (someone) to make a mistake by distracting his attention or cause to be wrong, inaccurate † *These continual interruptions have thrown me out.* † *These new statistics have thrown out all our calculations.* **2** Make (someone) leave (job, place) † *He was thrown out of work when the factory closed down.* † *He was thrown out of the library for singing.* [NOTE: Violence is normally implied only in active sentences † *If you don't shut up, I'll throw you out of the house.*] **3** Make (a suggestion, etc) casually † *You don't have to do as I say. I just threw out the idea as a possible solution.*

throw over Abandon, break off relations with † *They were to be married to-day, but last week she suddenly threw him over.*

throw together 1 Put together hurriedly (of things) † *There was no time to prepare the exhibition properly. We had to throw everything together at the last minute.* 2 Bring together haphazardly, by chance † *During the war, people were thrown together from all walks of life.*

throw up 1 Give up (a job) suddenly, abruptly † *He threw up his job and went off to Australia.* 2 Vomit † *The piles of rubbish were so disgusting that I almost threw up (what I had eaten).*

THUMB *n.*

under someone's thumb Under his control † *He wouldn't dare do anything without his wife's agreement. He is under her thumb.* † *He doesn't like his staff to show any independence. He wants all the work to be under his thumb.*

THUNDER *n.*

steal someone's thunder Take credit for something by anticipating a rival's work or proposals and publishing or acting before him.

TICK *n.*

in a tick Colloquial expression for in a moment, in a short time.

on tick Colloquial expression meaning on credit terms † *Can I have the sugar on tick? I've left my purse at home.*

TICK *v.i. & t.*

what makes someone (it) tick What impulses govern his behaviour, attitudes; what makes a machine, etc work † *He continually surprises me. I wish I could find out what makes him tick.*

tick off 1 Check (names, items) against a list by writing a tick ($\checkmark$).
2 Reprimand, tell off (*See* **tell off**).

tick over Originally of a car engine still running with the gears disconnected, but now used generally for continuing without incident, progress † *Hardly anyone has come into the shop this week. We are just ticking over until the Christmas rush.*

TIDE *v.t.*

tide over Enable (someone) to overcome or pass through (a difficult period; usually used financially) † *Would you lend me £5 to tide me over until I am paid?*

TIE *v.t. & i.*

be (get) tied up 1 Be (become) engaged, busy † *Will you ring back later? I'm tied up at the moment.* 2 Be (become) confused, muddled † *Can you explain to me what this tax form means? I always get tied up by figures.*

be (get) tied up with Be (become) connected with (particularly of arrangements

between companies, etc) † *His firm is tied up with a big American
company* (which owns shares in it, etc). [ALSO: **tie-up** *n*. Business
arrangement of this kind, merger between companies.]

TIGHT *adj*.
1 Drunk. 2 Mean, miserly. [ALSO: **tight-fisted** *adj*. (of a person).] 3 In
short supply, hard to obtain (of money) † *It's very difficult to get a loan
from the bank at present. Money is very tight.*

sit tight Not move, not commit oneself † *We'll have to sit tight until the storm
passes.* † *The project is still too risky for me to invest in it. I'll sit tight for
a time.*

TILL *prep*.
(*See* **until**).

TILT *n*.
(at) full tilt At great speed; with great force (used of collisions involving
people) † *I turned the corner and walked full tilt into a lamp-post.*

TIME *n*.
at one time During a period in the past, known but not specified † *That's
James Robinson. At one time he was engaged to my sister.* [NOTE: The
phrase is often used with *used to*, implying *in the past, but not now*.]

at the best of times When conditions are most favourable † *He is very quiet
today, but he doesn't say much at the best of times.*

at the same time 1 Together, simultaneously † *We arrived at the same time.*
2 Nevertheless † *I don't think there is any excuse for his behaviour. At the
same time, we should listen to what he has to say.*

for the time being Until there is some change, until a new arrangement is
made † *We are staying with my parents for the time being.*

from time to time Occasionally, now and then † *We used to be close friends,
and I still see him from time to time.*

in time (for) 1 Not too late (for), with enough time to spare † *I arrived in time
to catch the train.* † *Am I in time for tea?* (Is there still time for me to have
tea?) 2 Eventually † *You will find it difficult at first, but you'll get used to
it in time.* [ALSO: **all in good time** When the time is right (particularly in
asking someone to be patient, etc) † *You'll have a chance to express your
point of view, all in good time.*]

in (out of) time Keeping (failing to keep) musical time when playing an
instrument, dancing, etc.

in no time Very soon, very quickly † *Just wait here a moment. I'll be back in
no time.*

in one's time In the course of one's life † *He's a good player, but I've met
better in my time.*

in one's own time 1 In one's leisure hours † *He wasn't able to finish the job at* *the office, so he had to do it in his own time.* **2** At a time convenient to one † *Don't rush the job. Let me have it in your own time.*

on time At the time specified, not late † *The train arrived on time.* [NOTE: The difference between *on time* and *in time* **1** (above) should be clear from the definitions given. *In time* always implies with enough time at one's disposal to do something where *on time* implies the actual time of day, etc.]

to time In accordance with the scheduled timetable † *Are the trains running to time this morning?*

once upon a time At a certain time in the past (standard opening for a fairy tale and only used there or in imitation).

time and again, time after time, times without number Repeatedly † *I've told you time and again to take off your dirty boots before you come in.*

time out of mind, time immemorial A period longer than anyone can remember † *The family have lived in the district since time immemorial.*

bide one's time Wait for a better opportunity † *There's no point in rushing things. Bide your time (until you get a better offer).*

do time Serve a period of time in prison.

have a good (bad) time Enjoy (not enjoy) oneself † *Did you have a good time on holiday?* [ALSO: **have the time of one's life** Enjoy oneself more than at any other time.]

keep time Not get out of tune, step, when playing a musical instrument, dancing.

keep good time (of clocks, etc) Be accurate † *My watch keeps good time.*

kill time Find ways of passing the time to avoid being bored † *While I was waiting for her, I killed time by looking in shop-windows.*

take one's time Not hurry, take as much time as one needs † *You needn't make a decision immediately. Take your time.*

take up someone's time (*See* **take up 1**).

TIP *n.*

on the tip of one's tongue On the point of saying something † *The manager of the shop was so casual that I had it (it was) on the tip of my tongue to tell him off.* † *What's that man's name? I have it (it is) on the tip of my tongue* (i.e. I can almost remember it, but not quite).

TIP *v.t.*

tip off Warn (someone) or give him a hint † *The police set a trap for the thief, but someone must have tipped him off because he did not appear.* [ALSO: **tip-off** *n.* Warning, hint.]

TO *prep.*

1 Indicating destination or point reached † *I am going to London.* † *When you get to the main road, turn right.* † *At last, the performance came to an end.* **2** In the direction of, towards † *'Who's that?' he asked,* *pointing to a man who was talking to my wife.* † *Throw the ball to Johnny* (so that he can catch it). [NOTE: *To* emphasises the direction with verbs like *throw*, whereas *at* emphasises the target one is aiming at † *He pointed the gun at me* (threatening to shoot me). † *Don't throw stones at other children* (in order to hit them).] **3** Towards, involving contact with † *He raised the glass to his lips.* **4** As far as † *I will go with you to the door.* † *I counted to three and then pressed the button.* **5** Indicating the extent, limit of something † *To the best of my knowledge, this is the oldest building in the town* (as far as I know). **6** Until † *I shall be staying from Monday to Friday.* † *The office is open from 9.30 to 5.30 every day.* **7** Indicating the result of calculation, etc, a total † *The bill came to £5.* † *The price has gone up to £1.* **8** Indicating person or thing to which activity or wish is directed (objective use) † *He spoke to me about the meeting.* † *Are you going to write to your father?* † *Let us now drink to the happy couple* (drink their health). [ALSO: **talk to, shout to, call to,** etc.] **9** Indicating indirect object † *Give it to me.* † *I showed the photographs to my wife.* **10** In an objective sense after certain adjectives † *She was very kind to me.* † *You mustn't be rude to your aunt.* **11** Defining the adjective before it more precisely † *The examination is open to students whose native language is not English.* **12** Indicating opinion, attitude or person referred to †) *To my mind, the best thing to do would be to ring.*) *Do what you like. It's all the same to me* (as far as I am concerned). **13** Indicating reaction, emotion resulting from † *To my surprise, he said nothing about the argument we had had.* † *He announced his engagement to the delight of everyone present.* **14** Indicating relative position (in prepositional phrases) † *He sat down next to me.* † *He lives in the house opposite to my uncle's.* **15** Indicating correspondence, conformity with † *The novel is true to life.* † *The steak was cooked to order.* **16** Indicating comparison, ratio † *I prefer tennis to golf.* † *We won the match by three goals to one.* **17** Indicating attachment to a person or object † *The shelves are fixed to the wall.* † *He is tied to his job in London and cannot move to another part of the country.* **18** Indicating change † *There has been a change to decimal currency in Britain.* **19** To the accompaniment of (music, etc) † *We danced to the music of the band.*

TOE *n.*

on one's toes Alert, ready for action † *A number of firms are in competition with us, so we have to be on our toes.*

tread on someone's toes Offend him by doing, saying something that goes against his beliefs, idea of his responsibility † *I hope I am not treading on the toes of any doctors present in saying that the standards of the hospital should be improved.*

TOGETHER WITH *prep.*
1 Combined with † *The latest report from the Medical Council, together with evidence from other parts of the world, establishes that smoking is a danger to health.* **2** Accompanied by † *I enclose the manuscript of my book, together with a list of illustrations.*

TONE *v.t. & i.*
tone down Modify (the force, intensity of statements, colours, etc) † *Your article puts the case in very strong language. We will have to tone it down.*

TONGUE *n.*
with one's tongue in one's cheek Ironically, not intending that it should be taken at its face value † *He asked her if she was celebrating her third marriage or her second divorce. Of course, he was speaking with his tongue in his cheek.* [ALSO: **tongue-in-cheek** *adj. & adv.* Ironic(ally).]
bite one's tongue off (after 'could') Immediately regret something one has said † *When I saw she had been hurt by my remarks, I could have bitten my tongue off.*
have a tongue in one's head Be capable of speaking (used when one is surprised, annoyed by a person's remaining silent) † *Have you nothing to say in your defence? Come on, you have a tongue in your head, haven't you?*
hold one's tongue Remain silent deliberately † *I would like to have told the boss that he was a fool, but thought it wiser to hold my tongue.*
lose (find) one's tongue Be unable to find words to express oneself (suddenly find something to say after remaining silent) because of shyness, fear, etc. [ALSO: **tongue-tied** *adj.* Silent in such a situation † *He was so nervous that he stood in front of the examiner tongue-tied.*]

TOOTH *n.*
in the teeth of In spite of the force of (criticism, opposition, etc) † *He stood firm in the teeth of the criticism made of his policies.*

TOP *n.*
on top of *prep. phr.* **1** Over and above † *He behaved very badly at the party and on top of that refused to pay for the glasses he broke.* **2** Coming after and adding to the effect of † *The news of his friend's death, on top of the troubles he already had, was a terrible blow.*
get on top of Dominate; depress † *At first we could not cope with so much extra work, but now we are getting on top of it.* † *I'm afraid I've let the work get on top of me.*

TOP *v.t.*
top up Fill to the top (a container which is partly empty) † *There's a lot of*

froth in this glass of beer. Drink a little and I'll top it up for you (to give you the right quantity).

TOSS *v.t. & i.*

toss up Throw (a coin) into the air to decide something (which side is to begin a game, etc). [ALSO: **it's a toss-up** *n.* The chances are equal † *I don't know who will win the election. It's a toss-up (between Smith and Brown).*]

TOUCH *n.*

in (out of) touch (with) (people) (No longer) in communication (with); (events) (no longer) informed (about) † *I haven't seen him since he went to Australia but we keep in touch.* † *I don't know anything about modern theatre. I've got out of touch since we moved to the country.*

TOUCH-AND-GO *adj.*

Uncertain (of the situations, events which are exciting or emotionally important and could result in one of two ways) † *It was touch-and-go which team would win until the last minute of the game.* † *It is touch-and-go whether he will live or die.*

TOUCH *v.t. & i.*

touch someone (for money) Beg from someone known to one (not usually with the intention of paying him back) † *He spent all his money and went to his uncle's house to touch him for a few pounds.*

touch down (of an aeroplane) Land † *The plane touched down five minutes ago.* [ALSO: **touch-down** *n.* Landing.]

touch off Cause to fire, explode (of cannon, explosive) or begin (a (violent) series of events) † *The arrest of the students' leader touched off demonstrations all over the country.*

touch on Mention briefly † *His lecture was mainly about 'Hamlet', but he also touched on 'Macbeth'.*

touch up Make small changes to (piece of writing, painting, etc) to finish, improve it † *It's a good picture but it needs touching up.*

TOW *n.*

in tow Following along behind (originally of boat attached by rope or chain, but now used more widely) † *The Prime Minister arrived with various advisers in tow.*

TOWARDS *prep.*

1 In the direction of † *We were travelling towards London when the accident occurred (See to 1 and 2).* [NOTE: *Towards* differs from *to* in that the emphasis is placed on the route, not the destination. The example above does not necessarily mean that we intended to go to London.]
2 Near (of place or time) † *Towards the top of the hill the road is wider.*

† *We reached the village towards evening.* **3** In the direction of a purpose
† *I can put £1,000 towards the price of the house and will borrow the*
rest. **4** In relation to person or thing † *What are his feelings towards*
me? † *What is his attitude towards the plan?*

TOWN *n.*

go to town Do something expensively, lavishly † *She wanted a quiet wedding*
but her mother went to town over it and invited 200 people.

paint the town red Enjoy oneself in a public place in a wild, noisy manner
† *I'm tired of sitting at home watching the television. Let's go out and*
paint the town red.

TRACK *n.*

off the track Away from the point, subject † *I think you're getting off the*
track. That isn't the problem.

off the beaten track Away from the familiar, conventional path † *I'm fed up*
with this office job. I'd like to get off the beaten track and do something
exciting. [ALSO: **on the right** (**wrong**) **track** Going in the right (wrong)
direction (in action, argument, as well as of place).]

on the track of Pursuing (and helped by evidence) † *The police are on the*
track of the bank robbers. † *We have not yet found a way of curing the*
disease, but our research suggests we are on the track of it.

TRADE *v.i. & t.*

trade in Exchange (a used article in part payment for a new one) † *I traded in*
my old car when I bought this one. [NOTE: *In* is stressed with this
meaning, but not in the phrase *trade in old clothes*, where *trade in* means
buy and sell.] [ALSO: **trade-in** *n.* Thing so exchanged.]

trade on Take advantage of for one's own benefit (implying criticism) † *He*
wrote one good novel twenty years ago and has been trading on its
reputation ever since (by publishing inferior work).

TRAIL *n.*

blaze a trail Literally, show the way by marking trees so that others can follow,
but used to mean be the first to do something and in this way inspire others
to follow † *He was one of the early pioneers who blazed a trail across the*
country. † *This company blazed a trail in the field of electronics which*
others have followed.

TRAIN *n.*

in train Proceeding and expected to be complete by the time required (of
preparations, negotiations, etc) † *The preparations for the Queen's visit*
are in train and I am confident that everything will go well.

TREAT *v.t. & i.*

treat someone (to) Pay for something pleasurable for him when this is not expected of one † *If you're a good boy, I'll treat you to an ice-cream.* † *I felt in a very good mood today so I treated myself to a bottle of wine with my lunch.* [ALSO: **treat** *n*. Unexpected source of pleasure † *We took the children to the circus as a Christmas treat.*]

TREE *n*.

bark up the wrong tree Guess, think mistakenly † *I know you think it was my fault, but you're barking up the wrong tree.*

TRIAL *n*.

on trial 1 (of people) Being tried in a court of law † *He is on trial for murder.* **2** (of things) Being tested or tried out on approval † *The new machine is on trial.* † *Take the television set on a week's trial and see if you like it.*

TRIANGLE *n*.

the eternal triangle Set phrase describing situation where two people of one sex are in love with the same person of the other (particularly husband/wife/lover). [ALSO: **triangle drama** Novel, play, etc based on this theme.]

TRICK *n*.

do the trick Achieve one's purpose (particularly in solving problem, etc) † ⟩ *Have you anything in the house for a headache?* ⟩ *Yes, these aspirins should do the trick.*

TRUCK *n*.

have no truck with Have no dealings with † *I'm not having any truck with people of his kind.*

TRUMPET *n*.

blow one's own trumpet Praise one's own achievements, good qualities, etc, to others † *Perhaps you will accuse me of blowing my own trumpet, but the fact is that I am the best man for the job.*

TRUST *v.t. & i.*

trust someone (to) (imperative) He is to be relied on to (ironic) † *Trust him to lead the way to the nearest pub* (implying that he is fond of drink). † *I must have forgotten to put a stamp on the letter. Trust me!* (implying I am careless by nature).

TRY *v.i. & t.*

try on Put on (coat, dress, shoe, etc) to see if it fits or is suitable † *She tried on ten hats before she found one that she liked.*

try it on Do something to see if it will deceive someone (but without much planning or fear of punishment) † ⟩ *I can't go to see that film because I'm only 17.* ⟩ *If they stop you, say you are 18. You can try it on and see what* *happens.* [NOTE: Certain films in Britain have an 'X' certificate and no one under 18 is allowed into the cinema when they are shown.]

try out Test (an idea, theory) in practice or (*See* **try on 1** above) test (a machine, car, etc) to see if it works satisfactorily, is suitable, etc † *These exercises seem a good way of teaching the present tense. Try them out in your class.* † *Before you buy the car, try it out* (take it for a trial run).

TUCK *v.t. & i.*

tuck in (into) Eat heartily † *It's nice to see the children tucking in at Christmas* (or *tucking into their Christmas dinner*).

TUMBLE *v.i. & t.*

tumble to Suddenly realise † *I wondered why there was a hole in the road until I tumbled to the fact that they were connecting the water supply to the new flats.*

TUNE *n.*

to the tune of To the cost of (implying that it is too high) † *I received an income tax demand to the tune of £50 yesterday.*

change one's tune Change one's attitude, approach (because it has proved ineffective, unpopular) † *Seeing that I was not frightened by his manner, he changed his tune and tried to appeal to my generosity.*

TURN *v.i. & t.*

turn down **1** Reject † *His proposals were turned down.* † *They turned him down for the job because of his age.* **2** Reduce (*See* **turn on**).

turn in **1** Go to bed † *I'm tired. I think I'll turn in.* **2** Return (equipment, property, etc belonging to employer) † *When I left the army I turned in my rifle and uniform.* **3** Tell authorities (police, etc) where to find (an escaped prisoner, suspected criminal) (used in contexts suggesting that prisoner has asked for protection, etc) † *I found the man hiding in a shed in the garden, and he begged me not to turn him in.*

turn into (*See* **turn to**).

turn off (*See* **turn on**).

turn on **1** Turn a switch or tap to cause (electrical current, water, gas, etc) to flow † *Turn the light on, please. I can't see what I'm doing.* [NOTE: A number of other prepositions are used in conjunction with *turn* in this context. *Turn off* is the opposite of *turn on*, meaning stop the flow of (water, gas, etc) but *turn out* is preferred where the meaning is extinguish † *Turn the light out. Turn up* and *turn down* mean increase/reduce the flow of (gas) or power, number of (lights on) † *Turn the gas down or the dinner will be cooked too quickly.* † *He turned the lights down to provide a more romantic atmosphere.*] **2** Centre on, be decided on the basis of † *The decision between the two candidates turned on which one had the more agreeable personality.* **3** Attack suddenly and unexpectedly (implying an attack on a friendly person) † *The dog turned on me and bit my hand.* † *It was horrible to see him turn on a man who had been so kind to him.*

turn out 1 Produce (particularly goods) † *The factory turns out 100 cars a day.* 2 Prove (to be) in the end † *The weather turned out fine.* † *We thought the party would be boring, but it turned out better than we had expected.* † *We waited for him at the station, but afterwards it turned out that he had come by car* (it became known). 3 Come out (to see); (make an effort to) attend † *Thousands of people turned out to watch the procession.* † *It's unreasonable to expect many people to turn out in this weather.* [ALSO: **turn-out** *n.* Attendance † *There was a good turn-out at the annual reunion of the regiment.*] 4 Take everything out of (pockets, drawer, etc) † *I turned out all my pockets but couldn't find my keys.* [ALSO: **turn-out** *n.* Action in emptying drawers, cupboards, etc either to find something or, particularly, to see what can be thrown away † *There are piles of old papers in my desk. It's about time I had a good turn-out.*] 5 Expel † *He was turned out (of his flat) for not paying the rent.* † *The landlord turned him out (of the pub) because he was drunk.* 6 (almost always in passive) Dress † *Her children are always well turned out.* [ALSO: **turn-out** *n.* Appearance (of dress) † *The officer congratulated the men on their turn-out.*] 7 Extinguish (*See* **turn on**).

turn over 1 Hand over † *He has retired and turned over the business to his son.* 2 Do business to the amount of † *The shop turns over £1,000 a week.* [ALSO: **turnover** *n.* 1 Amount of money passing through a business over a period of time † *The firm has an annual turnover of £10 million, which gives a profit of £1 million.* 2 Extent to which men leave employment and are replaced † *There is a high turnover of staff in this industry.*]

turn to 1 Apply to (for help, comfort, advice) † *She hadn't a friend to turn to.* 2 Change from one (occupation, state) to another † *He could not earn a living as a novelist so he turned to journalism.* † *It is getting colder. I think the rain will soon turn to snow.* [NOTE: *Turn to* expresses change, whereas *turn into* indicates transformation, the result of the change † *At 0°C, water turns to ice* (in the sense that ice is still composed of water) but *turns into solid form.* † *The witch turned the prince into a dog.*] 3 Set to work † *We turned to and cleared up the mess.* [NOTE: In usage 3, *to* is emphasised in speech (tu:, not tu or te.]

turn up 1 Arrive, appear † *I was wondering when you would turn up.* † *He is looking for a job, but so far nothing has turned up.* 2 Be found (by chance) † *Don't waste any more time trying to find it. It will turn up somewhere.* 3 Increase (*See* **turn on** 1).

TURN *n.*

at every turn Wherever one looks, goes, etc. The phrase combines the idea of frequency with changes of direction, plan, etc † *We are doing our best to produce the goods on time, but we are running into obstacles at every turn.*

by turns Alternately † *While he was waiting for the examination result he was confident and despondent by turns.*

in turn One after the other (in a sequence) † *He asked each of the boys in turn whether they had taken the book.*

out of turn 1 Out of the correct order or sequence † *You have played your card out of turn.* 2 At an inappropriate time or in an inappropriate situation † *The Prime Minister was angry with a member of the Government who had spoken out of turn* (by telling people the Government's plans before they became official, for example).

to a turn (of things being cooked) Exactly, to the right degree † *Take the chicken out of the oven now. It is done to a turn.*

(do someone) a good (bad) turn (Do him) a helpful (unhelpful) action † *I am grateful to him for the good turn he did me.*

(give someone) a turn (Give him) a sudden shock † *It gave me (quite) a turn to see the child balancing on the high wall.*

serve one's turn Meet one's need (for the time being) † *The firm have lent me a car which will serve my turn (until mine is repaired).*

take turns at Do (something) in turn † *We took turns at steering the boat.*
[ALSO: **take it in turn to** Same meaning † *We took it in turn to shoot at the target.* **take a turn at (with)** Do one's part of a task ordered in rotation, sequence † *Take a turn at the wheel, will you?*]

take a turn for (the better, the worse, etc) Indicating a change in condition † *He was very ill yesterday, but now he's taken a turn for the better.*

TWICE *adv.*

think twice Hesitate, think carefully † *I would think twice before spending so much money on a car.*

TWO *n.*

put two and two together Relate separate pieces of information to infer something else † *I knew he had gone away for the weekend and when I found she was away, too, I put two and two together and decided she must have gone with him.*

UNDER *prep.*

1 In or to a position lower than, beneath † *The dog is lying under the table.* † *The road runs under the bridge.* [NOTE: *Under* and *beneath* are interchangeable in a physical sense (see examples above) though *under* is more commonly used, but figurative expressions (examples below) and (*See* **beneath**) set phrases have grown up where only one of the two prepositions is acceptable. There are grounds for confusion, however, between the following 1 † *He thought we were all beneath him.* † *He has a large staff under him.* Here *beneath* indicates the man's attitude (he despised us), while *under* simply means the staff were under his authority. 2 † *He felt the remark was beneath his notice.* † *He is under notice to leave our employment. Beneath* again indicates an attitude (he felt the remark was not worthy of notice) while *under notice* (*See* **under 6**) means 'he had been given notice that his employment was to end within a certain time'.] **2** Below the surface of † *He is swimming under the water.* † *Under his calm manner he is a very excitable person.* **3** Close against (implying shelter, protection) † *Stand here under the wall and you will be protected from the rain.* **4** Less than † *People under 18 are not allowed to buy alcoholic drink in a pub.* † *We did the journey in under an hour.* † *He bought the house for under £5,000.* **5** Subject to the authority of † *He has a large staff under him.* † *The regiment is under the command of Colonel Smith.* † *She has been under the doctor for several weeks.* **6** By the authority of † *Under the terms of the contract, he cannot be dismissed without three months' notice.* **7** Subjected to, bound by † *He is under a strain because of his wife's illness* (undergoing anxiety). † *He is under arrest* (has been arrested). † *I am under oath not to disclose any information to the press.* † *I feel under an obligation to her.* **8** Indicating a classification, heading, etc in a book, list, etc † *In this book, 'turn the tables on' is listed under 'table', not under 'turn'.* **9** Indicating a name taken to disguise one's real identity † *The group sing under the name of the Beatles.* **10** In process of † *The road is under repair.* † *The matter is under review.* [NOTE: In this construction, the meaning is equivalent to a passive verb (being repaired, being reviewed, etc).]

UNDER-DOG *n.*

The person expected to lose a contest, game, etc † *It is traditional at*

Wimbledon (tennis championship) for the spectators to take the side of the under-dog.

UNDERNEATH *prep.*

Under (*See* **beneath 1** and **under 1** and **2**) (particularly used when it implies hidden or obscured by) † *I found the letter underneath a pile of papers on my desk.* † *Underneath his rough way of speaking, he is essentially a kind man.*

UNDERSTUDY *n.*

(*See* **stand-in**).

UNTIL *prep.*

1 Up to (the event or time stated) † *Until his marriage, he lived with his parents.* † *The museum will be open until 7 o'clock.* **2** Before (a time or event stated) (usually in negative sentences) † *I won't see him until tomorrow.* [NOTE: *Until* and *till* are interchangeable, though *until* is preferred at the beginning of a sentence.]

UNTIL *conj.*

1 and **2** As preposition (above) † *I did nothing about it until I received my instructions.* **3** With the same basic meaning, but implying a result † *He was so funny that I laughed until I cried* (i.e. my laughter made me cry, rather than 'first I laughed and then I cried').

UP *prep.*

1 Indicating movement to a higher point, position † *He walked up the hill.* † *Arsenal won their match on Saturday and moved up the league table* (classification of football teams playing each other). **2** Along † *He came up the street towards me.* [NOTE: This example assumes the street is level. *Up the street* and *down the street* are obviously acceptable with their literal meaning if the street runs up, down a hill. (*See* also **3** below).] **3** Indicating movement towards a more important place from the speaker's point of view † *There has been an accident up the line which has blocked the railway* (on part of the line nearer the more important terminus station). [NOTE: This usage often conflicts with geography, but in such cases overrules it. In the same way, we say *I went up to London*, whether we travel from north or south, mountain or seaside, etc, because London is the most important city in England. It is also possible to find *down* used to mean along – *I met him coming down the corridor* – within definition **3**. The speaker means along the corridor, away from some more important place (the main half of a school, the managing director's office, etc).]

UP *adv. part.*

1 Happening, going on (implying something unusual or wrong) † *I knew from the noise that something was up.* † *What's up (with you)?* (What is

201

the matter?) † *Is anything up?* (Is anything wrong, strange happening?). **2** Out of bed † *What time did you get up?* † *Is he up yet?* † *We stayed up all night.* [ALSO: **up and about** Out of bed after an illness and able to go out of the house.] **3** As in **up** *prep.* **1** † *He is up on the roof.* † *The price of apples has gone up.* **4** As in **up** *prep.* **3** † *He went up to London on business.* [NOTE: While the distinction regarding the importance of a place to the speaker always applies, *up* also suggests north, *down* south † *I went up to Glasgow.* † *I went down to Brighton.*] **5** Indicating completion or finality † *Time is up. Hand your papers to the teacher.* † *Eat up your dinner* (leave nothing uneaten). † *I'm not going to buy any more sugar until we have used up this packet.* [NOTE: In general, the element of completion or finality is all that distinguishes a number of verbs + *up* from the verb used alone. Some further comparisons, however, are useful † *She has torn her dress.* † *He tore up his manuscript and threw it away* (tore it to pieces so that it was unusable). † *The chair is broken.* † *They broke up the chair for firewood.* † *Have you locked the door?* † *Have you locked up the house?* (locked all the doors, windows, etc). **6** Indicating greater force, intensity † *Speak up! I can't hear you* (Speak more loudly).

up against Faced with (difficulties, opposition) † *We were up against one of the best teams in the country.*

up against it In a difficult situation † *We're up against it at the moment. We have a lot of work and half the staff are away ill.*

up and down In one direction and then the opposite † *He travels up and down to London every day.* † *He walked up and down the room, thinking.* [ALSO: **ups and downs** *n.* Good and bad conditions, situations † *Every job has its ups and downs.*]

up to *prep.* **1** Indicating movement to a higher point or one of more importance to the speaker (*See* **up** *prep.*) † *We climbed up to the summit of the mountain.* † *We went up to London yesterday.* **2** Until (the time or event stated) † *Up to now I've had a very easy life.* **3** Indicating a limit † *We can take up to 30 people on the excursion, but no more.* † *Up to a point, I agree with you, but not entirely.*

up to *adv.* **1** Doing, busy with † *What is he up to?* **2** Equal to † *He's not up to the job.* † *I don't think she is up to the journey.* **3** Indicating responsibility, duty, choice † *It's up to you to decide what is to be done.* † ⟩ *Which would you prefer?* ⟩ *It's up to you.*

(all) up (with) Over, at an end (with) † *The game is up* (set phrase meaning pursuit (of criminal, etc) is over). † *It's all up with them. We cannot save them now.*

UP-AND-COMING *adj.*

Promising, likely to succeed † *He is regarded as an up-and-coming writer.*

UPON *prep.*
On [NOTE: *On* is preferred except in the set phrase † *Once upon a time* (*See* **once**).]

UPTAKE *n.*
quick (slow) on the uptake Quick (slow) to understand (something said or suggested) † *You will have to be patient with him. He's not very quick on the uptake.*

USE *n.*
in (out of) use Used, or being used (no longer) † *The equipment in use at present is out of date.* [ALSO: **come into (go out of) use** Become (cease to be) used.]
of use Useful † *Would you like to borrow this book? It may be of use to you in your studies.*
of no use Not useful.
no use No good † *It's no use turning the light on. The electricity is not connected.* [NOTE: The same distinction applies to **of any use/any use** and **of what use/what use** † *Is this of any use to you?* (Could you find a use for it?) † *Is it any use writing to him? He never replies.* (Is it any good, is it worthwhile?).]

USED TO *anom. fin.*
Indicating existence or practice in the past (which is no longer the case) † *I used to live in France* (but now I live somewhere else) † *He used to come to see me every week when he lived near here.*
be (get) used to *p.p.* Be (become) accustomed to † *He is used to a high standard of living.* † *It's not a difficult job, once you get used to it.* † *It took him a long time to get used to working at night.* [NOTE: Although the difference in meaning is quite clear, the two forms of *used to* are often confused. The anomalous finite only exists in the past tense and must be followed by a verb in the infinitive. The participle appears with all tenses of the verbs *be get, become* and can have a direct object or be followed by a gerund. Two further examples may illustrate this † *Your father used to work hard at the factory* (but he is now dead, retired or in another job). † *He was used to working hard* (or *used to hard work*) *so he didn't mind the long hours at the factory* (He had always worked hard and was accustomed to it).]

VAIN *adj.*

in vain 1 To no effect, without success † *He tried in vain to convince her that she was wrong.* † *All our efforts were in vain.*

take someone's name in vain Use it without obtaining his permission (to support one's argument, cause, etc) † ⟩ *I'm sure many of you here – Professor Jones, for example – will agree with me.* ⟩ *Now then, don't take my name in vain* (don't use my name to strengthen your case without asking me). [ALSO: **take the name of God in vain** Use it without reverence, respect (by swearing).]

VENGEANCE *n.*

with a vengeance Thoroughly, to a much greater degree than expected † *They used not to mind if people arrived late at the office, but now they are checking up with a vengeance.*

VERY *adv.*

very well All right (indicating agreement, acceptance) † ⟩ *Your shoes will be ready tomorrow.* ⟩ *Very well, I'll call for them then.* † *I can see that you don't want my advice. Very well, do as you think best (if that is your attitude).* [ALSO: **all very well** All right (for you, as far as it goes, etc) (used ironically) † ⟩ *He thinks there should be much higher taxes for motorists.* ⟩ *That's all very well for him. He hasn't got a car.*]

VICIOUS *adj.*

vicious circle Situation in which a cause produces a bad effect which in turn produces the cause † *We can't do research to find out if the theory will work unless they give us the money. They won't give the money for research unless they know it will work. It's a vicious circle.*

VIEW *n.*

in (out of) view In sight (no longer) † *We waved goodbye to them until the ship was out of view.* [NOTE: **come into view** (not *in*) Come into sight.]

(have) in view (Have) in mind, in prospect † *He says he wants to merge his company with ours to fight foreign competition, but he may have something else in view.* † *I wonder if he has anything in view now that he has resigned from the Government* (i.e. any prospect of another appointment).

in view of Taking into consideration, into account † *In view of his long experience, he is well qualified to speak on the subject.* † *In view of the fact that he has given back the money he stole, we shall not tell the police.*

in one's view In one's opinion † *In my view, we ought to take action as quickly as possible.*

on view On display † *The latest model of the car is on view at our showrooms.*

with a view to Indicating intention, purpose † *I am sending the manuscript to you with a view to its publication (its being published).*

V.I.P. *n.*

Abbreviation for Very Important Person, meaning person who receives special treatment because of his rank, fame, etc † *There is a special lounge at the airport reserved for V.I.P.s.* † *Is he well enough known to be given V.I.P. treatment?* (receive special consideration).

VIRTUE *n.*

by virtue of By right of (implying justification) † *By virtue of the authority vested in me, I here pronounce you man and wife.*

in virtue of Because of and in recognition of † *In virtue of his services to his country, we have decided to put up a statue to him.*

WADE *v.i. & t.*

wade in (into) Attack (someone) vigorously † *The two men waded in (into each other), exchanging blows.*

wade through Move through (something that makes progress difficult) (from walking through water, but also used of books, papers, etc) † *I don't know if I'll have time to wade through this pile of documents.*

WAKE *n.*

in the (its, someone's) wake (of) After, following (it, him) (from *wake* = track left by a ship in water) † *The storm left a trail of destruction in its wake* (behind it). † *Once the new territory was opened up, thousands of farmers arrived in the wake of the explorers.*

WALK *v.i. & t.*

walk off (away) with 1 Carry off (by mistake or intentionally) † *Someone must have walked off with my umbrella.* 2 Win (a prize, etc) (implying little effort) † *He only entered the competition at the last minute but he walked off with the first prize.*

walk out (on) Leave, desert (a job or person) † *He lost his temper and walked out.* † *He walked out on her and left her to bring up the children alone.*

walk over Defeat very easily or by default. [ALSO: **walk-over** *n.* Success obtained either easily or by default † *The examination was a walk-over* (very easy). † *Because of his injury, he had to give his opponent a walk-over* (i.e. allow him to win without playing).

WALK *n.*

walk of life Profession, occupation † *The audience was composed of people from all walks of life.*

WALL *n.*

with (have) one's back to the wall With (have) no means of escape † *We had our backs to the wall. The only thing we could do was to fight.*

drive up the wall Drive (someone) mad † *If the baby goes on crying, it will drive me up the wall.*

(the weakest) go to the wall (The weakest) are sacrificed, destroyed, etc (particularly in this phrase) † *In a competitive business like this, the weakest (the small firms) go to the wall.*

WANT *v.t. & i.*

1 Need (*See* **need** (NOTE 3)) † *Your shoes want mending.* † *What he wants is a firm hand.* [ALSO: **what do you want with?** Why do you need? † *What do you want with those old books? You'll never read them again.*]
2 Should, ought to (particularly in 2nd person) † *You want to be careful. If the boss saw you doing that, you'd get the sack.* † *To see Spain at its best, you want to go in the early summer.*

want for Lack † *He wants for nothing.* [ALSO: **be wanting in** (continuous tenses only) Lack † *He is wanting in common-sense.*]

be found wanting Be unequal to the need † *We train our men thoroughly so that they will not be found wanting in an emergency.*

WANT *n.*

for want of Because of the lack of † *I failed, but it was not for want of trying* (not because I didn't try hard enough).

in want In need (of help, money, etc) (particularly of people who are hungry, poor) † *While you enjoy a high standard of living, millions of people all over the world are in want.*

WAR *n.*

cold war Situation where two opposing sides actively work against one another and maintain a state of preparation for war without fighting openly.

hot war (shooting war) (USA) War which develops out of a cold-war situation without formal declaration.

WARM *v.t. & i.*

warm to 1 (work, task, etc) Begin to do it with more enthusiasm, energy † *I wasn't very keen on the job at first, but I soon warmed to the task.* 2 (a person) Find him more agreeable, sympathetic † *He seemed an unattractive character, but I found myself warming to him as I listened to his story.*

warm up 1 (food, drink) Warm it again after it has gone cold † *I'll warm up what is left of the pie from yesterday and have it for lunch.* 2 Make warm or become warm † *Put the fire on. It will soon warm up the room (The room will soon warm up).* 3 Practise strokes, shots, etc, do exercises, before a game begins † *The two teams are warming up and the game will soon begin.* [ALSO: **warm-up** *n.* Practice of this kind.]

WASH *v.t. & i.*

it (that) won't wash It (that) is not a convincing excuse † ⟩ *Couldn't we tell the teacher we are late because the bus broke down?* ⟩ *That won't wash.*

washed out *adj.* Exhausted, without any energy † *I didn't get much sleep last night and I feel washed out.* [ALSO: **wash-out** *n.* Failure, disappointment † *The film was a wash-out.*]

wash up Clean the plates, etc after a meal † *Will you help me to wash up?* [NOTE: If there is only one article to be washed, *up* is not used † *Would you mind washing this cup?*]

WASH *n.*

come out in the wash Eventually resolve itself, become clear † *Don't worry about it. It will all come out in the wash.*

WATER *n.*

in deep water(s) In a difficult situation † *I'm afraid he's in deep waters. He hasn't paid his income tax and he's spent all his money.*

get into hot water Get into trouble (not implying serious punishment, etc) † *I'd get into hot water if the boss knew I'd been using his telephone for a private call.*

hold water (of theories) Prove sound when tested † *The prisoners could not have escaped without the help of the guards. No other explanation holds water.*

throw cold water on (a plan, proposal, etc) Discourage it † *The Minister said the plan was impracticable and threw cold water on it.*

WATER *v.t. & i.*

water down Make (a story, scene, etc) less vivid (for fear of offending

207

people) † *The article he wrote criticised the Government in such strong language that the Editor decided to water it down.*

WAY *n.*

by way of 1 Via, passing through (on the way to somewhere else) † *The train goes to London by way of St. Albans.* 2 As a kind of, serving as † *Before I begin my lecture on Shakespeare, I would like to say something by way of introduction about the age he lived in.*

by the way 1 In passing † *I don't want to discuss that point at length. I just mentioned it by the way in case you were interested.* 2 Used in the course of a conversation to introduce a thought one has just been reminded of, incidental remark, etc † *I spent the week-end with John Brown. By the way, did you know that his wife has left him?*

in a way From one point of view; to a certain extent † *He didn't like being moved to a smaller office, but in a way he is better off because there is less noise there.*

in a big (small) way On a large (small) scale † *We are a big company and we do everything in a big way.*

in the (someone's) way (of) 1 Causing an obstruction (to) (him) † *Get that box out of the corridor. It's in the way (of people trying to pass through).* † *He tried to run after her, but there were too many people in his way.* † *I'm not in the way, am I?* (not an inconvenience to you, preventing you from working, etc). 2 In the nature of † *There isn't much in the way of comfort for smokers in the doctors' report.* 3 In the (normal) course of † *It's in the way of business for the public to get tired of a product after a time.*

in someone's (own) way 1 Obstructing him (*See* **in the way**). 2 Within the limitations of his personality † *He's rather nice in his (own) way, if you can get used to his casual manner.*

on the (someone's) way 1 In the course of a (his) journey † *I met him on the (my) way to the station.* 2 Coming † *I am sure that better times are on the way.*

on the way out Ceasing to be fashionable, common practice, etc † *People are saying that the mini-skirt is on the way out.* [NOTE: **way-out** *adj.* Recently come into use with the meaning of 'original', 'unusual'. It is used as a term of praise, primarily by people who consider themselves to be 'way out' (pop singers, hippies, etc).]

out of the (someone's) way (of) 1 In or to a place where no obstruction is caused † *Would you mind moving out of the way?* 2 Out of the reach of † *There's a dangerous dog in the garden. Keep out of its way.* [ALSO: **out-of-the-way** *adj.* Not easy to reach † *He lives in an out-of-the-way place, miles from the nearest town.*]

under way In progress, movement † *Once the party is under way, I'll find a* quiet corner where we can talk.   † *The ship slowly got under way* (started moving).

give way (to) 1 Concede all or part (of demand)   † *If we give way on this point, we shall be forced to accept whatever they decide.* 2 Allow (emotions) to dominate one   † *Don't give way. Try to keep your dignity.* 3 Allow to pass   † *Give way to traffic coming from the right.* 4 Collapse, break † *The floor gave way under me.* 5 Be followed or replaced by   † *The sunshine gave way to showers of rain.*

go one's own way Act independently   † *It's no use trying to advise him. He'll go his own way, whatever you say.*

go out of one's way (to) Make a special effort (in order to)   † *He went out of his way to help us.*

have (get) one's own way Get, do what one wants   † *It's bad for the child to have his own way all the time.*

have it your own way! Indicating that one prefers to let someone win the argument rather than argue any longer   † *Have it your own way! It was my fault, if it makes you happy to think so.*

have it both ways Make either side of an argument, etc fit one's case   † *You can't have it both ways. She is either lying or she's not.*   [ALSO: **there are no two ways about it** There is no alternative in the matter (especially in argument, etc)   † *There are no two ways about it. If she doesn't come back to work tomorrow, I will sack her.*]

make way (for) 1 Get out of the way (to allow someone, something to pass) † *The cars had to make way for the ambulance to get through. It's time he retired and made way for a younger man.*

pave the way for Prepare for, make it easier for (someone to take the place of another, changes in law, etc)   † *He paved the way for his successor by making the country strong and peaceful.*   † *This law will pave the way for more radical reforms.*

put in the way of Help to get (business, etc)   † *I might be able to put you in the way of a contract.*   [ALSO: **put in someone's way** Give him the opportunity (of doing business, etc).]

put out of the way Get rid of (someone) (by killing him, putting him in prison, etc)   † *It would be a good thing for society if we could put someone like him out of the way for a few years, or, even better, for ever.*

WEAR *v.t. & i.*

wear down Reduce gradually but consistently (strength, opposition, energy, etc)   † *We wore the enemy down with daily bombing.*   † *Over the years the opposition to co-educational schools* (boys and girls together) *has been worn down.*   † *She has been worn down by the continual worry* (Her energy has gone, nerves have been affected, etc).

wear off Gradually disappear, fade, etc   † *My tooth is aching again because the* *effect of the aspirin I took is wearing off.* † *The coat of paint I put on the door is wearing off.*

wear on Continue (towards the end) (used only of periods of time) † *As the year wore on, the leaves on the trees turned brown.* † *The night wore on, but there was no sign of the discussion's coming to an end.*

wear out 1 Use up, exhaust (strength, energy); make useless by wear (articles of clothing, machines, etc) † *Looking after so many children wears me out.* † *I feel worn out* (exhausted). † *He wears out his shoes in a few weeks.* † *My clothes are worn out.* **2** Become useless through wear † *Clothes seem to wear out more quickly than they did when I was a boy.* [NOTE: **outwear** Outlast, last longer than † *For the sword outwears its sheath. And the soul wears out the breast* (Byron, 'So We'll Go No More A-Roving'). The contrast between *outwear* and *wear out* **1** is apparent here.]

WEAR *n.*

wear and tear Deterioration through wear † *Gears on buses need replacing frequently, because they suffer a lot of wear and tear.*

the worse for wear In poor condition because of constant use, etc (often used humorously of people to suggest exhausted by one's efforts, etc) † *The car looked the worse for wear after being driven over such bad roads.* † *I was up all night at a party and feel the worse for wear.*

WEATHER *n.*

under the weather Not very well † *I don't think I'll go out today. I'm a bit under the weather.*

make heavy weather of Find (more) difficulty (than would be expected) in doing † *It's a simple task. I don't understand why you made such heavy weather of it.*

WEDGE *n.*

the thin end of the wedge 1 Action, change, etc, which may not be important in itself but is seen as a sign of precedent for further changes † *The Government accept that the Union's demand for higher wages is reasonable, but fear it may be the thin end of the wedge.* **2** Lesser portion of something (usually desirable) † *Lower-paid workers get the thin end of the wedge when percentage pay rises are awarded.*

WEIGH *v.t. & i.*

weigh up Consider, estimate † *Your proposal seems attractive, but I shall need time to weigh up its advantages.*

weigh with Influence (someone, in making a decision, etc) † *It was his enthusiasm for the job that weighed most with me when I decided to appoint him.*

WEIGHT *n.*

pull one's weight Make the proper effort to do one's share (of a job, etc)
† *Most of you work hard, but there are some who are not pulling their
weight.*

throw one's weight about Make people unpleasantly aware of one's strength,
influence † *Just because he is the boss's son, he likes to throw his weight
about and give people orders.*

WELL *adv.*

well out of Fortunate to be no longer involved in † *The firm got into a mess
after I had left. I was well out of it.*

well up in Very knowledgeable about † *He's well up in legal matters.*

as well (as) **1** Too, in addition (to) † *She came to the cinema with me, and her
brother and sister came as well.* † *You must take the oral examinations as
well as the written.*

just as well Used to imply 'a good thing in the circumstances' † ⟩ *It's stopped
raining.* ⟩ *Just as well. I didn't bring my umbrella.* † *It's just as well that
he couldn't come to the meeting. We had nothing new to tell him.*

may (might) (just) as well **1** May, without fear of error, bad result † *There is
no point in our waiting any longer. We may as well go without him* (We
shall lose nothing by going). **2** Might (more often than *may*, because it is
usually found in a conditional sense) as easily or with equal justification
† *It's ridiculous to say all wives are jealous. You might (just) as well say
that all husbands are intelligent.*

do well to Indicating acting wisely, skilfully or luckily † *I would have made a
foolish mistake if you had not spoken to me. You did well to warn me*
(You were right or thoughtful). † *He is a very fast runner and I will do
well to keep up with him* (I will be lucky or will use my limited ability
well). † *I don't think he will pass the examination. He will do well to
answer any of the questions* (be lucky if he can answer).

WELL *predic. adj.*

well off Rich, fortunately placed † *He buys a new car every year. He's quite
well off.* † *He doesn't know when he's well off* (doesn't recognise his good
fortune in a situation).

WELL *int.*

Used as an exclamation to express a variety of emotions and reactions
1 *Well, look who's here! I thought you were in America* (surprise).
2 *Well! What have you got to say for yourself?* (expectancy). **3** *Well! It
can't be helped* (resignation). **4** *Well! That's that. The job's finished*
(relief). **5** *Well, if that's what you want, I suppose I must let you do it*
(concession). [NOTE: *Well* is used more often than not with none of these
implications, either to relate something that is said to what has gone

before or simply to indicate that the speaker is thinking about what he is going to say next, is in doubt, etc † *You know Charlie Robinson, the fellow who used to work here. Well, they say he has been sent to prison.* † *Will I see you tomorrow? Well, I'm not sure* (or *Well, that depends*).]

WEST *adv.*

go west Die, be lost for ever (used humorously) † *The horses I bet on never win. That's another five pounds that has gone west.*

WHAT *pron.*

what about? **1** Used in making a suggestion † *I'm so thirsty. What about a drink?* (Shall we have . . . ?). † *What about going to Brighton for the weekend?* (Shall we go . . . ?). **2** Used in making an objection to a proposal † *I don't see how we can go away for a week. What about the children?* (What is going to happen to them?). [NOTE: The phrase is also used in making a question in reply to a statement. This can imply that the speaker thinks the statement is impertinent or unnecessary † *I wanted to ask you about my salary. What about it?* (i.e. What do you want to know? or What do you expect me to say?).]

what . . . for? **1** What is the purpose of † *What is that machine for?* **2** Why † *What did you do that for?* [NOTE: **give someone what for** *n.* Tell him off or chastise him † *If you don't wash your hands immediately Johnny, I'll give you what for.*] **what of it?** Why should I worry? What does that matter to me? † *The boss is on his way here? What of it?* [ALSO: **so what?** Used in the same way.]

or what Used as a shortened form of *or what the reason is, or what I ought to do* etc † *He didn't speak to me this morning. I don't know whether I have upset him, or what* (the cause of it was). † *I'm not sure whether he didn't give me the money, or I lost it, or what* (happened to it).

I know (I'll tell you) what Used when one has had an idea, is making a suggestion † *I know what. Let's go to the seaside!* † *I'll tell you what. If you pay half the expenses, I'll pay the other half.*

and what not And other things of the same kind † *He only came for the weekend, but he brought his tennis racket, his golf clubs and what not.* [ALSO: **and I don't know what else** Used with the same meaning but stronger emphasis.]

what's-his (her, its)-name Used when the speaker cannot remember the name of someone, something † *I gave it to What's-his-name, the fellow who works in the same office as you.* † *I put it on the what's-its-name, near the window.* [ALSO: **what-d'you-call-him (it)** Used with the same meaning.]

WHAT *rel. pron.*

what with . . . and (with) Indicating a combination of causes, circumstances † *What with the rent and the gas bill and the telephone to pay there is* *hardly enough money left for food.* † *What with one thing and another, I haven't got round to painting the kitchen.*

have (got) what it takes Have whatever qualities are necessary for the purpose
† *I'm sure he'll be a success. He's got what it takes (to get to the top).*

WHEEL *n.*

wheels within wheels Implying a complicated system of influences behind the apparent state of affairs † *When the managing director approved, I thought the matter was settled. Naturally, but there are wheels within wheels in this organisation.*

WHISTLE *v.i. & t.*

whistle for Go without, since there is no way of getting † *He says you owe him money. He can whistle for it. I'm not going to pay him.*

WHITEWASH *v.t.*

Make appear more virtuous than is true by covering up or excusing faults
† *The new biography of Byron attempts to whitewash him by blaming his behaviour on his wife.*

WHOLE *adj.*

the whole The entire, the complete † *The whole affair makes me sick.*

the whole of All of (as compared to part of) † *I didn't stay to hear the whole of the story.*

(taken) as a whole (Considered) in its entirety † *There are a few errors in the first paragraph, but taken as a whole it is a good essay.*

on the whole (Considered) from every point of view, in all aspects, etc † *Some parts of your essay could be improved, but on the whole it is a good effort.* [NOTE: The difference between *as a whole* and *on the whole* is that the first implies looking at something as an entity, not at its separate parts, while the second means considering all the parts and reaching an overall conclusion as a result.]

WILD *adj.*

wild (about) 1 Angry (about) † *It makes me wild to see young people with long hair.* † *He is wild about the television's breaking down.*
2 Enthusiastically in favour of, madly attracted to † *He is wild about opera.* † *Do you love me? I'm wild about you* (See **crazy**).

WILL *anom. fin.*

[NOTE: Grammarians have spent a great deal of time on the question of whether *will* or *shall* is to be preferred in a given context and most English speakers have difficulty in distinguishing between them at times. The object of the examples given here is merely to emphasise cases where only one of the alternatives is acceptable and where an English person would find the use of the other meaningless, confusing or objectionable. In general terms, however, there are two fundamental questions to be considered. The more important of the two is that a distinction exists between *will* and *shall* in that *will* (in the 1st person) implies what we are willing to do (what we wish or consent to) or what we have the will (determination, moral conviction) to do, while *shall* implies duty, necessity, etc imposed on us from outside. Therefore, in the marriage service, the bridegroom is asked *Will you honour (the bride), love her, etc?* and replies *I will* (It is my wish or I am determined to do so). But *Shall I open the window?* means Do you wish me to open it? For the same reason, where *shall* replaces *will* in the 2nd and 3rd persons, it is because what is to happen to the person is controlled or influenced by the speaker † *You shall have whatever you wish* means I will ensure that this is so. *They shall not pass* means We will prevent them from passing. The second question that causes confusion is whether *shall* or *will* should be used in the 1st person purely to express the future. *Will* is, of course, the only form acceptable here in the 2nd and 3rd persons. Here, usage is changing and *will* is gradually replacing *shall*, almost certainly because of the social changes that have taken place in the past fifty years by which more and more people have grown used to thinking of the future as being determined as much by their own wishes (*I will*) as by outside influences (*I shall*). At the present time, either form is acceptable simply to express the future and in any case, both are contracted in spoken English to *I'll*.]

will (only)

1 As polite request, in 2nd or 3rd person, having the force of *please* † *Will you help me with this heavy case?* (or, would you?, more polite). † *Give me your telephone number again, will you?* (or, more polite, would you? or Would you mind giving me your number again?). † *Will Dr Jones please go to the theatre manager's office? There is an urgent call for him.* (But *See* **shall**). 2 As polite invitation, in 2nd (or possibly 3rd) person † *Will you have coffee or tea?* (more polite, would you like?). † *Will he have some more tea?* (do you think he would like?). 3 In 1st person, indicating a firm promise or offer (expressing determination or willingness) † *I won't do it again, I promise.* † *I will carry that case for you.* † *I will not listen to your insults any longer.* 4 In 2nd or 3rd person, indicating what is inevitable, the way things are † *It couldn't be helped.* † *Accidents will happen.* † *You will do as you think best. It's in your nature.* [NOTE: In these examples *will* is stressed and cannot be shortened to *'ll*.] 5 In negative, indicating refusal † *So you won't do anything to help me?* † *This window is stuck and won't open* (I cannot open it). [NOTE: This usage is common in connection with inanimate objects which seem to resist control.] 6 Indicating a custom, habit † *He will sit for hours in silence, looking out of the window.* 7 Indicating probability † *I can hear*

the noise of a car stopping. That will be John coming home from work.
(That must be or I believe that is).

shall (only)

    1 In 1st person, making an offer, suggestion † *You look cold. Shall I put
the fire on?* (would you like me to?). † *There is a good film at the Palace
this week. Shall we go?* **2** In 2nd or 3rd person, indicating that the speaker
intends to ensure that something will or will not happen † *You shall have
everything you want* (I will give it to you, make sure that you get it). †
Don't worry, Madam. It shall be done (I will make myself responsible for
ensuring that your orders are carried out). † *Government of the people,
by the people, for the people, shall not perish from this earth* (Lincoln) (we
will ensure that it does not disappear). [NOTE: *Shall* cannot be shortened
to *'ll* in any of these examples.]

    WILL *n.*

at will When and how one pleases † *I have an office here but I can come and
go at will.*

with a will With determination, enthusiasm † *He set to work with a will and
soon finished the job.*

    WIN *v.t. & i.*

win over Persuade (someone) to change his mind in favour of, to change sides
in an argument, etc † *Her father didn't like him at first, but the affection
the boy showed his daughter won him over.* † *He is not sure which way to
vote. If you speak to him, you may win him over* (to our side).

    WIND [wind]

in the wind Being planned or considered, but not yet stated openly † *The
Government have not yet announced their plans for the industry, but there
is something in the wind.*

get wind of Find out about, learn of (by indirect means) † *How did you
manage to get wind of their intentions?*

take the wind out of someone's sails Prevent him from saying something either
by saying it first oneself or giving information which would make his
remark pointless, inappropriate, etc † *He was about to say that the Chief
of Police should be dismissed because the murderer had not been caught,
when the news of the man's capture arrived. That took the wind out of his
sails.*

    WIND [waind] *v.i. & t.*

wind up **1** Bring to an end † *I would like to wind up my speech by thanking
the organisers of the Conference.* † *He lost all his money and his business
was wound up.* **2** Put in order before bringing to an end (of business

affairs) † *The lawyers are winding up the estate* (making a list of property, etc so that someone's will may be proved). **3** End (intransitive) † *The meeting wound up at 6 o'clock.*

be (get) wound up Be (become) tense with excitement, emotion † *Actors often get wound up before a performance.*

WINK *v.i. & t.*

wink at Deliberately overlook, pretend not to see † *If the police didn't wink at some small motoring offences, they would have to stop everyone driving.*

WIPE *v.t. & i.*

wipe off Remove (a debt) † *I have owed him money for a long time and I'm anxious to wipe off the debt.*

wipe out Destroy totally † *The whole population of the village was wiped out by a hurricane.*

WIRE *n.*

1 Telegram † *I'll send you a wire as soon as I have news.* [ALSO: **wire** *v.i. & t.* Send a telegram (to someone) † *I'll wire (you) as soon as I have news.*]

a live wire A person of great energy, enthusiasm, etc † *He's very good at organising parties. He is such a live wire.*

WISE *adj.*

put wise to Inform (someone) of (what is going on) † *Put me wise to what has happened in my absence.* [ALSO: **get wise to** Inform oneself of, realise.]

WISH *v.t. & i.*

wish on Curse with † *What a hopeless secretary you have! Who wished her on you?* (Who was responsible for your being so unfortunate as to have her?) † *It's a terrible disease. I wouldn't wish it on my worst enemy.*

WISHFUL *adj.*

wishful thinking Believing that what one wishes were true really is true † *He thinks she is in love with him, but that's wishful thinking.*

WIT *n.*

have (keep) one's wits about one Be (stay) alert (in all circumstances) † *He may ask you some awkward questions. You'll have to keep your wits about you.*

be at one's wits' end Not know what to do, having tried every solution one can think of † *I'm at my wits' end. The child refuses to eat anything I cook for him.*

WITCH-HUNT *n.*

Originally with literal meaning, but now attempt to discredit people for

political, commercial advantage, etc † *The official enquiry into the
disaster has turned into a witch-hunt. The press are anxious to find
someone to blame.*

WITH *prep.*

1 In the company of, in the presence of † *Were you with John when you
met her?* † *Mr Smith is with the manager at the moment.* **2** Having as a
possession or characteristic † *A man with a bald head.* † *A girl with a
beautiful mouth.* † *A house with two bathrooms, and with a large
garden.* † *A man with more money than sense.* **3** Carrying, bringing,
etc † *The postman came with some letters in his hand.* † *There is
someone outside with a message for you.* **4** Indicating instrument, tool,
constituents used for an action † *He hit me with a stick.* † *He wrote the
letter with his new pen.* † *She made the cake with butter, eggs and
flour.* **5** Indicating coincidence of time † *With the death of his father, he
found himself responsible for all the family affairs.* † *With that, he walked
out, banging the door behind him* (when that happened or having said
that). **6** Indicating relationship between action and time (*keeping up with,*
etc) † *We must change with the times.* † *She tries to keep up with the
fashion.* **7** In the same direction as † *He likes to go with the crowd.* † *It
is easier to swim with the current than against it.* **8** Indicating activity
involving two people, sides † *Come and play with me.* † *I will discuss the
matter with you another time.* † *Is she still living with her parents?* **9** As
far as someone is concerned † *What's wrong with him?* † *I don't know if
he's happy or sad. I never know with him.* **10** Indicating association
between or support for † *I agree with you.* † *We're with you on this
matter* (we are on your side). † *Do you think this tie goes with my jacket?*
(does it match, is it in harmony with?). **11** Showing an objective
relationship between the noun following it and verb preceding it † *Do
you want me to deal with it?* † *What are you going to do with that old
picture?* **12** After an adjective or participial adjective, indicating a
subjective relationship † *The floor was covered with books* (Books
covered the floor). † *I'm not happy with my job* (My job does not make
me happy). † *I was disappointed with my work* (My work disappointed
me). **13** Indicating cause † *He trembled with rage.* † *She shivered with
cold.* **14** Indicating the manner in which something is done † *He walked
with an affected air.* † *He lay on the bed with his feet turned upwards.*
15 Indicating circumstances or state attendant on † *It's difficult to drive
fast, with ice on the roads.*

with all In spite of † *With all his faults, he still attracts me.*

with it This expression has recently come into fashion. It is used adjectivally to
mean aware of what is going on around one and therefore, in the fashion,
in harmony with what is considered modern. [NOTE: Someone who is

unaware, behind the times, old-fashioned, etc is described as **not with it**, not *without it*.]

WITHIN *prep.*
1 Not beyond (the limits, scope of) † *I am willing to do anything within my power.* † *He was within reach of his objective.* **2** In not more than (a period of time) † *I will see you again within an hour.* **3** In not more than (a period of time) after an event † *We called the doctor and he came within a quarter of an hour.* **4** Indicating the limits of distance from † *We were within a mile of the town when the car broke down* (not more than a mile away from). **5** Inside (a group) † *There is said to be disagreement within the Government.* [NOTE: We no longer use *within* to mean *inside* a place.]

WITHOUT *prep.*
1 Not accompanied by † *What are you doing here without your mother?* **2** Not having, lacking, free from † *I came without my umbrella.* † *He entered the examination without hope of success.* † *I want the lecture to be heard without interruptions.* **3** Not doing or forgetting to do something † *He passed the driving test without making a mistake.* † *He left without saying goodbye.* [NOTE: Since *without* carries a negative meaning a sentence of this kind with the main verb in the negative automatically has a positive meaning † *Don't go without saying goodbye* (Say goodbye before you go). † *I wouldn't invite him without asking you* (I would ask your opinion before inviting him).

WOLF *n.*
a wolf in sheep's clothing Someone with bad or dangerous intentions who pretends to be friendly, harmless.
keep the wolf from the door Earn enough, get enough food to save one's family from hunger (often used humorously to mean only to save someone from hunger) †) *How much do you earn.*) *Not much, but enough to keep the wolf from the door.* † *Eat this. It will keep the wolf from the door.*

WONDER *n.*
no wonder It is not surprising (that) †) *The children were very happy on Christmas morning.*) *No wonder! They had so many presents.*

WONDER *v.i. & t.*
wonder (about) Ask oneself (about), be curious (about) † *I've been wondering about what you told me yesterday. Did you really mean it?* † *I wonder where she is* (I am curious to know).
wonder (at) Be surprised (at) † *I wonder at her lack of concern for her children.* † *I don't wonder that she refused to speak to you, after the way you treated her.*

WOOD *n.*

out of the wood Clear of difficulties, trouble † *The firm lost a lot of money last year, but now we are out of the wood.*

be unable to see the wood for the trees Be unable to form a clear picture of the situation, plan, etc as a whole because one concentrates too much on details † *He can't make a decision about the project because he can't see the wood for the trees.*

touch wood (in USA **knock on wood**) Superstitious gesture for luck, also used as phrase meaning 'I'm glad to say, and hope this luck will continue' † *The children haven't had a cold so far this winter, touch wood.*

WOOL *n.*

pull the wool over someone's eyes Trick, deceive him.

WORD *n.*

word for word 1 In exactly the same words † *I gave him your message word for word.* 2 (in translation) Literally (translating each word in turn and not the general sense).

the last word 1 (in comfort, elegance, etc) The most modern up-to-date † *His house is the last word in comfort.* 2 (on the subject, etc) Final statement (either of one's attitude, position or in settling an argument, deciding something) † *That is my last word on the matter. You can take it or leave it.* [ALSO: **have the last word** Make the final statement (implying victory in an argument, etc or a determination to express one's point of view after a decision has been taken) † *Don't think it is settled yet, the Director always has the last word.* † *He always insists on having the last word* (on refusing to give up the argument or on appearing to have been the one who took the decision).]

by word of mouth In spoken, not written, words † *It is not enough to have his promise by word of mouth. To prove it in Court you must have something in writing.*

in a word In brief (summarising what is meant or has been said) † *There has not been time for us to express our admiration for your discovery. In a word, we are delighted at its success.*

eat one's words Admit that one was wrong (and apologise) † *They said it was impossible for anyone to climb that mountain, but now they will have to eat their words.*

have a word with Speak to (often implying something more serious) † *I told the boss that you want a rise in salary and he said he would have a word with you about it.*

have words (with) Quarrel (with) † *My wife was annoyed about it and we had words. (She had words with me).*

put in (say) a good word for Say something in (a person's) favour † *If you want to work here, I could put in a good word for you.* † *He was so* *unpopular that no one could be found to say a good word for him.* [NOTE: The difference is slight. *Put in* suggests a voluntary act, *say* implies when asked.]

take someone at his word Trust him and act on the assumption that he means what he says † *He said he would deliver the goods yesterday and I took him at his word.*

take someone's word for Believe him † *If you say it's true, I'll take your word for it.* † *Take my word for it* (Believe me), *this will lead to trouble.*

WORK *n.*

at work 1 At the place where one works † *If I don't answer the 'phone at home, ring me at work.* 2 Working at the place where one works † *My husband is at work.* 3 (**on**) Working (on a task of any kind) † *He is at work on a novel.* † *Don't interrupt him. He is hard at work* (busy with a task).

in (out of) work In employment (unemployed) † *Those who have always been in regular work do not know how hard it is to have no job.* † *If the factory is closed down, hundreds of people will be out of work.*

off work Away from one's place of work (through illness, etc) † *He is off work because he has broken his arm.*

all in a day's work (Acceptable as) part of one's normal job, routine † *As a policeman, I have to be prepared to deal with traffic as well as catch thieves. It's all in a day's work.*

have one's work cut out Be tested to the limits of one's ability (to do something) † *He will have his work cut out to do better than the man who had the job before him.*

make short work of Finish (a job) quickly (often humorous) † *The boys made short work of that cake.*

WORK *v.i. & t.*

it works It functions properly or it is effective † *The lift is not working* † ⟩ *I tried the cure for colds you sold me and it worked.* ⟩ *You're lucky. It didn't work with me.*

work at (*See* **work on** 1).

work for 1 Be employed by † *He works for the Electricity Council.* 2 Work in order to get † *I'm not going to work for nothing.* † *He deserves his promotion. He worked for it.* † *They are working for peace.*

work in 1 (usually passive) Accustom to routine, method of working † *We have a lot of new operators and they're not worked in (to the system) yet.* 2 Penetrate (and form part of) † *Can you see how this nail has worked in (to my shoe)?* [ALSO: **work one's way in** Gradually penetrate into (usually for dishonest reasons) † *He worked his way into my confidence by pretending to sympathise with me.*]

work off 1 Repay (a debt) by working for nothing. 2 Use up (one's anger, energy) † *He was afraid to tell the boss what he thought of him, so he worked off his frustration on the rest of us.* † *Let the child run about. He has so much energy that he has to work it off somehow.* 3 Gradually disappear, through use, activity † *My jaw felt dead after the injection, but the numbness (lack of feeling) worked itself off in an hour or so.*

work on 1 Be busy with (*See* **at work** 3) † *We haven't found the solution to the problem yet. We are still working on it.* [NOTE: **work at** Similar meaning, but implies activity (*at work on*) where *work on* simply states the kind of work.] 2 Work sustained by (food) † *Go to work on an egg* (advertising slogan) (i.e. Have an egg for breakfast). 3 Use as a basis for work, action † *The police are investigating the crime but so far they have no evidence to work on.* 4 Try to influence † *If she won't listen to you, let me work on her.*

work out 1 Calculate † *Can you work the sum out in your head?* 2 Amount to, by calculation † *If we sell 20 machines for £1,000, that works out at £50 each.* 3 Produce a result, by calculation † *This equation doesn't work out.* 4 Devise † *We have worked out a system for improving the delivery of materials.* 5 Result, turn out † *There was trouble in the beginning, but in the end everything worked out according to plan.* 6 Train (for a sporting event, etc) † *The boxer worked out for half-an-hour on the day before the fight.* [ALSO: **work-out** *n*. Training session.]

work up 1 Gradually build up by work (a business, etc) † *From small beginnings he has worked up the business to its present size.* 2 Develop, produce within oneself † *I couldn't work up the energy to play tennis today.* 3 Excite † *He worked up the crowd into a rage by his speech.* † *She was very worked up when she heard the news* (in a nervous, excited state). [ALSO: **get worked up** Become excited † *Don't get so worked up about it. It's no longer important.*]

work up (in)to Gradually increase (in power, speed, emotion, etc) to; excite to the point of † *The play worked up to a climax.* † *Don't work yourself up into a rage.*

WORLD *n*.

a world of A great deal of † *There's a world of sense in what he says.*

the world and his wife Everyone (especially within 'high society') † *It was a very fashionable wedding. The world and his wife were there.*

a man of the world A man who has wide experience of the world (and who is therefore supposed to be urbane, sophisticated) † *I don't think he would be shocked by the film. After all, he's a man of the world.*

nothing (who) in the world Used for emphasis † *Nothing in the world would persuade me to tell you* (no threat, punishment of any kind, etc). † *Who in the world could have told you that?* (who on earth?).

be all the world to Mean everything to † *He loves her dearly. She is all the world to him.*

for all the world like (as if) Exactly like (as if) † *It was for all the world as if I had dreamed the whole affair and nothing had really happened.*

for the world (usually in negative sentences) For anything, any reason † *I wouldn't harm the child for the world.*

on top of the world In very good spirits (and health) † *I feel on top of the world this morning.*

the best of both worlds Advantages from both sides (of a situation, etc) † *He wants to get the credit for the job without doing the work. That would mean getting the best of both worlds.*

third world Used when referring to uncommitted nations in terms of the two opposing 'worlds' of West and East (the American and Soviet blocs) and particularly to countries which have openly stressed their neutrality in the Cold War (*See* **war**).

WORRY *v.t. & i.*

worry out (a problem) Continue to attack it until one solves it.

WORSE *adv.*

worse off Not in such a good position as before, poorer (*See* **well off**) † *If prices go up but income does not, people are worse off.*

none the worse Not suffering or worse off, as a result † *The children were caught in a storm, but fortunately are none the worse for it.*

WORST *n.*

the worst of it is The most unfortunate part of the matter, etc is † *He is out visiting his uncle and the worst of it is that they have no telephone so we can't contact him.*

if the worst comes to the worst If what is feared eventually takes place † *They promised to reconnect the electricity this afternoon but if the worst comes to the worst, we'll have to sit in the dark* (i.e. if, as I fear, they don't come).

at (the) worst If the worst happens † *At best we shall be lucky to make a profit. At worst we could lose all our money.*

get the worst of it Be defeated (in a fight, etc).

WORTH *predic. adj.*

for all one is worth With all one's energy † *He ran for all he was worth when he saw the bus.*

for what it is worth In so far as it has any use or value † *That's my opinion, for what it is worth.*

WOULD *anom. fin.*

[NOTE: Apart from serving as the auxiliary of the conditional tense and (+ *have*) of the conditional perfect, *would* replaces *will* to show future in the past † *He will be late.* † *She said that he would be late.* This applies to all the examples given under *will* † e.g. *He would sit for hours looking out of the window* means it was his custom, habit to do this (*See* **will** (only) **6**). Whether *shall* or *will* should be used in the 1st person purely to express the future is covered in the NOTE to **will**. The same question may be raised over *should* and *would*, complicated by the fact that the 1st person in the future tense will change to 3rd person in reported speech (*shall, will* to *would*). All the examples listed under **will** (only) change to *would* in all persons in reported speech; those listed under **shall** (only) change to *should*.]

WOULD-BE *adj.*
Wishing or imagining oneself to be † *the would-be President* (used in describing a candidate for the Presidency). † *He is a would-be novelist, but he has never published anything.*

WRAP *v.t. & i.*
be wrapped (up) in **1** Be hidden by, enveloped in † *The negotiations were wrapped (up) in secrecy.* **2** Be completely involved in † *He is wrapped up in his work and has no time for anything else.* **3** Be absorbed by † *He is too wrapped up in himself to worry about anyone else's problems.*

WRITE *v.i. & t.*
write off **1** Write (to someone) without delay † *I saw that his book had been published and wrote off (to the publishers) for a copy.* **2** (a debt) Cancel (write down in a book as lost) † *We have no hope of being paid, so we must write the debt off (as a loss).* **3** Consider as loss (in value) † *You can write £100 off the value of a new car as soon as you buy it.* **4** Regard as unworthy of consideration † *He has made so many mistakes as a Minister that the party have written him off as a future leader.* [ALSO: **write-off** *n.* Object (especially car, aeroplane, etc) considered worthless, useless † *The car was a complete write-off after the crash.*]

write up Write a description of, but in neat written form † *He wrote up the Conference for his newspaper.* † *The students wrote up their lecture notes.* [ALSO: **write-up** *n.* Written account, report.]

WRONG *n.*
(put someone) in the wrong (Cause him to appear) at fault, to blame † *You are both in the wrong. He knew he was to blame himself, but he tried to put me in the wrong.*

on the wrong side of (an age) Over † *He is on the wrong side of 40.*

get on the wrong side of (a person) Make him angry, become out of favour with him † *He has a bad temper. Don't get on the wrong side of him.*

go wrong Fail, make a mistake † *The party was a failure. Everything went wrong.* † *I cannot solve this problem, but I don't see where I've gone wrong (in my calculations).*

what's wrong with that? Often used as rhetorical question, meaning Why not? Why shouldn't that be so? † *He has made a profit by selling his house, but it was his property, so what's wrong with that?*

two wrongs don't make a right To revenge oneself for a bad action by doing something equally bad is not justified † *He had reason to feel the boss had been unfair to him, but that doesn't justify his hitting the man. Two wrongs don't make a right.*

YELLOW *adj.*
Cowardly † *You're afraid to fight me. Admit that you're yellow.*

YES *particle.*
yes and no Indicating that the speaker is in favour from one point of view but opposed from another † 〉 *Would you like to live in the country* 〉 *Yes and no. I like fresh air, but I also like a lot of company.*

YES-MAN *n.*
Person ready to agree with anything his superiors say in order to obtain their favour.